W9-BGG-094

How to Think Straight About Psychology

TENTH EDITION

Keith E. Stanovich

University of Toronto

Boston   Columbus   Indianapolis   New York   San Francisco   Upper Saddle River
Amsterdam   Cape Town   Dubai   London   Madrid   Milan   Munich   Paris   Montréal   Toronto
Delhi   Mexico City   São Paulo   Sydney   Hong Kong   Seoul   Singapore   Taipei   Tokyo

Editorial Director: Craig Campanella
Editor in Chief: Jessica Mosher
Executive Editor: Stephen Frail
Editorial Assistant: Crystal McCarthy
Director of Marketing: Brandy Dawson
Managing Editor: Denise Forlow
Production Project Manager:
  Maria Piper
Senior Operations Supervisor:
  Mary Fischer
Operations Specialist: Diane Peirano
Art Director, Cover: Janye Conte

Cover Designer: Suzanne Duda
Cover Art: Shutterstock
Senior Digital Media Editor:
  Peter Sabatini
Full-Service Project Management:
  Integra Software Services, Pvt. Ltd.
Composition: Integra Software
  Services, Pvt. Ltd.
Printer/Binder: STP/RRD/
  Harrisonburg
Cover Printer: STP/RRD/
  Harrisonburg

Credits and acknowledgments borrowed from other sources and reproduced, with permission, in this textbook appear on the appropriate page within text [or on page 229].

Copyright © 2013, 2010, 2007 Pearson Education, Inc. All rights reserved. Manufactured in the United States of America. This publication is protected by Copyright, and permission should be obtained from the publisher prior to any prohibited reproduction, storage in a retrieval system, or transmission in any form or by any means, electronic, mechanical, photocopying, recording, or likewise. To obtain permission(s) to use material from this work, please submit a written request to Pearson Education, Inc., Permissions Department, One Lake Street, Upper Saddle River, New Jersey 07458, or you may fax your request to 201-236-3290.

Many of the designations by manufacturers and sellers to distinguish their products are claimed as trademarks. Where those designations appear in this book, and the publisher was aware of a trademark claim, the designations have been printed in initial caps or all caps.

Library of Congress Cataloging-in-Publication Data
Stanovich, Keith E.
  How to think straight about psychology/Keith E. Stanovich.—10th ed.
    p. cm.
  Includes bibliographical references and index.
  ISBN-13: 978-0-205-91412-8 (alk. paper)
  ISBN-10: 0-205-91412-8 (alk. paper)
  1. Psychology—Research—Methodology.   2. Mass media—Psychological
  aspects.   3. Mass media—Objectivity.   I. Title.
  BF76.5.S68 2013
  150.72—dc23

                                              2012027520

10 9 8 7 6 5 4 3 2

Student Version:
ISBN 10: 0-205-91412-8
ISBN-13: 978-0-205-91412-8

To Paula, who taught me how to think straight about life

Contents

Preface

New to the Tenth Edition

The tenth edition of *How to Think Straight About Psychology* has no major structural revisions because a chapter reorganization occurred in a previous edition. The content and order of the chapters remain the same. At the request of reviewers and users, this edition remains at the same length as the ninth edition. Readers and users have not wanted the book to lengthen and, indeed, it has not. I have continued to update and revise the examples that are used in the book (while keeping those that are reader favorites). Some dated examples have been replaced with more contemporary studies and issues. I have made a major effort to use contemporary citations that are relevant to the various concepts and experimental effects that are mentioned. A large number of new citations appear in this edition (172 new citations, to be exact!), so that the reader continues to have up-to-date references on all of the examples and concepts.

The goal of the book remains what it always was—to present a short introduction to the critical thinking skills that will help the student to better understand the subject matter of psychology. During the past decade and a half there has been an increased emphasis on the teaching of critical thinking in universities (Abrami et al., 2008; Sternberg, Roediger, & Halpern, 2006). Indeed, some state university systems have instituted curricular changes mandating an emphasis on critical thinking skills. At the same time, however, other educational scholars were arguing that critical thinking skills should not be isolated from specific factual content. *How to Think Straight About Psychology* combines these two trends. It is designed to provide the instructor with the opportunity to teach critical thinking within the rich content of modern psychology.

Readers are encouraged to send me comments at: keith.stanovich@ utoronto.ca.

There exists a body of knowledge that is unknown to most people. This information concerns human behavior and consciousness in their various forms. It can be used to explain, predict, and control human actions. Those who have access to this knowledge use it to gain an understanding of other human beings. They have a more complete and accurate conception of what determines the behavior and thoughts of other individuals than do those who do not have this knowledge.

Surprisingly enough, this unknown body of knowledge is the discipline of psychology.

What can I possibly mean when I say that the discipline of psychology is unknown? Surely, you may be thinking, this statement was not meant to be taken literally. Bookstores contain large sections full of titles dealing with psychology. Television and radio talk shows regularly feature psychological topics. Magazine articles quote people called psychologists talking about a variety of topics. Nevertheless, there is an important sense in which the *field* of psychology is unknown.

Despite much seeming media attention, the discipline of psychology remains for the most part hidden from the public. The transfer of "psychological" knowledge that is taking place via the media is largely an illusion. Few people are aware that the majority of the books they see in the psychology sections of many bookstores are written by individuals with absolutely no standing in the psychological community. Few are aware that many of the people to whom television applies the label *psychologist* would not be considered so by the American Psychological Association or the Association for Psychological Science. Few are aware that many of the most visible psychological "experts" have contributed no information to the fund of knowledge in the discipline of psychology.

The flurry of media attention paid to "psychological" topics has done more than simply present inaccurate information. It has also obscured the very real and growing knowledge base in the field of psychology. The general public is unsure about what is and is not psychology and is unable to independently evaluate claims about human behavior. Adding to the problem is the fact that many people have a vested interest in a public that is either without evaluative skills or that believes there is no way to evaluate psychological claims. The latter view, sometimes called the "anything goes" attitude, is one of the fallacies discussed in this book, and it is particularly costly to the public. Many pseudosciences are multimillion-dollar industries that depend on the lack of public awareness that claims about human behavior can be tested. The general public is also unaware that many of the claims made by these pseudosciences (e.g., astrology, psychic surgery, speed reading, biorhythms, therapeutic touch, subliminal self-help tapes, facilitated communication, and psychic detectives) have been tested and proved false. The existence of the pseudoscience industry, which is discussed in this book, increases the media's tendency toward sensationalistic reporting of science. This tendency is worse in psychology than in other sciences, and understanding the reasons why this is so is an important part of learning how to think straight about psychology.

This book, then, is directed not at potential researchers in psychology but at a much larger group: the consumers of psychological information. The target audience is the beginning psychology student and the general reader who have encountered information on psychological issues in the general media and have wondered how to go about evaluating its validity.

This book is not a standard introductory psychology text. It does not outline a list of facts that psychological research has uncovered. Indeed, telling everyone to take an introductory psychology course at a university is probably not the ultimate solution to the inaccurate portrayal of psychology in the media. There are many laypeople with a legitimate interest in psychology who do not have the time, money, or access to a university to pursue formal study. More importantly, as a teacher of university-level psychology courses, I am forced to admit that my colleagues and I often fail to give our beginning students a true understanding of the science of psychology. The reason is that lower-level courses often do not teach the critical analytical skills that are the focus of this book. As instructors, we often become obsessed with "content"—with "covering material." Every time we stray a little from the syllabus to discuss issues such as psychology in the media, we feel a little guilty and begin to worry that we may not cover all the topics before the end of the term.

Consider the average introductory psychology textbook. Many now contain between 600 and 800 multicolumned pages and reference literally hundreds of studies in the published literature. Of course, there is nothing wrong with such books containing so much material. It simply reflects the increasing knowledge base in psychology. There are, however, some unfortunate side effects. Instructors are often so busy trying to cram their students full of dozens of theories, facts, and experiments that they fail to deal with some of the fundamental questions and misconceptions that students bring with them to the study of psychology. Rather than dealing directly with these misconceptions, the instructors (and the introductory textbook authors) often hope that if students are exposed to enough of the empirical content of psychology, they will simply *induce* the answers to their questions. In short, the instructors hope that students will recognize the implicit answers to these questions in the discussions of empirical research in several content areas. All too often this hope is frustrated. In a final review session—or in office hours at the end of the term—instructors are often shocked and discouraged by questions and comments that might have been expected on the first day of the course but not after 14 weeks: "But psychology experiments aren't real life; what can they tell us?"; "Psychology just can't be a *real* science like chemistry, can it?"; "But I heard a therapist on TV say the opposite of what our textbook said"; "I think this theory is stupid—my brother behaves just the opposite of what it says"; "Psychology is nothing more than common sense, isn't it?"; "Everyone knows what anxiety is—why bother defining it?" For many students, such questions are not implicitly answered merely by a consideration of the content of psychology. In this book, I deal explicitly with the confusions that underlie questions and comments such as these.

Unfortunately, research has shown that the average introductory psychology course does surprisingly little to correct some of entering students' misconceptions about the discipline (Keith & Beins, 2008; Kowalski & Taylor, 2009; Standing & Huber, 2003; Taylor & Kowalski, 2004). This unfortunate fact provides the rationale for this book. Psychology students need explicit instruction in the critical thinking skills that will make them into independent evaluators of psychological information.

Years after students have forgotten the content of an introductory psychology course, they will still use the fundamental principles covered in this book to evaluate psychological claims. Long after Erikson's stages of development have been forgotten, students will be using the thinking tools introduced in this text to evaluate new psychological information encountered in the media. Once acquired, these skills will serve as lifelong tools that will aid in the evaluation of knowledge claims. First, they provide the ability to conduct an initial gross assessment of plausibility. Second, these skills provide some criteria for assessing the reliability of "expert" opinion. Because the need to rely on expert opinion can never be eliminated in a complex society, the evaluation of an expert's credibility becomes essential to knowledge acquisition. Although these critical thinking skills can be applied to any discipline or body of knowledge, they are particularly important in the area of psychology because the field is so often misrepresented in the general media.

Many psychologists are pessimistic about any effort to stem the tide of misinformation about their discipline. Although this pessimism is, unfortunately, often justified, this "consumer's guide" to psychology was motivated by the idea that psychologists must not let this problem become a self-fulfilling prophecy.

Although I have welcomed the opportunity to prepare several editions of *How to Think Straight About Psychology*, it is unfortunately true that the reasons for the book's existence are just as applicable today as they were when I wrote the first edition. Media presentations of psychology are just as misleading as they ever were, and students in introductory psychology courses enter with as many misconceptions as they ever did. Thus, the goals of all subsequent editions have remained the same. These goals are shared by an increasing number of psychology instructors. Stanford University psychologist Roger Shepard (1983) echoed all the concerns that motivated the writing of the first edition of this text: "Although most undergraduate psychology students may not go on to scientific careers, one hopes that they acquire some facility for the critical evaluation of the incomplete, naive, confused, or exaggerated reports of social science 'findings' to which they will continue to be exposed by the popular media.... Widespread notions that human behavior and mental phenomena can be adequately understood through unaided common sense or, worse, by reference to nonempirical pseudosciences, such as astrology, present us with a continuing challenge" (p. 855).

The goal of this book is to present a short introduction to the critical thinking skills that will help students to better understand the subject matter of psychology and better understand events in the world in which they live.

Acknowledgments

Many of the individuals I have acknowledged in earlier editions continue to contribute ideas for the book. However, I must single out Richard West of James Madison University, who has been a most valuable continuing contributor to the book's evolution. A humane scholar and a true friend, his intellectual and emotional support is much appreciated.

Several other scholars have provided valuable feedback on this and earlier editions. These include Wayne Bartz, American River College; Christopher Bauer, University of New Hampshire; Ludy Benjamin, Texas A&M University; Angela M. Birkhead-Flight, University of Cincinnati; Virginia Blankenship, University of Northern Arizona; Edward C. Chang, Northern Kentucky University; Michael Choban, West Virginia Wesleyan University; James Clark, University of Winnipeg; Jim Coan, University of Arizona; Ellen Cole, Alaska Pacific University; Ellen Cotter, Georgia Southwestern State University; Anne Cunningham, University of California, Berkeley; Ian Deary, University of Edinburgh; Julie Deisinger, Saint Xavier University; David DiBattista, Brock University; Wallace Dixon, Heidelberg College; Mark Fineman, Southern Connecticut State University; Herbert Fink, SUNY–Brockport; Heinz Fischer, Long Beach City College; Ronald Gandelman, Rutgers University; Michael Gasser, University of Northern Iowa; Traci A. Giuliano, Southwestern University; William Graziano, Purdue University; Nancy J. Gussett, Baldwin-Wallace College; Gordon Hammerle, Adrian College; Randy Hansen, Oakland University; William L. Hathaway, Regent University; George Heise, Indiana University; Albert Heldt, Grand Rapids Junior College; Dori Henderson, Metropolitan State University; George Howard, University of Notre Dame; Barry Kendall; Bernie Koenig, Fanshawe College; Victor Koop, Goshen College; Andy Kwong, University of New South Wales; P. A. Lamal, University of North Carolina, Charlotte; Stephen Louisell, Kalamazoo Community College; Gwen Lupfer-Johnson, University of Alaska, Anchorage; Margaret Matlin, State University of New York-Geneseo; Douglas Mook, University of Virginia; Timothy Moore, York University; Edward Morris, University of Kansas; Joseph E. Morrow, California State University at Sacramento; Michael O'Boyle,

Iowa State University; Blaine Peden, University of Wisconsin, Eau Claire; John F. Pfister, Dartmouth College; Sam Rakover, University of Haifa; Richard Redding, Hahneman University; Michael Ross, University of Waterloo; John Ruscio, Elizabethtown College; Walter Sa, Grand Valley State University; Allen Salo, University of Maine at Presque Isle; Frank Schieber, University of South Dakota; Jillene Grover Seiver, Bellevue College; Marjorie Semonick, University of Minnesota; David Share, University of Haifa; Jeffrey Sherman, Northwestern University; Linda Siegel, University of British Columbia; Norman Silverman, University of Illinois, Chicago; Frank Smoll, University of Washington; Paul Solomon, Williams College; Mike Stadler, University of Missouri; Maggie Toplak, York University; Larry Vandervert, Spokane Falls Community College; John Vokey, University of Lethbridge; Carol Wade, College of Marin; Marty Wall, University of Toronto; Barbara Wanchisen, Baldwin-Wallace College; Toni G. Wegner, University of Virginia; Edward Wisniewski, Northwestern University; Murray S. Work, California State University at Sacramento; and Edward Zuckerman, Guilford Press.

The insights from many discussions about teaching methodology with Ted Landau, Larry Lilliston, and Dean Purcell, all of Oakland University, were incorporated into the book. Reviewers of recent editions who were particularly helpful include Michael Choban, West Virginia Wesleyan University; David DiBattista, Brock University; Steven Isonio, Golden West College; John Ruscio, Elizabethtown College; Allen Salo, University of Maine at Presque Isle; Cindy Sifonis, Oakland University; Michael Tagler, Nebraska Wesleyan University; and Chris Ward, Stonehill College.

My editor at Pearson, Stephen Frail, has provided guidance, enthusiasm, and support for the book, as has his editorial assistant, Madelyn Schricker. Robyn Macpherson is thanked for her diligent library and reference assistance on several editions prior to this one.

Finally, I wish to thank Paula J. Stanovich for more than just the emotional support that is routinely alluded to in acknowledgments. Her concern for all human beings, particularly those less fortunate, is an inspiration to all who know her. A view we both share is that all human beings should have the opportunity to utilize their full potential. This book attests to the fact that I have had such an opportunity. Paula works to speed the day when this opportunity will be fully extended to all individuals with disabilities.

CHAPTER 1

Psychology Is Alive and Well (and Doing Fine Among the Sciences)

The Freud Problem

Stop 100 people on the street and ask them to name a psychologist, either living or dead. Record the responses. Of course, Dr. Phil, Wayne Dyer, and other "media psychologists" would certainly be named. If we leave out the media and pop psychologists, however, and consider only those who have made a recognized contribution to psychological knowledge, there would be no question about the outcome of this informal survey. Sigmund Freud would be the winner hands down. B. F. Skinner would probably finish a distant second. No other psychologist would get enough recognition even to bother about. Thus, Freud, along with the pop psychology presented in the media, largely defines psychology in the public mind.

The notoriety of Freud has greatly affected the general public's conceptions about the field of psychology and has contributed to many misunderstandings. For example, many introductory psychology students are surprised to learn that if all the members of the American Psychological Association (APA) who were concerned with Freudian psychoanalysis were collected, they would make up less than 10 percent of the membership. In another major psychological association, the Association for Psychological Science, they would make up considerably less than 5 percent (Engel, 2008). One popular introductory psychology textbook (Wade & Tavris, 2008) is over 700 pages long, yet contains only 15 pages on which either Freud or psychoanalysis is mentioned—and these 15 pages often contain criticism ("most Freudian concepts were, and still are, rejected by most empirically

1

oriented psychologists," p. 19). The authors of one survey of trends in psychology have summarized the situation by noting that "psychoanalytic research has been virtually ignored by mainstream scientific psychology over the past several decades" (Robins, Gosling, & Craik, 1999, p. 117).

In short, modern psychology is not obsessed with the ideas of Sigmund Freud (as are the media and some humanities disciplines), nor is it largely defined by them. Freud's work is an extremely small part of the varied set of issues, data, and theories that are the concern of modern psychologists. This larger body of research and theory encompasses the work of five Nobel Prize winners (David Hubel, Daniel Kahneman, Herbert Simon, Roger Sperry, and Torsten Wiesel) and a former director of the National Science Foundation (Richard Atkinson), all of whom are virtually unknown to the public.

It is bad enough that Freud's importance to modern psychology is vastly exaggerated. What makes the situation worse is that Freud's methods of investigation are completely unrepresentative of how modern psychologists conduct their research. In fact, the study of Freud's methods gives an utterly misleading impression of psychological research. For example, Freud did not use controlled experimentation, which, as we shall see in Chapter 6, is the most potent weapon in the modern psychologist's arsenal of methods. Freud thought that case studies could establish the truth or falsity of theories. We shall see in Chapter 4 why this idea is mistaken. As one historian of psychotherapy has noted, "If Freud himself was a scientist, it was a strange science he was promulgating.... Psychoanalysis contained theories and hypotheses, but it lacked a method of empirical observation" (Engel, 2008, p. 17).

Finally, a critical problem with Freud's work concerns the connection between theory and behavioral data. As we shall see in Chapter 2, for a theory to be considered scientific, the link between the theory and behavioral data must meet some minimal requirements. Freud's theories do not meet these criteria (Dufresne, 2007; Engel, 2008). To make a long story short, Freud built an elaborate theory on a database (case studies and introspection) that was not substantial enough to support it. Freud concentrated on building complicated theoretical structures, but he did not, as modern psychologists do, ensure that they would rest on a database of reliable, replicable behavioral relationships. In summary, familiarity with Freud's style of work can be a significant impediment to the understanding of modern psychology.

In this chapter, we shall deal with the Freud problem in two ways. First, when we illustrate the diversity of modern psychology, the rather minor position occupied by Freud will become clear. Second, we shall discuss what features are common to psychological investigations across a wide variety of domains. A passing knowledge of Freud's work has obscured from the general public what is the only unifying characteristic of modern psychology: the quest to understand behavior by using the methods of science.

The Diversity of Modern Psychology

There is, in fact, a great diversity of content and perspectives in modern psychology. This diversity drastically reduces the coherence of psychology as a discipline. Henry Gleitman (1981), winner of the American Psychological Foundation's Distinguished Teaching Award, characterized psychology as "a loosely federated intellectual empire that stretches from the domains of the biological sciences on one border to those of the social sciences on the other" (p. 774).

Understanding that psychology is composed of an incredibly wide and diverse set of investigations is critical to an appreciation of the nature of the discipline. Simply presenting some of the concrete indications of this diversity will illustrate the point. The APA has 54 different divisions, each representing either a particular area of research and study or a particular area of practice (see Table 1.1). From the table, you can see the range of subjects studied by psychologists, the range of settings involved, and the different aspects of behavior studied. The other large organization of psychologists—the Association for Psychological Science—is just as diverse. Actually, Table 1.1 understates the diversity within the field of psychology because it gives the impression that each division is a specific specialty area. In fact, each of the 54 divisions listed in the table is a broad area of study that contains a wide variety of subdivisions! In short, it is difficult to exaggerate the diversity of the topics that fall within the field of psychology.

TABLE 1.1 *Divisions of the American Psychological Association*

1. General Psychology
2. Teaching of Psychology
3. Experimental Psychology
5. Evaluation, Measurement, and Statistics
6. Behavioral Neuroscience and Comparative Psychology
7. Developmental Psychology
8. Personality and Social Psychology
9. Psychological Study of Social Issues
10. Psychology of Aesthetics, Creativity, and the Arts
12. Clinical Psychology
13. Consulting Psychology
14. Industrial and Organizational Psychology
15. Educational Psychology
16. School Psychology
17. Counseling Psychology
18. Psychologists in Public Service
19. Military Psychology
20. Adult Development and Aging
21. Applied Experimental and Engineering Psychology
22. Rehabilitation Psychology

(continued)

TABLE 1.1   *Divisions of the American Psychological Association (continued)*

23. Consumer Psychology
24. Theoretical and Philosophical Psychology
25. Behavior Analysis
26. History of Psychology
27. Community Psychology
28. Psychopharmacology and Substance Abuse
29. Psychotherapy
30. Psychological Hypnosis
31. State Psychological Association Affairs
32. Humanistic Psychology
33. Intellectual and Developmental Disabilities
34. Population and Environmental Psychology
35. Psychology of Women
36. Psychology of Religion
37. Child and Family Policy and Practice
38. Health Psychology
39. Psychoanalysis
40. Clinical Neuropsychology
41. Psychology and Law
42. Psychologists in Independent Practice
43. Family Psychology
44. Psychological Study of Lesbian, Gay, and Bisexual Issues
45. Psychological Study of Ethnic Minority Issues
46. Media Psychology
47. Exercise and Sport Psychology
48. Peace Psychology
49. Group Psychology and Group Psychotherapy
50. Addictions
51. Psychological Study of Men and Masculinity
52. International Psychology
53. Clinical Child and Adolescent Psychology
54. Pediatric Psychology
55. Pharmacotherapy
56. Trauma Psychology

Note: There is no Division 4 or 11.

Implications of Diversity

Many people come to the study of psychology hoping to learn the one grand psychological theory that unifies and explains all aspects of human behavior. Such hopes are often disappointed, because psychology contains not one grand theory, but many different theories, each covering a limited aspect of behavior (Griggs, Proctor, & Bujak-Johnson, 2002). The diversity of psychology guarantees that the task of theoretical unification will be immensely difficult. Indeed, many psychologists would argue that such a unification is impossible. Others, however, are searching for greater unification within the field (Cacioppo, 2007a, 2007b; Cleeremans, 2010; Gray, 2008; Henriques, 2011; Sternberg, 2005). For example, the coherence of psychology as a discipline has increased over the last two decades due to the theoretical efforts of evolutionary psychologists. These researchers have tried to bring unification to our conceptualization of human psychological processes by viewing them as mechanisms serving critical evolutionary functions such as kinship recognition, mate selection, cooperation, social exchange, and child rearing (Buss, 2005, 2011; Cartwright, 2008; Ellis & Bjorklund, 2005; Geary, 2005, 2008). Likewise, Cacioppo (2007b) points to subfields such as social cognitive neuroscience as tying together numerous specialty areas within psychology—in this case, cognitive psychology, social psychology, and neuropsychology.

Some researchers see the diversity of psychology as reflecting an underlying strength of the discipline (Cacioppo, 2007a; Gray, 2008). For example, Cacioppo (2007a) views psychology as a so-called hub discipline—a science whose findings have unusually wide implications for other fields. He cites evidence indicating that, compared with other sciences, psychological findings have quite broad implications for other sciences.

No matter what their position on the issue of the coherence of the subject matter of psychology, all psychologists agree that theoretical unification will be an extremely difficult task. The lack of theoretical integration leads some critics of psychology to denigrate the scientific progress that psychology has made. Such criticism often arises from the mistaken notion that all true sciences must have a grand, unifying theory. It is a mistaken notion because many other sciences also lack a unifying conceptualization. Harvard psychologist William Estes (1979) has emphasized this point:

> The situation in which the experimental psychologists find themselves is not novel, to be sure, nor peculiar to psychology. Physics during the early twentieth century subdivided even at the level of undergraduate teaching into separate disciplines. Thus I was introduced to that science through separate university courses in mechanics, heat, optics, acoustics, and electricity. Similarly, chemistry has branched out, evidently irreversibly, into inorganic, organic, physical, and biochemical specialties, among which there may be no more communication than among some of the current subdisciplines of psychology. In both cases, unity has reemerged only at the level of abstract mathematical theory. Medicine has similarly fragmented into specialties, but is like psychology in that there has been no appearance of a new unity. (pp. 661–662)

Once we acknowledge the implications of the social and historical factors that determine the structure of disciplines, we can recognize that it is illogical to demand that all fields be unified. Indeed, many scholars have argued that the term "psychology" implies a coherence of subject matter that is not characteristic of the discipline. As a result, a number of leading university departments in the United States have been changing their names to Department of Psychological Sciences (see Jaffe, 2011). The term "sciences" conveys two important messages of this chapter. That it is plural signals the point about the diversity of content in the discipline that we have been discussing. The term "sciences" also signals where to look for the unity in the discipline of psychology—not to its content, but instead to its *methods*. Here is where we can hope to find more unity of purpose among investigators. But here, in the domain of the methods that psychologists use to advance knowledge, is where we also find some of the greatest misunderstandings of the discipline.

Unity in Science

Simply to say that psychology is concerned with human behavior does not distinguish it from other disciplines. Many other professional groups and disciplines—including economists, novelists, the law, sociology, history, political science, anthropology, and literary studies—are, in part, concerned with human behavior. Psychology is not unique in this respect.

Practical applications do not establish any uniqueness for the discipline of psychology either. For example, many university students decide to major in psychology because they have the laudable goal of wanting to "help people." But helping people is an applied part of an incredibly large number of fields, including social work, education, nursing, occupational therapy, physical therapy, police science, human resources, and speech therapy. Similarly, the goal of training applied specialists to help people by counseling them does not demand that we have a discipline called psychology. Helping people by counseling them is an established part of many fields, including education, social work, police work, nursing, pastoral work, occupational therapy, and many others.

It is easy to argue that there are really *only* two things that justify psychology as an independent discipline. The first is that psychology studies the full range of human and nonhuman behavior with the techniques of science. The second is that the applications that derive from this knowledge are *scientifically* based. Were this not true, there would be no reason for psychology to exist.

Psychology is different from other behavioral fields in that it attempts to give the public two guarantees. One is that the conclusions about behavior that it produces derive from scientific evidence. The second is that practical applications of psychology have been derived from and tested by scientific methods. Does psychology ever fall short of these goals? Yes, quite often (Lilienfeld, 2007; Lilienfeld, Ruscio, & Lynn, 2008). This book is about how we might better attain them. I will return in Chapter 12 to the issue of psychologists themselves undermining their own legitimacy by not meeting appropriate scientific standards. But, in principle, these are the standards that justify psychology as an independent field. If psychology ever decides that these goals are not worth pursuing—that it does not wish to adhere to scientific standards—then it might as well fold its tent and let its various concerns devolve to other disciplines because it would be a totally redundant field of intellectual inquiry.

Clearly, then, the first and most important step that anyone must take in understanding psychology is to realize that its defining feature is that it is the data-based scientific study of behavior. Comprehending all of the implications of this fact will occupy us for the rest of this book, because it is the primary way that we develop the ability to think straight about psychology. Conversely, the primary way that people get confused in their thinking about psychology is that they fail to realize that it is a scientific discipline. For example, it is quite common to hear people outside the discipline voice the opinion that psychology is not a science. Why is this a common occurrence?

Attempts to convince the public that psychology cannot be a science stem from a variety of sources. As will be discussed in later chapters, much confusion about the actual discipline of psychology is deliberately fostered by purveyors of bogus psychology. There has grown up in our society a considerable industry of pseudoscientific belief systems that have a vested interest in convincing the public that anything goes in psychology and that there are no rational criteria for evaluating psychological claims. This is the perfect atmosphere in which to market such offers as "Lose weight through hypnosis," "Develop your hidden psychic powers," and "Learn French while you sleep," along with the many other parts of the multibillion-dollar self-help industry that either are not based on scientific evidence or, in many cases, are actually contradicted by much available evidence.

Another source of resistance to scientific psychology stems from the tendency to oppose the expansion of science into areas where unquestioned authorities and "common sense" have long reigned. History provides many examples of initial public resistance to the use of science rather than philosophical speculation, theological edict, or folk wisdom to explain the natural world. Each science has gone through a phase of resistance to its development. Learned contemporaries of Galileo refused to look into his new telescope because the existence of the moons of Jupiter would have violated their philosophical and theological beliefs. For centuries, the understanding of human anatomy progressed only haltingly because of lay and ecclesiastical prohibitions of the dissection of human cadavers (the Christian view was that the interior of the body was "God's province"; see Grice, 2001). Charles Darwin was repeatedly denounced. Paul Broca's Society of Anthropology was opposed in France in the nineteenth century because knowledge about human beings was thought to be subversive to the state.

Each scientific step to greater knowledge about human beings has evoked opposition. This opposition eventually dissipated, however, when people came to realize that science does not defile humanity by its investigations but contributes to human fulfillment by widening the sphere of knowledge. Who now believes that astronomy's mapping of the galaxies and its intricate theories about the composition of distant stars destroy our wonder at the universe? Who would substitute the health care available in their community for that available before human cadavers were routinely dissected? An empirical attitude toward the stars or the human body has not diminished humanity. More recently, Darwin's evolutionary synthesis laid the foundation for startling advances in genetics and biology. Nevertheless, as we get closer to the nature of human beings and their origins, vestiges of opposition remain. In the United States, some politicians continue to press for the teaching of creationism in the public schools, and surveys show that the scientific fact that humans evolved by natural selection is not accepted by a large portion of the U.S. (though not the European and Canadian) public (Barnes, Keilholtz, & Alberstadt, 2008; Frazier, 2009, 2010; Laden, 2008). If evolutionary biology, with its long and impressive record of scientific achievements, still engenders public opposition, is it any wonder that psychology, the most recent discipline to bring long-held beliefs about human beings under scientific scrutiny, currently provokes people to deny its validity?

What, Then, Is Science?

In order to understand what psychology is, we must understand what science is. We can begin by dealing with what science is not. First, science is not defined by subject matter. Any aspect of the universe is fair game for the development of a scientific discipline, including all aspects of human behavior. We cannot divide the universe into "scientific" and "nonscientific" topics. Although strong forces throughout history have tried to place human beings outside the sphere of scientific investigation, they have been unsuccessful, as we shall see. The reactions against psychology as a scientific discipline probably represent the modern remnants of this ancient struggle.

Science is also not defined by the use of particular experimental apparatus. It is not the test tube, the computer, the electronic equipment, or the investigator's white coat that defines science. These are the trappings of science but are not its defining features. Science is, rather, a way of thinking about and observing the universe that leads to a deep understanding of its workings.

In the remainder of this chapter, we shall discuss three important and interrelated features that define science: (1) the use of systematic empiricism; (2) the production of public knowledge; and (3) the examination of solvable problems. Although we shall examine each feature separately, remember that the three connect to form a coherent general structure. (For a more detailed discussion of the general characteristics of a science, see the works of Bronowski, Haack, Medawar, Popper, and Sagan listed in the references section of this book.)

Systematic Empiricism

If you look up the word empiricism in any dictionary, you will find that it means "the practice of relying on observation." Scientists find out about the world by examining it. The fact that this point may seem obvious to you is an indication of the spread of the scientific attitude in the past couple of centuries. In the past, it has not always seemed so obvious. Recall the example of Galileo. With his primitive telescope, Galileo claimed to have seen moons around the planet Jupiter at a time when it was thought by learned people that there were only seven "heavenly bodies" (five planets, the sun, and the moon). This was at a time when it was thought that knowledge was best obtained through pure thought or through appeal to authority. Some contemporary scholars refused to look into Galileo's telescope. Others said the telescope was designed to trick. Still others said that it worked on Earth but not in the sky (Shermer, 2011). Another scholar, Francesco Sizi, attempted to refute Galileo, not with observations, but with the following argument:

> There are seven windows in the head, two nostrils, two ears, two eyes and a mouth; so in the heavens there are two favorable stars, two unpropitious, two luminaries, and Mercury alone undecided and indifferent. From which and many other similar phenomena of nature such as the seven metals, etc., which it were tedious to enumerate, we gather that the number of planets is necessarily seven.... Besides, the Jews and other ancient nations, as well as modern Europeans, have adopted the division of the week into seven days, and have named them from the seven planets; now if we increase the number of planets, this whole system falls to the ground.... Moreover, the satellites are invisible to the naked eye and therefore can have no influence on the earth and therefore would be useless and therefore do not exist. (Holton & Roller, 1958, p. 160)

The point is not that the argument is laughably idiotic, but that it was seen as a suitable rebuttal to an actual observation! We laugh now because we have the benefit of hindsight. Three centuries of the demonstrated power of the empirical approach give us an edge on poor Sizi. Take away those years of empiricism, and many of us might have been there nodding our heads and urging him on. No, the empirical approach is not necessarily obvious, which is why we often have to teach it, even in a society that is dominated by science.

Empiricism pure and simple is not enough, however. Note that the heading for this section is "*Systematic* Empiricism." Observation is fine and necessary, but pure, unstructured observation of the natural world will not lead to scientific knowledge. Write down every observation you make from the time you get up in the morning to the time you go to bed on a given day. When you finish, you will have a great number of facts, but you will not have a greater understanding of the world. Scientific observation is termed *systematic* because it is structured so that the results of the observation reveal something about the underlying nature of the world. Scientific observations are usually theory driven; they test different explanations of the nature of the world. They are structured so that, depending on the outcome of the observation, some theories are supported and others rejected.

Publicly Verifiable Knowledge: Replication and Peer Review

Scientific knowledge is public in a special sense. By *public*, we, of course, do not mean that scientific observations are posted on community center bulletin boards. Instead, we refer to the fact that scientific knowledge does not exist solely in the mind of a particular individual. In an important sense, scientific knowledge does not exist at all until it has been submitted to the scientific community for criticism and empirical testing by others. Knowledge that is considered "special"—the province of the thought processes of a particular individual, immune from scrutiny and criticism by others—can never have the status of scientific knowledge.

Science makes the idea of public verifiability concrete via the procedure of *replication*. In order to be considered in the realm of science, a finding must be presented to the scientific community in a way that enables other scientists to attempt the same experiment and obtain the same results. When this occurs, we say that the finding has been replicated. Scientists use replication to define the idea of public knowledge. Replication ensures that a particular finding is not due simply to the errors or biases of a particular investigator. In short, for a finding to be accepted by the scientific community, it must be possible for someone other than the original investigator to duplicate it. When a finding is presented in this way, it becomes public. It is no longer the sole possession of the original researcher; it is instead available for other investigators to extend, criticize, or apply in their own ways.

The poet John Donne told us that "no man is an island." In science, no researcher is an island. Each investigator is connected to the scientific community and its knowledge base. It is this interconnection that enables science to grow cumulatively. Researchers constantly build on previous knowledge in order to go beyond what is currently known. This process is possible only if previous knowledge is stated in such a way that any investigator can use it to build on.

By *publicly verifiable knowledge*, then, we mean findings presented to the scientific community in such a way that they can be replicated, criticized, or extended by anyone in the community. This is a most important criterion not only for scientists but also for the layperson, who, as a consumer, must evaluate scientific information presented in the media. As we shall see in Chapter 12, one important way to distinguish charlatans and practitioners of pseudoscience from legitimate scientists is that the former often bypass the normal channels of scientific publication and instead go straight to the media with their "findings." One ironclad criterion that will always work for the public when presented with scientific claims of uncertain validity is the question, Have the findings been published in a recognized scientific journal that uses some type of peer review procedure? The answer to this question will almost always separate pseudoscientific claims from the real thing.

Peer review is a procedure in which each paper submitted to a research journal is critiqued by several scientists, who then submit their criticisms to an editor. The editor is usually a scientist with an extensive history of work in the specialty area covered by the journal. The editor decides whether the weight of opinion warrants publication of the paper, publication after further experimentation and statistical analysis, or rejection because the research is flawed or trivial. Most journals carry a statement of editorial policy in each issue, so it is easy to check whether a journal is peer reviewed.

Not all information in peer-reviewed scientific journals is necessarily correct, but at least it has met a criterion of peer criticism and scrutiny. Peer review is a minimal criterion, not a stringent one, because most scientific disciplines publish dozens of different journals of varying quality. Most scientific ideas can get published somewhere in the legitimate literature if they meet some rudimentary standards. The idea that only a narrow range of data and theory can get published in science is false. This is an idea often suggested by purveyors of bogus remedies and therapies who try to convince the media and the public that they have been shut out of scientific outlets by a conspiracy of "orthodox science." But consider for a minute just how many legitimate outlets there are in a field like psychology. The APA database *PsycINFO* summarizes articles from over 2,000 different journals. Most of these journals are peer reviewed. Virtually all halfway legitimate theories and experiments can find their way into this vast array of publication outlets.

Again, I am not suggesting that all ideas published in peer-reviewed psychological journals are necessarily valid. On the contrary, I emphasized earlier that this is only a minimal criterion. However, the point is that the failure of an idea, a theory, a claim, or a therapy to have adequate documentation in the peer-reviewed literature of a scientific discipline is a very sure sign. Particularly when the lack of evidence is accompanied by a media campaign to publicize the claim, *it is a sure sign that the idea, theory, or therapy is bogus.* For example, in a famous Pennsylvania court case in 2005 regarding attempts to teach creationism in school biology classes, one of the witnesses advocating for intelligent design (a form of creationism) admitted that "he was unable to name any peer-reviewed research generated by intelligent design, though the movement has been around for more than a decade" (Talbot, 2005, p. 68).

The mechanisms of peer review vary somewhat from discipline to discipline, but the underlying rationale is the same. Peer review is one way (replication is another) that science institutionalizes the attitudes of objectivity and public criticism. Ideas and experimentation undergo a honing process in which they are submitted to other critical minds for evaluation.

Ideas that survive this critical process have begun to meet the criterion of public verifiability. The peer review process is far from perfect, but it is really the only consumer protection that we have. To ignore it is to leave ourselves at the mercy of the multimillion-dollar pseudoscience industries that are so good at manipulating the media to their own ends (see Chapter 12). In subsequent chapters, we will discuss in much more detail the high price we pay for ignoring the checks and balances inherent in the true scientific practice of psychology.

Empirically Solvable Problems: Scientists' Search for Testable Theories

Science deals with solvable, or specifiable, problems. This means that the types of questions that scientists address are potentially answerable by means of currently available empirical techniques. If a problem is not solvable or a theory is not testable by the empirical techniques that scientists have at hand, then scientists will not attack it. For example, the question "Will three-year-old children given structured language stimulation during day care be ready for reading instruction at an earlier age than children not given such extra stimulation?" represents a scientific problem. It is answerable by currently available empirical methods. The question "Are human beings inherently good or inherently evil?" is not an empirical question and, thus, is simply not in the realm of science. Likewise, the question "What is the meaning of life?" is not an empirical question and so is outside the realm of science.

Science advances by positing theories to account for particular phenomena in the world, by deriving predictions from these theories, by testing the predictions empirically, and by modifying the theories based on the tests. The sequence might be portrayed as follows: theory → prediction → test → theory modification. So what a scientist often means by the term *solvable problem* is "*testable* theory." What makes a theory testable? The theory must have specific implications for observable events in the natural world; this is what is meant by *empirically testable*. This criterion of testability is often called the *falsifiability criterion*, and it is the subject of Chapter 2.

By saying that scientists tackle empirically solvable problems, we do not mean to imply that different classes of problems are inherently solvable or unsolvable and that this division is fixed forever. Quite the contrary: Some problems that are currently unsolvable may become solvable as theory and empirical techniques become more sophisticated. For example, decades ago historians would not have believed that the controversial issue of whether Thomas Jefferson fathered a child by his slave Sally Hemings was an empirically solvable question. Yet, by 1998, this problem had become solvable through advances in genetic technology, and a paper was published in the journal *Nature* (Foster et al., 1998) indicating that it was highly probable that Jefferson was the father of Eston Hemings Jefferson.

This is how science in general has developed and how new sciences have come into existence. There is always ample room for disagreement about what is currently solvable. Scientists themselves often disagree on this point as it relates to a particular problem. Thus, although all scientists agree on the solvability criterion, they may disagree on its specific applications. Nobel laureate Peter Medawar titled one of his books *The Art of the Soluble* (1967) to illustrate that part of the creativity involved in science is finding the problem on the farthest edge of the frontier of human knowledge that will yield to empirical techniques.

Psychology itself provides many good examples of the development from the unsolvable to the solvable. There are many questions (such as "How does a child acquire the language of his or her parents?" "Why do we forget things we once knew?" "How does being in a group change a person's behavior and thinking?") that had been the subjects of philosophical speculation for centuries before anyone recognized that they could be addressed by empirical means. As this recognition slowly developed, psychology coalesced as a collection of problems concerning behavior in a variety of domains. Psychological issues gradually became separated from philosophy, and a separate empirical discipline evolved.

Cognitive psychologist Steven Pinker (1997) discusses how ignorance can be divided into *problems* and *mysteries.* In the case of problems, we know that an answer is possible and what that answer might look like even though we might not actually have the answer yet. In the case of mysteries, we can't even conceive of what an answer might look like. Using this terminology, we can see that science is a process that turns mysteries into problems. In fact, Pinker (1997) noted that he wrote his book *How the Mind Works* "because dozens of mysteries of the mind, from mental images to romantic love, have recently been upgraded to problems" (p. ix).

Psychology and Folk Wisdom: The Problem With "Common Sense"

We all have implicit models of behavior that govern our interactions and our thoughts about ourselves and other people. Indeed, some social, personality, and cognitive psychologists study the nature of these implicit psychological theories. Rarely do we state our theories clearly and logically. Instead, we usually become aware of them only when attention is drawn to them or when we find them challenged in some way. Actually, our personal models of behavior are not really coherent in the way that an actual theory would have to be. Instead, we carry around a ragbag of general principles, homilies, and clichés about human behavior that we draw on when we feel that we need an explanation. The problem with this commonsense knowledge about behavior is that much of it contradicts itself and is, therefore, unfalsifiable (the principle of falsifiability is the topic of the next chapter).

Often a person uses some folk proverb to explain a behavioral event even though, on an earlier occasion, this same person used a directly contradictory folk proverb to explain the same type of event. For example, most of us have heard or said, "look before you leap." Now there's a useful, straightforward bit of behavioral advice—except that I vaguely remember admonishing on occasion, "he who hesitates is lost." And "absence makes the heart grow fonder" is a pretty clear prediction of an emotional reaction to environmental events. But then what about "out of sight, out of mind"? And if "haste makes waste," why do we sometimes hear that "time waits for no man"? How could the saying "two heads are better than one" not be true? Except that "too many cooks spoil the broth." If I think "it's better to be safe than sorry," why do I also believe "nothing ventured, nothing gained"? And if "opposites attract," why do "birds of a feather flock together"? I have counseled many students to "never to put off until tomorrow what you can do today." But I hope my last advisee has never heard me say this, because I just told him, "cross that bridge when you come to it."

The enormous appeal of clichés like these is that, taken together as implicit "explanations" of behavior, they cannot be refuted. No matter what happens, one of these explanations will be cited to cover it. No wonder we all think we are such excellent judges of human behavior and personality. We have an explanation for anything and everything that happens. Folk wisdom is cowardly in the sense that it takes no risk that it might be refuted.

That folk wisdom is "after the fact" wisdom, and that it actually is useless in a truly predictive sense, is why sociologist Duncan Watts titled one of his books: *Everything Is Obvious—Once You Know the Answer* (2011). Watts discusses a classic paper by Lazarsfeld (1949) in which, over 60 years ago, he was dealing with the common criticism that "social science doesn't tell us anything that we don't already know." Lazarsfeld listed a series of findings from a massive survey of 600,000 soldiers who had served during World War II; for example, that men from rural backgrounds were in better spirits during their time of service than soldiers from city backgrounds. People tend to find all of the survey results to be pretty obvious. In this example, for instance, people tend to think it obvious that rural men would have been used to harsher physical conditions and thus would have adapted better to the conditions of military life. It is likewise with all of the other findings—people find them pretty obvious. Lazarsfeld then reveals his punchline: All of the findings were the opposite of what was originally stated. For example, it was *actually* the case that men from city backgrounds were in better spirits during their time of service than soldiers from rural backgrounds. The last part of the learning exercise is for people to realize how easily they would have explained just the opposite finding. In the case of the actual outcome, people tend to explain it (when told of it first) by saying that they expected it because city men are used to working in crowded conditions and under hierarchical authority. They never realize how easily they would have concocted an explanation for exactly the opposite finding.

So sometimes our implicit psychological theories can't be refuted. We will see in the next chapter why this inability to be refuted makes such theories not very useful. However, a further problem occurs even in cases in which our folk beliefs do have some specificity, that is, even when they are empirically testable. The problem is that psychological research has shown that, when many common cultural beliefs about behavior are subjected to empirical test, they turn out to be false.

It is not difficult to generate instances of folk beliefs (or "common sense") that are wrong. Take, for example, the idea that children who excel academically or who read a lot are not socially or physically adept. This idea still circulates in our society even though it is utterly false. There is voluminous evidence that, contrary to "commonsense" folk belief, readers and academically inclined individuals are more physically robust and are more socially involved than are people who do not read (Zill & Winglee, 1990). For example, children high in scholastic achievement are more likely to be accepted by their peers than children low in achievement. People who are avid readers are more likely to play sports, jog, camp, hike, and do car repair than are people who do not read very much.

Many of our folk beliefs about behavior arise and take on a life of their own. For example, throughout the 1990s the folk belief developed in our society and in schools that low self-esteem was a cause of aggression. But empirical investigations indicated that there was no connection between aggression and low self-esteem (Baumeister, Campbell, Krueger, & Vohs, 2003, 2005; Krueger, Vohs, & Baumeister, 2008). If anything, the opposite appeared to be the case—aggression is more often associated with high self-esteem. Likewise, an extremely popular hypothesis for the past couple of decades has been that school achievement problems are the result of low self-esteem in students. In fact, it turns out that the relationship between self-esteem and school achievement is more likely to be in the opposite direction from that assumed by educators and parents. It is superior accomplishment in school (and in other aspects of life) that leads to high self-esteem and not the reverse.

Consider another commonplace expression of folk wisdom: "children bring happiness to their parents." This statement might have some degree of truth if used to refer to how we view the effects of our children from the vantage point of retirement. People do indeed *look back* on their children as having brought them great happiness. The problem is that people tend to confuse the perspective of looking back on an event with the actual experience of the event. Having children turns out to be a case where the two perspectives are very different. Looking back on having children from old age does indeed make people happy. However, in terms of ongoing, moment-to-moment happiness (as opposed to retrospectively looking back), children actually make people less happy. There is now a fairly sizable literature using so-called experience-sampling methods to look at how happy people are at various points in time (Brooks, 2008; Gilbert, 2006; Gorchoff, John, & Helson,

2008; Lyubomirsky & Boehm, 2010; Wargo, 2007), and this research shows a number of trends, for example, that getting married increases happiness. This literature also shows that parental happiness drops with the arrival of the first child. It rebounds a little until the first child reaches adolescence, and then it drops even further. Marital happiness returns to childless levels only when the last child leaves home.

In short, the folk wisdom "children bring happiness to their parents," when subjected to scientific examination, turns out to have a number of complications. It is true only from the retrospective standpoint—"children bring happiness" when they have finally left home and we can appreciate the accomplishment of raising them! This is not, though, what the phrase is often used to imply. It is often used to imply that having children will bring you happiness right *now*—in your short-term future. This is where this "folk wisdom" is most egregiously wrong.

Another example of folk wisdom gone wrong is the common admonition to students that if they become unsure about an answer that they have given on a multiple-choice test they should never switch from their original choice. Not only do most students think that they should not switch when uncertain of an answer, but even Barron's Guide to GRE Preparation advises "Exercise great caution if you decide to change an answer. Experience indicates that many students who change answers change to the wrong answer" (Kruger, Wirtz, & Miller, 2005, p. 725). This advice is completely wrong. The advice is wrong because the folk myth that changing answers decreases a person's score is dead wrong. Actual research has shown that when doubts about a multiple-choice answer arise, students are better off switching from their first answer (Kruger et al., 2005; Lilienfeld, Lynn, Ruscio, & Beyerstein, 2010).

A case where we can really see folk wisdom run amok is in the folk myth that we use only 10 percent of our brainpower. Despite having absolutely no basis in cognitive neuroscience (Boyd, 2008; Lilienfeld et al., 2010), this one has been around for decades and has taken on the status of what has been termed a "psycho-fact"—a statement about psychology that is not true but which has been repeated so much that the average person thinks that it is a fact. It is likewise with the belief that some people are "left-brained" and other people are "right-brained"; or that certain aspects of personality are controlled by the left side of the brain and other aspects of personality by the right side. Although modern neuroscience research does show subtle specializations throughout the brain, the strongly stated popularizations of this idea in terms of "left" or "right" are invariably nonsense—particularly in the context of the finding that our brains work in an integrated fashion (Lilienfeld et al., 2010; Radford, 2011).

Folk beliefs are not always immune to evidence. Sometimes, when the contradictory evidence becomes too widely known, folk psychology ("common sense") does change. For example, years ago, one widely held cliché about children was "Early ripe, early rot" (Fancher, 1985, p. 141).

The cliché reflected the belief that childhood precocity was associated with adult abnormality, a belief sustained by many anecdotes about childhood prodigies who came to ruin in later life. In this case, the psychological evidence documenting the inaccuracy of the cliché has been absorbed into the general culture, and you will almost never hear this bit of folk "wisdom" anymore.

This last example also carries a warning by reminding us to beware of today's "common sense"—because it is not difficult to show that yesterday's common sense has often turned into today's nonsense. After all, common sense is what "everybody knows," right? Right. Well, everybody knows that women shouldn't be able to vote, right? Everybody knows that African Americans shouldn't be taught to read, right? Everybody knows that individuals with disabilities should be institutionalized out of the sight of society, right? In fact, 150 years ago, all of these beliefs were what "everybody knew." Of course, we now recognize this common sense of the past as nonsense—as beliefs based on totally unverified assumptions. But in these examples we can see the critical role that psychology plays vis-à-vis common sense. Psychology tests the empirical basis of the assumptions of common sense. Sometimes the assumptions do not hold up when tested, as we saw in many of the previous examples. From the examples discussed—and many more could be cited—we can see that psychology's role as the empirical tester of much folk wisdom often brings it into conflict with many widely held cultural beliefs. Psychology is often the bearer of the "bad tidings" that comfortable folk beliefs do not stand up to the cold light of day. Perhaps it is not surprising that many people would like not only to ignore the message but also to do away with the messenger.

Psychology as a Young Science

There has always been opposition to an empirically based psychology. Just a little more than 100 years ago, Cambridge University refused to establish a psychophysics laboratory because the study of such a topic would "insult religion by putting the human soul on a pair of scales" (Hearst, 1979, p. 7). Psychology's battle to establish its problems as empirically solvable has only recently been won. But as the science progresses, psychologists will address more and more issues that are the subject of strongly held beliefs about human beings because many of these problems are empirically testable. Psychologists now study such highly charged topics as the development of moral reasoning, the psychology of romantic love, the nature of racial prejudice, the efficacy of prayer, and the psychological and social determinants of religious beliefs. Studies of childhood sexual activity have incited much controversy (Lilienfeld, 2010; Rind, 2008). Some people object to empirical investigation in these areas; yet there has been scientific progress in each one of them.

Past president of the APA Gerald Koocher (2006) boldly warned us about the nature of psychological research by titling one of his presidential columns "Psychological Science is not Politically Correct." In the article, he discussed research on topics such as the causes of obesity, what determines political attitudes, the relation between religion and sexual behavior, and domestic violence. He pointed out that the research findings on each of these topics have proved controversial, but that "psychological science cannot be held to a standard of political correctness by social liberals or conservatives" (p. 5).

Psychology is often in a no-win situation as a discipline. On one hand, some people object to calling psychology a science and deny that psychologists can establish empirical facts about behavior. On the other hand, there are those who object to the investigation of certain areas of human behavior because they fear that facts uncovered by psychology might threaten their beliefs. Skinnerian psychologists regularly deal with these contradictory criticisms. For instance, critics have argued that the laws of reinforcement formulated by behaviorists do not apply to human behavior. At the same time, other critics are concerned that the laws will be used for the rigid and inhumane control of people. Thus, the behaviorists are faced with some critics who deny that their laws can be applied and others who charge that their laws can be applied too easily!

Examples such as this arise because the relatively new science of psychology has just begun to uncover facts about aspects of behavior that have previously escaped study. The relative youth of psychology as a science partially explains why many people are confused about the discipline. Nevertheless, during the past several decades, psychology has become firmly established in the interconnecting structure of knowledge that we call science. Failure to appreciate this fact is the source of almost all of the confused thinking about psychology that you will encounter.

Summary

Psychology is an immensely diverse discipline covering a range of subjects that are not always tied together by common concepts. Instead, what unifies the discipline is that it uses scientific methods to understand behavior. The scientific method is not a strict set of rules; instead it is defined by some very general principles. Three of the most important are that (1) science employs methods of systematic empiricism; (2) it aims for knowledge that is publicly verifiable; and (3) it seeks problems that are empirically solvable and that yield testable theories (the subject of the next chapter). The structured and controlled observations that define systematic empiricism are the subject of several later chapters of this book. Science renders knowledge public by procedures such as peer review and mechanisms such as replication.

Psychology is a young science and, thus, is often in conflict with so-called folk wisdom. This conflict is typical of all new sciences, but understanding it helps to explain some of the hostility directed toward psychology as a discipline. This characteristic of questioning common wisdom also makes psychology an exciting field. Many people are drawn to the discipline because it holds out the possibility of actually testing "common sense" that has been accepted without question for centuries.

CHAPTER 2

Falsifiability: How to Foil Little Green Men in the Head

In 1793, a severe epidemic of yellow fever struck Philadelphia. One of the leading doctors in the city at the time was Benjamin Rush, a signer of the Declaration of Independence. During the outbreak, Rush was one of the few physicians who were available to treat literally thousands of yellow fever cases. Rush adhered to a theory of medicine that dictated that illnesses accompanied by fever should be treated by vigorous bloodletting (the removal of blood from the body either by using an instrument such as a lancet or by the application of leeches). He administered this treatment to many patients, including himself when he came down with the illness. Critics charged that his treatments were more dangerous than the disease. However, following the epidemic, Rush became even more confident of the effectiveness of his treatment, even though many of his patients had died. Why?

One writer summarized Rush's attitude this way: "Convinced of the correctness of his theory of medicine and lacking a means for the systematic study of treatment outcome, he attributed each new instance of improvement to the efficacy of his treatment and each new death that occurred despite it to the severity of the disease" (Eisenberg, 1977, p. 1106). In other words, if the patient got better, this improvement was taken as proof that bloodletting worked. If instead the patient died, Rush interpreted this to mean that the patient had been too ill for *any* treatment to work. We now know that Rush's critics were right: His treatments were as dangerous as the disease. In this chapter, we will discuss how Rush went wrong. His error illustrates one of the most important principles of scientific thinking, one that is particularly useful in evaluating psychological claims.

In this chapter, we focus in more detail on the third general characteristic of science that we discussed in Chapter 1: Scientists deal with solvable problems. What scientists most often mean by a *solvable problem* is a "testable theory." The way scientists make sure they are dealing with testable theories is by ensuring that their theories are falsifiable, that is, that they have implications for actual events in the natural world. We will see why what is called *the falsifiability criterion* is so important in psychology.

Theories and the Falsifiability Criterion

Benjamin Rush fell into a fatal trap when assessing the outcome of his treatment. His method of evaluating the evidence made it impossible to conclude that his treatment did not work. If the recovery of a patient meant confirmation of his treatment (and, hence, his theory of medicine), then it only seems fair that the death of a patient should have meant disconfirmation. Instead, he rationalized away these disconfirmations. By interpreting the evidence as he did, Rush violated one of the most important rules regarding the construction and testing of theories in science: He made it impossible to falsify his theory.

Scientific theories must always be stated in such a way that the predictions derived from them could potentially be shown to be false. Thus, the methods of evaluating new evidence relevant to a particular theory must always include the possibility that the data will falsify the theory. This principle is often termed the *falsifiability criterion,* and its importance in scientific progress has been most forcefully articulated by Karl Popper, a philosopher of science whose writings are read widely by working scientists.

The falsifiability criterion states that, for a theory to be useful, the predictions drawn from it must be specific. The theory must go out on a limb, so to speak, because in telling us what *should* happen, the theory must also imply that certain things will *not* happen. If these latter things *do* happen, then we have a clear signal that something is wrong with the theory: It may need to be modified, or we may need to look for an entirely new theory. Either way, we shall end up with a theory that is nearer to the truth. By contrast, if a theory does not rule out any possible observations, then the theory can never be changed, and we are frozen into our current way of thinking, with no possibility of progress. Thus, a successful theory is not one that accounts for every possible outcome because such a theory robs itself of any predictive power.

Because we shall often refer to the evaluation of theories in the remainder of this book, we must clear up one common misconception surrounding the word *theory*. The misconception is reflected in the commonly used phrase "Oh, it's only a theory." This phrase captures what *laypeople* often mean when they use the word *theory*: an unverified hypothesis, a mere guess, a hunch. It implies that one theory is as good as another. This is most definitely *not* the way the word *theory* is used in science! When scientists refer to theories, they do not mean unverified guesses.

A theory in science is an interrelated set of concepts that is used to explain a body of data and to make predictions about the results of future experiments. *Hypotheses* are specific predictions that are derived from theories (which are more general and comprehensive). Currently viable theories are those that have had many of their hypotheses confirmed. The theoretical structures of such theories are, thus, consistent with a large number of observations. However, when the database begins to contradict the hypotheses derived from a theory, scientists begin trying to construct a new theory (or, more often, simply make adjustments in the previous theory) that will provide a better interpretation of the data. Thus, the theories that are under scientific discussion are those that have been verified to some extent and that do not make many predictions that are contradicted by the available data. They are *not* mere guesses or hunches.

The difference between the layperson's and the scientist's use of the word *theory* has often been exploited by some religious fundamentalists who want creationism taught in the public schools (Miller, 2008; Scott, 2005). Their argument often is "After all, evolution is only a theory." This statement is intended to suggest the *layperson's* usage of the term *theory* to mean "only a guess." However, the theory of evolution by natural selection is not a theory in the layperson's sense (to the contrary, in the layperson's sense, it would be called a fact; see Randall, 2005). Instead, it is a theory in the *scientific* sense. It is a conceptual structure that is supported by a large and varied set of data (Dawkins, 2010; Shermer, 2006; Wilson, 2007). It is not a mere guess, equal to any other guess. Instead, it interlocks with knowledge in a host of other disciplines, including geology, physics, chemistry, and all aspects of biology. The distinguished biologist Theodosius Dobzhansky (1973) made this point in a famous article titled "Nothing in Biology Makes Sense Except in the Light of Evolution."

The Theory of Knocking Rhythms

A hypothetical example will show how the falsifiability criterion works. A student knocks at my door. A colleague in my office with me has a theory that makes predictions about the rhythms that different types of people use to knock. Before I open the door, my colleague predicts that the person behind it is a female. I open the door and, indeed, the student is a female. Later I tell my colleague that I am impressed, but only mildly so because he had a 50 percent chance of being correct even without his "theory of knocking rhythms"—actually even higher, because on most campuses females outnumber males. He says he can do better. Another knock comes. My colleague tells me it is a male under 22 years old. I open the door to find a male student whom I know to be just out of high school. I comment that I am somewhat impressed because our university has a considerable number of students over the age of 22. Yet I still maintain that, of course, young males are quite common on campus. Thinking me hard to please, my colleague proposes one last test. After the next knock, my colleague predicts, "Female, 30 years old, 5 feet 2 inches tall, carrying a book and a purse in the left hand and knocking with the right." After opening the door and confirming the prediction completely, I have quite a different response. I say that, assuming my colleague did not play a trick and arrange for these people to appear at my door, I am now in fact extremely impressed.

Why the difference in my reactions? Why do my friend's three predictions yield three different responses, ranging from "So what?" to "Wow!"? The answer has to do with the specificity and precision of the predictions. The more specific predictions made a greater impact when they were confirmed. Notice, however, that the specificity varied directly with the falsifiability. The more specific and precise the prediction was, the more potential observations there were that could have falsified it. For example, there are a lot of people who are *not* 30-year-old females and 5 feet 2 inches tall. Note that implicitly, by my varied reactions, I signaled that I would be more impressed by a theory that made predictions that maximized the number of events that should *not* occur.

Good theories, then, make predictions that expose themselves to falsification. Bad theories do not put themselves in jeopardy in this way. They make predictions that are so general that they are almost bound to be true (e.g., the next person to knock on my door will be less than 100 years old) or are phrased in such a way that they are completely protected from falsification (as in the Benjamin Rush example). In fact, a theory can be so protected from falsifiability that it is simply no longer considered scientific at all. Indeed, it was philosopher Karl Popper's attempt to define the criteria that separate science from nonscience that led him to emphasize the importance of the falsifiability principle. There is a direct link here to psychology and to our discussion of Freud in Chapter 1.

Freud and Falsifiability

In the early decades of the twentieth century, Popper was searching for the underlying reasons that some scientific theories seem to lead to advances in knowledge and others lead to intellectual stagnation (Hacohen, 2000). Einstein's general relativity theory, for example, led to startlingly new observations (for instance, that the light from a distant star bends when it passes near the sun) precisely because its predictions were structured so that many possible events could have contradicted them and, thus, falsified the theory.

Popper reasoned that this is not true of stagnant theories—and pointed to Freudian psychoanalysis as an example. Freudian theory uses a complicated conceptual structure that explains human behavior after the fact—that is, after it has occurred—but does not predict things in advance. In short,

Freudian theory can explain everything. However, as Popper argued, it is precisely this property that makes it scientifically useless. It makes no specific predictions. Adherents of psychoanalytic theory spend much time and effort in getting the theory to explain every known human event, from individual quirks of behavior to large-scale social phenomena. But their success in making the theory a rich source of after-the-fact explanation robs it of any scientific utility. Freudian psychoanalytic theory currently plays a much larger role as a spur to the literary imagination than as a theory in contemporary psychology. Its demise within psychology can be traced in part to its failure to satisfy the falsifiability criterion (Wade & Tavris, 2008).

But the existence of such unfalsifiable theories does real damage. For example, explanations for the cause of autism (in part a genetically determined disorder) were led down a blind alley by psychoanalytic explanations for the condition. Influenced by psychoanalytic ideas, psychologist Bruno Bettelheim popularized the now-discredited notion of "refrigerator mothers" as the cause and thought that "the precipitating factor in infantile autism is the parent's wish that his child should not exist" (Offit, 2008, p. 3). Ideas like this not only did damage, but they set back the study of autism.

As another example, consider the history of Gilles de la Tourette syndrome. This is a disorder characterized by physical tics and twitches that may involve any part of the body, as well as vocal symptoms such as grunts and barks, echolalia (involuntary repetition of the words of others), and coprolalia (compulsive repetition of obscene words). Tourette syndrome is an organically based disorder of the central nervous system and is now often successfully treated with drug therapies (Scahill et al., 2006; Smith, Polloway, Patton, & Dowdy, 2008). Throughout history, individuals with Tourette syndrome have been persecuted—earlier as witches by religious authorities, and in more modern times by being subjected to exorcisms (Hines, 2003). Importantly, understanding of the cause and treatment of the disorder was considerably hampered from 1921 to 1955, when explanations and treatments for Tourette syndrome were dominated by psychoanalytic conceptualizations (see Kushner, 1999). Author after author presented unfalsifiable psychoanalytic explanations for the syndrome. The resulting array of vague explanations created a conceptual sludge that obscured the true nature of the syndrome and probably impeded scientific progress toward an accurate understanding of it. For example, according to one author,

> [Tourette syndrome is] a classic example of the retrogressive effect of psychoanalysis on the investigation of brain disease. La Tourette had attributed the disease to a degenerative process of the brain. After Freud's theories became fashionable in the early decades of the present century, attention in such conditions was deflected from the brain.... The consequence of this retrograde movement was that patients tended to be referred to psychiatrists (usually of a psychoanalytic persuasion) rather than to neurologists, so that physical examinations and investigation were not performed. (Thornton, 1986, p. 210)

Shapiro, Shapiro, Bruun, and Sweet (1978) described one psychoanalyst who thought that his patient was "reluctant to give up the tic because it became a source of erotic pleasure to her and an expression of unconscious sexual strivings." Another considered the tics "stereotyped equivalents of onanism....The libido connected with the genital sensation was displaced into other parts of the body." A third considered the tic a "conversion symptom at the anal-sadistic level." A fourth thought that a person with Tourette syndrome had a "compulsive character, as well as a narcissistic orientation" and that the patient's tics "represent[ed] an affective syndrome, a defense against the intended affect."

In fact, these examples were numerous and typical in their uninformed overconfidence. Developmental psychologist Jerome Kagan (2006) tells us how "Sandor Ferenczi, a disciple of Freud *who had never seen a patient with Tourette's syndrome* [italics added], made an equally serious error when he wrote that the frequent facial tics of people with Tourette's were the result of a repressed urge to masturbate" (p. 179).

The summary by Shapiro et al. (1978) of the resulting theoretical situation demonstrates quite well the harmful effects of ignoring the falsifiability criterion:

> Psychoanalytic theorizing of this kind in effect leaves no base untouched. Tics are a conversion symptom but not hysterical, anal but also erotic, volitional but also compulsive, organic but also dynamic in origin....These psychological labels, diagnoses, and treatments were unfortunately imposed on patients and their families, usually with little humility, considerable dogmatism, and with much harm....These papers, because of their subsequent widespread influence, had a calamitous effect on the understanding and treatment of this syndrome. (pp. 39–42, 50, 63)

Progress in the treatment and understanding of Tourette syndrome began to occur only when researchers recognized that the psychoanalytic "explanations" were useless. These explanations were enticing because they seemed to explain things. In fact, they explained everything—after the fact. However, the explanations they provided created only the illusion of understanding. By attempting to explain everything after the fact, they barred the door to any advance. Progress occurs only when a theory does not predict *everything* but instead makes specific predictions that tell us—in advance—something specific about the world. The predictions derived from such a theory may be wrong, of course, but this is a strength, not a weakness.

The Little Green Men

It is not difficult to recognize unfalsifiable conceptualizations when one is detached from the subject matter and particularly when one has the benefit of historical hindsight (as in the Benjamin Rush example). It is also easy to detect unfalsifiable conceptualizations when the instance is obviously concocted. For example, it is a little known fact that I have discovered the underlying brain mechanism that controls behavior. You will soon be reading about this discovery (in the *National Enquirer*, available at your local supermarket). In the left hemisphere of the brain, near the language areas, reside two tiny green men. They have the power to control the electrochemical processes taking place in many areas of the brain. And, well, to make a long story short, they basically control everything. There is one difficulty, however. The little green men have the ability to detect any intrusion into the brain (surgery, X-rays, etc.), and when they do sense such an intrusion, they tend to disappear. (I forgot to mention that they have the power to become invisible.)

I have no doubt insulted your intelligence by using an example more suitable for elementary school students. I have obviously concocted this example so that my hypothesis about the little green men could never be shown to be wrong. However, consider this. As a lecturer and public speaker on psychological topics, I am often confronted by people who ask me why I have not lectured on all the startling new discoveries in extrasensory perception (ESP) and parapsychology that have been made in the past few years. I have to inform these questioners that most of what they have heard about these subjects has undoubtedly come from the general media rather than from scientifically respectable sources. In fact, some scientists have looked at these claims and have not been able to replicate the findings. I remind the audience that replication of a finding is critical to its acceptance as an established scientific fact and that this is particularly true in the case of results that contradict either previous data or established theory.

I further admit that many scientists have lost patience with ESP research. Although one reason is undoubtedly that the area is tainted by fraud, charlatanism, and media exploitation, perhaps the most important reason for scientific disenchantment is the existence of what Martin Gardner (1972) years ago called the catch-22 of ESP research.

It works as follows: A "believer" (someone who believes in the existence of ESP phenomena before beginning an investigation) claims to have demonstrated ESP in the laboratory. A "skeptic" (someone who doubts the existence of ESP) is brought in to confirm the phenomena. Often, after observing the experimental situation, the skeptic calls for more controls (controls of the type we will discuss in Chapter 6), and though these are sometimes resisted, well-intentioned believers often agree to them. When the controls are instituted, the phenomena cannot be demonstrated (Farha, 2007; Kelly, 2005; Milton & Wiseman, 1999; Park, 2008; Wiseman, 2011). The skeptic, who correctly interprets this failure as an indication that the original demonstration was due to inadequate experimental control and, thus, cannot be accepted, is often shocked to find that the believer does not regard the original demonstration as invalid. Instead, the believer invokes the catch-22 of ESP: Psychic powers, the believer maintains, are subtle, delicate, and easily disturbed. The "negative vibes" of the skeptic were probably responsible for the disruption of the "psi powers." The believer thinks that the powers will undoubtedly return when the negative aura of the skeptic is removed.

This way of interpreting failures to demonstrate ESP in experiments is logically analogous to my story about the little green men. ESP operates just as the little green men do. It's there as long as you don't intrude to look at it carefully. When you do, it disappears. If we accept this explanation, it will be impossible to demonstrate the phenomenon to any skeptical observers. It appears only to believers. Of course, this position is unacceptable in science. We do not have the magnetism physicists and the nonmagnetism physicists (those for whom magnetism does and does not "work"). Interpreting ESP experiments in this way makes the hypothesis of ESP unfalsifiable just as the hypothesis of the little green men is. Interpreting the outcomes in this way puts it outside the realm of science.

Not All Confirmations Are Equal

The principle of falsifiability has important implications for the way we view the confirmation of a theory. Many people think that a good scientific theory is one that has been confirmed repeatedly. They assume that the amount of confirming evidence is critical in the evaluation of a theory. But falsifiability implies that the number of times a theory has been confirmed is not the critical element. The reason is that, as our example of the "theory of knocking rhythms" illustrated, not all confirmations are equal. Confirmations are more or less impressive depending on the extent to which the prediction exposes itself to potential disconfirmation. One confirmation of a highly specific, potentially falsifiable prediction (for instance, a female, 30 years old, 5 feet 2 inches tall, carrying a book and a purse in the left hand and knocking with the right) has a greater impact than the confirmation of 20 different predictions that are all virtually unfalsifiable (for instance, a person less than 100 years old).

Thus, we must look not only at the *quantity* of the confirming evidence, but also at the *quality* of the confirming instances. Using the falsifiability criterion as a tool to evaluate evidence will help the research consumer resist the allure of the nonscientific, all-explaining theory that inevitably hinders the search for deeper understanding. Indeed, such theoretical dead ends are often tempting precisely because they can never be falsified. They are islands of stability in the chaotic modern world.

Popper often made the point that "the secret of the enormous psychological appeal of these [unfalsifiable] theories lay in their ability to explain everything. To know in advance that whatever happens you will be able to understand it gives you not only a sense of intellectual mastery but, even more important, an emotional sense of secure orientation in the world" (Magee, 1985, p. 43). However, the attainment of such security is not the goal of science, because such security would be purchased at the cost of intellectual stagnation. Science is a mechanism for continually challenging previously held beliefs by subjecting them to empirical tests in such a way that they can be shown to be wrong. This characteristic often puts science—particularly psychology—in conflict with so-called folk wisdom or common sense (as we discussed in Chapter 1).

Falsifiability and Folk Wisdom

Psychology is a threat to the comfort that folk wisdom provides because, as a science, it cannot be content with explanations that cannot be refuted. The goal of psychology is the empirical testing of alternative behavioral theories in order to rule out some of them. Aspects of folk wisdom that are explicitly stated and that do stand up to empirical testing are, of course, welcomed, and many have been incorporated into psychological theory. However, psychology does not seek the comfort of explanatory systems that account for everything after the fact but predict nothing in advance. It does not accept systems of folk wisdom that are designed never to be changed and that end up being passed on from generation to generation. It is self-defeating to try to hide this fact from students or the public. Unfortunately, some psychology instructors and popularizers are aware that psychology's threat to folk wisdom disturbs some people, and they sometimes seek to soothe such feelings by sending a false underlying message that implies, "You'll learn some interesting things, but don't worry—psychology won't challenge things you believe in strongly." This is a mistake, and it contributes to confusion both about what science is and about what psychology is. Psychology establishes facts about sexual behavior, intelligence, crime, financial behavior, the effects of marriage, child rearing, and many other topics that people feel strongly about. It would be amazing if the investigation of subjects such as these failed to uncover something that did not upset *somebody*!

Science seeks conceptual change. Scientists try to describe the world as it really is, as opposed to what our prior beliefs dictate it should be. The dangerous trend in modern thought is the idea that people must be shielded from the nature of the world—that a veil of ignorance is necessary to protect a public unequipped to deal with the truth. Psychology is like other sciences in rejecting the idea that people need to be shielded from the truth.

Furthermore, we all lose when we are surrounded by others who hold incorrect views of human behavior. Our world is shaped by public attitudes toward education, crime, health, industrial productivity, child care, and many other critical issues. If these attitudes are the products of incorrect theories of behavior, then we are all harmed.

The Freedom to Admit a Mistake

Scientists have found that one of the most liberating and useful implications of the falsifiability principle is that, in science, making a mistake is not a sin. Philosopher Daniel Dennett (1995) has said that the essence of science is "making mistakes in public—making mistakes for all to see, in the hopes of getting the others to help with the corrections" (p. 380). By the process of continually adjusting theory when data do not accord with it, scientists collectively arrive at theories that better reflect the nature of the world.

In fact, our way of operating in everyday life might be greatly improved if we could use the falsifiability principle on a personal level. This is why the word *liberating* was used in the opening sentence of this section. It has a personal connotation that was specifically intended—because the ideas developed here have implications beyond science. We would have many fewer social and personal problems if we could only understand that, when our beliefs are contradicted by evidence in the world, it is better to adjust our beliefs than to deny the evidence and cling tenaciously to dysfunctional ideas.

How many times have you been in an intense argument with someone when right in the middle—perhaps just as you were giving a heated reply and defending your point of view—you realized that you were wrong about some critical fact or piece of evidence? What did you do? Did you back down and admit to the other person that you had assumed something that wasn't true and that the other person's interpretation now seemed more correct to you? Probably not. If you are like most of us, you engaged in endless rationalization. You tried to extricate yourself from the argument without admitting defeat. The last thing you would have done was admit that you were wrong. Thus, both you and your partner in the argument became a little more confused about which beliefs more closely tracked the truth. If refutations never become public (as they do in science), if both true and false beliefs are defended with equal vehemence, and if the correct feedback about the effects of argument is not given (as in this example), there is no mechanism for getting beliefs more reliably in synch with reality. This is why so much of our private and public discourse is confused and why the science of psychology is a more reliable guide to the causes of behavior than is so-called common sense.

We perhaps would find it easier to change our beliefs in the face of evidence if we understood how historically contingent our beliefs are—that is, how much they simply result from the accident of where and when we grew up. Research indicates, though, that this is insufficiently appreciated by many people. In my own lab we have collected data from questionnaires designed to assess people's ability to appreciate the historical contingency of their beliefs. One item on this questionnaire is the following statement, to which the subject must agree or disagree strongly, moderately, or mildly: "Even if my environment (family, neighborhood, schools) had been different, I probably would have had the same religious views." Religion of course is the classic case of an environmentally contingent belief (Christianity is clustered in Europe and the Americas, Islam in Africa and the Middle East, and Hinduism in India, etc.). Nevertheless, in several studies, my colleagues and I have repeatedly found that roughly 40–55% of a university student population will deny that their religious views are conditioned in any way by their historical circumstances (parents, country, education).

Why the falsifying attitude is useful in science itself is that, particularly in the early stages of investigating a problem, science advances by ruling out incorrect hypotheses rather than immediately zeroing in on the perfect theory. In fact, in many domains of life this is often the case as well. It is often difficult to specify what the best type of performance might be, but performance *errors* are much easier to spot. Essayist Neil Postman (1988) points out that doctors would find it hard to define "perfect health" but, despite this, they are quite good at spotting disease. Likewise, lawyers are much better at spotting injustice than at defining "perfect justice." The falsifying attitude is useful to scientists for just this reason. Particularly in the early stages of an investigation, a focus on what is wrong—on eliminating incorrect beliefs—is often a very fruitful approach for a scientist to take.

Many scientists have attested to the importance of understanding that making errors in the course of science is normal and that the real danger to scientific progress is our natural human tendency to avoid exposing our beliefs to situations in which they might be shown to be wrong. Scientists must avoid this tendency, and Nobel Prize winner Peter Medawar (1979) urged them to avoid it by remembering that *"the intensity of the conviction that a hypothesis is true has no bearing on whether it is true or not"* (p. 39; italics in original).

Here is a way of thinking about what Medawar is saying. On his show on October 17, 2005, comedian Stephen Colbert coined the term "truthiness" (Zimmer, 2010). Truthiness is the "quality of a thing *feeling* true without any evidence suggesting it actually was" (Manjoo, 2008, p. 189). What Medawar is saying is that science rejects truthiness. This often puts science at odds with modern society, where truthiness is more prevalent than ever.

Many of the most renowned scientists in psychology have followed Medawar's advice—"the intensity of the conviction that a hypothesis is true has no bearing on whether it is true or not." In an article on the career of noted experimental psychologist Robert Crowder, one of his colleagues, Mahzarin Banaji, is quoted as saying that "he is the least defensive scientist I know. If you found a way to show that his theory was wobbly or that his experimental finding was limited or flawed, Bob would beam with pleasure and plan the demise of his theory with you" (Azar, 1999, p. 18). Azar (1999) describes how Crowder developed a theory of one component of memory called precategorical acoustic storage and then carefully designed the studies that falsified his own model. Physician Jerome Groopman (2009) describes how practical and useful the falsifying attitude is in the process of medical diagnosis: "So a doctor learns to question the quality and significance of the data he extracts from the medical history.... The most instructive moments are when you are proven wrong, and realize that you believed you knew more than you did, wrongly dismissing a key bit of information that contradicted your presumed diagnosis or failed to consider that the patient had more than one malady" (p. 26).

Centuries before Darwin, Aristotle observed that "It is the mark of an educated mind to be able to entertain a thought without accepting it." More humorously, the economist John Maynard Keynes illustrated the falsifying attitude when, during the Great Depression, he replied to a critic, "When the facts change, I change my mind. What do you do, sir?" (Malabre, 1994, p. 220).

But the falsifying attitude doesn't always have to characterize each and every scientist for *science* to work. The unique power of science to reveal knowledge about the world does *not* arise because scientists are uniquely virtuous (that they are completely objective; that they are never biased in interpreting findings, etc.) but instead it arises because fallible scientists are immersed in a process of checks and balances—in a process in which other scientists are always there to criticize and to root out the errors of their peers. Philosopher Daniel Dennett (2000) has made the same point by arguing that it is not necessary for every scientist to display the objectivity of Robert Crowder. Dennett stresses that "scientists take themselves to be just as weak and fallible as anybody else, but recognizing these very sources of error in themselves and in the groups to which they belong, they have devised elaborate systems to tie their own hands, forcibly preventing their frailties and prejudices from infecting their results" (p. 42). The strength of science comes not because scientists are especially virtuous, but from a social process where scientists constantly cross-check each others' knowledge and conclusions.

Thoughts Are Cheap

Our earlier discussion of the idea of testing folk wisdom leads us to another interesting corollary of the falsifiability principle: Thoughts are cheap. To be specific, what we mean here is that certain *kinds* of thoughts are cheap. Biologist and science writer Stephen J. Gould (1987) illustrated this point:

> Fifteen years of monthly columns have brought me an enormous correspon-
> dence from nonprofessionals about all aspects of science....I have found that
> one common misconception surpasses all others. People will write, telling me
> that they have developed a revolutionary theory, one that will expand the
> boundaries of science. These theories, usually described in several pages of
> single-spaced typescript, are speculations about the deepest ultimate questions
> we can ask—what is the nature of life? the origin of the universe? the begin-
> ning of time? But thoughts are cheap. Any person of intelligence can devise his
> half dozen before breakfast. Scientists can also spin out ideas about ultimates.
> We don't (or, rather, we confine them to our private thoughts) because we
> cannot devise ways to test them, to decide whether they are right or wrong.
> What good to science is a lovely idea that cannot, as a matter of principle, ever
> be affirmed or denied? (p. 18)

The answer to Gould's last question is "No good at all." The type of thoughts that Gould is saying are cheap are those that we referred to in our discussion of Karl Popper's views: grand theories that are so global, complicated, and "fuzzy" that they can be used to explain anything—theories constructed more for emotional support because they are not meant to be changed or discarded. Gould was telling us that such theories are useless for scientific purposes, however comforting they may be. Science is a creative endeavor, but the creativity involves getting conceptual structures to fit the confines of empirical data. This is tough. These types of thoughts—those that explain the world as it *actually is*—are not cheap. Probably this is why good scientific theories are so hard to come by and why unfalsifiable pseudoscientific belief systems proliferate everywhere—the latter are vastly easier to construct.

Theories in science make contact with the world. They are falsifiable. They make specific predictions. Actually coming up with the theories that are truly scientific explanations is a difficult task. However, understanding the general logic by which science works is *not* so difficult. Indeed, there are plenty of materials about the logic of scientific thinking that have been written for children (Binga, 2009; Bower, 2009; Dawkins, 2012; Epstein, 2008; Swanson, 2001, 2004).

Errors in Science: Getting Closer to the Truth

In the context of explaining the principle of falsifiability, we have outlined a simple model of scientific progress. Theories are put forth and hypotheses are derived from them. The hypotheses are tested by a variety of techniques that we shall discuss in the remainder of this book. If the hypotheses are confirmed by the experiments, then the theory receives some degree of corroboration. If the hypotheses are falsified by the experiments, then the theory must be altered in some way, or it must be discarded for a better theory.

Of course, saying that knowledge in science is tentative and that hypotheses derived from theories are potentially false does not mean that everything is up for grabs. There are many relationships in science that have been confirmed so many times that they are termed *laws* because it is extremely doubtful that they will be overturned by future experimentation. It is highly unlikely that we shall find one day that blood does not circulate in the veins and arteries or that the earth does not orbit the sun. These mundane facts are not the type of hypotheses that we have been talking about. They are of no interest to scientists precisely because they are so well established. Scientists are interested only in those aspects of nature that are on the fringes of what is known. They are not interested in things that are so well confirmed that there is no doubt about them.

This aspect of scientific practice—that scientists gravitate to those problems on the fringes of what is known and ignore things that are well confirmed (so-called laws)—is very confusing to the general public. It seems that scientists are always emphasizing what they don't know rather than what is known. This is true, and there is a very good reason for it. To advance knowledge, scientists must be at the outer limits of what is known. Of course, this is precisely where things are uncertain. But science advances by a process of trying to reduce the uncertainty at the limits of knowledge. This can often make scientists look "uncertain" to the public. But this perception is deceiving. Scientists are *only* uncertain at the fringes of knowledge—where our understanding is currently being advanced. Scientists are *not* uncertain about the many facts that have been well established by replicable research.

It should also be emphasized that, when scientists talk about falsifying a theory based on observation and about replacing an old, falsified theory with a new one, they do not mean that all the previous facts that established the old theory are thrown out (we shall talk about this at length in Chapter 8). Quite the contrary, the new theory must explain all of the facts that the old theory could explain plus the new facts that the old theory could not explain. So the falsification of a theory does not mean that scientists have to go back to square one. Complex theories can be generally right without being perfectly right; and beliefs can be getting closer to the truth without being exactly true (Radcliffe Richards, 2000).

Science writer Isaac Asimov illustrated the process of theory revision very well in an essay titled "The Relativity of Wrong" (1989), in which he wrote about how we have refined our notions of the earth's shape. First, he warned us not to think that the ancient belief in a flat earth was stupid. On a plain (where the first civilizations with writing developed), the earth looks pretty flat, and Asimov urged us to consider what a quantitative comparison of different theories would reveal. First, we could express the different theories in terms of how much curvature per mile they hypothesized. The flat-earth theory would say that the curvature is 0 degrees per mile. This theory is wrong, as we know. But in one sense, it is close. As Asimov (1989) wrote,

> About a century after Aristotle, the Greek philosopher Eratosthenes noted that the sun cast a shadow of different lengths at different latitudes (all the shadows would be the same length if the earth's surface were flat). From the difference in shadow length, he calculated the size of the earthly sphere and it turned out to be 25,000 miles circumference. The curvature of such a sphere is about 0.000126 degrees per mile, a quantity very close to 0 per mile, as you can see.... The tiny difference between 0 and 0.000126 accounts for the fact that it took so long to pass from the flat earth to the spherical earth. Mind you, even a tiny difference, such as that between 0 and 0.000126, can be extremely important. The difference mounts up. The earth cannot be mapped over large areas with any accuracy at all if the difference isn't taken into account and if the earth isn't considered a sphere rather than a flat surface. (pp. 39–40)

But science, of course, did not stop with the theory that the earth was spherical. As we discussed earlier, scientists are always trying to refine their theories as much as possible and to test the limits of current knowledge.

For example, Newton's theories of gravitation predicted that the earth should not be perfectly spherical, and indeed this prediction has been confirmed. It turns out that the earth bulges a little at the equator and that it is a little flat at the poles. It is something called an *oblate spheroid*. The diameter of the earth from North Pole to South Pole is 7,900 miles, and the equatorial diameter is 7,927 miles. The curvature of the earth is not constant (as in a perfect sphere); instead, it varies slightly from 7.973 inches to 8.027 inches to the mile. As Asimov (1989) noted, "The correction in going from spherical to oblate spheroidal is much smaller than going from flat to spherical. Therefore, although the notion of the earth as a sphere is wrong, strictly speaking, it is not as wrong as the notion of the earth as flat" (p. 41).

Asimov's example of the shape of the earth illustrates for us the context in which scientists use such terms as "mistake," "error," or "falsified." Such terms do not mean that the theory being tested is wrong in every respect, only that it is incomplete. So when scientists emphasize that knowledge is tentative and may be altered by future findings, they are referring to a situation such as this example. When scientists believed that the earth was a sphere, they realized that, in detail, this theory might someday need to be altered. However, the alteration from spherical to oblate spheroidal preserves the "roughly correct" notion that the earth is a sphere. We do not expect to wake up one day and find that it is a cube.

Clinical psychologist Scott Lilienfeld (2005) contextualizes Asimov's point for the psychology student:

> When explaining to students that scientific knowledge is inherently tentative and open to revision, some students may mistakenly conclude that genuine knowledge is impossible. This view, which is popular in certain postmodernist circles, neglects to distinguish knowledge claims that are more certain from those that are less certain. Although absolute certainty is probably unattainable in science, some scientific claims, such as Darwin's theory of natural selection, have been extremely well corroborated, whereas others, such as the theory underpinning astrological horoscopes, have been convincingly refuted. Still others, such as cognitive dissonance theory, are scientifically controversial. Hence, there is a continuum of confidence in scientific claims; some have acquired virtual factual status whereas others have been resoundingly falsified. The fact that methodological skepticism does not yield completely certain answers to scientific questions—and that such answers could in principle be overturned by new evidence—does not imply that knowledge is impossible, only that this knowledge is provisional. (p. 49)

The mistaken notion the science must yield certain knowledge is often used to undermine science itself. Paleontologist Neil Shubin has described how creationists use this tactic. In an interview with science writer Natalie Angier (2007), Shubin notes how "creationists first try to paint science as a body of facts and certainties, and then they attack this or that 'certainty' for not being so certain after all. They cry 'Aha! You can't make up your mind.

You can't be trusted. Why should we believe you about anything?' Yet they are the ones who constructed the straw man of scientific infallibility in the first place" (p. 20).

Summary

What scientists most often mean by a *solvable problem* is a *testable theory*. The definition of a testable theory is a very specific one in science: It means that the theory is potentially falsifiable. If a theory is not falsifiable, then it has no implications for actual events in the natural world and, hence, is useless. Psychology has been plagued by unfalsifiable theories, and that is one reason why progress in the discipline has been slow.

Good theories are those that make specific predictions, and such theories are highly falsifiable. The confirmation of a specific prediction provides more support for the theory from which it was derived than the confirmation of a prediction that was not precise. In short, one implication of the falsifiability criterion is that all confirmations of theories are not equal. Theories that receive confirmation from highly falsifiable, highly specific predictions are to be preferred. Even when predictions are not confirmed (i.e., when they are falsified), this falsification is useful to theory development. A falsified prediction indicates that a theory must either be discarded or altered so that it can account for the discrepant data pattern. Thus, it is by theory adjustment caused by falsified predictions that sciences such as psychology get closer to the truth.

CHAPTER 3

Operationism and Essentialism: "But, Doctor, What Does It Really Mean?"

Do physicists really know what gravity is? I mean *really*. What is the real *meaning* of the term *gravity*? What is the underlying essence of it? What does it ultimately mean even to speak of gravity? When you get down to rock bottom, what is it all about?

Questions such as these reflect a view of science that philosopher Karl Popper called *essentialism.* This is the idea that the only good scientific theories are those that give ultimate explanations of phenomena in terms of their underlying essences or their essential properties. In this chapter, we will discuss why science does not answer essentialist questions such as this and why, instead, science advances by developing *operational definitions* of concepts.

Why Scientists Are Not Essentialists

Scientists, in fact, do not claim to acquire the type of knowledge that the essentialist seeks. The proper answer to the preceding questions is that physicists do *not* know what gravity is in this sense. Science does not attempt to answer "ultimate" questions about the universe. Biologist Peter Medawar (1984) wrote,

> There exist questions that science cannot answer and that no conceivable advance of science would empower it to answer. These are the questions that children ask—the "ultimate questions."...I have in mind such questions

as: How did everything begin? What are we all here for? What is the point of living? (p. 66)

However, the failure of science to answer questions about first and last things does not in any way entail the acceptance of answers of other kinds; nor can it be taken for granted that because these questions can be put they can be answered. So far as our understanding goes, they cannot. (p. 60)

Finally, however, there is no limit upon the ability of science to answer the kind of questions that science can answer....Nothing can impede or halt the advancement of scientific learning except a moral ailment such as the failure of nerve. (p. 86)

One reason that scientists are suspicious of claims that some person, theory, or belief system provides absolute knowledge about ultimate questions is that scientists consider questions about "ultimates" to be unanswerable. Scientists do not claim to produce perfect knowledge; the unique strength of science is not that it is an error-free process, but that it provides a way of eliminating the errors that are part of our knowledge base. Furthermore, claims of perfect or absolute knowledge tend to choke off inquiry. Because a free and open pursuit of knowledge is a prerequisite for scientific activity, scientists are always skeptical of claims that the ultimate answer has been found.

Essentialists Like to Argue About the Meaning of Words

A common indication of the essentialist attitude is an obsessive concern about defining the meaning of terms and concepts before the search for knowledge about them begins. "But we must first define our terms" is a frequent essentialist slogan. "What does that theoretical concept really *mean?*" The idea seems to be that, before a word can be used as a concept in a theory, we must have a complete and unambiguous understanding of all the underlying language problems involved in its usage. In fact, this is exactly the opposite of the way scientists work. Before they begin to investigate the physical world, physicists do not engage in debates about how to use the word *energy* or whether the word *particle* really captures the essence of what we mean when we talk about the fundamental constituents of matter.

The meaning of a concept in science is determined *after* extensive investigation of the phenomena the term relates to, not before such an investigation. The refinement of conceptual terms comes from the interplay of data and theory that is inherent in the scientific process, not from debates on language usage. Essentialism leads us into endless argument about words, and many scientists believe that such language games distract us from matters of substance. For example, concerning the question "What is the true meaning of the word *life?*" two biologists give the startling answer that "There is no true meaning. There is a usage that serves the purposes of working biologists well enough, and it is not the subject of altercation or dispute" (Medawar & Medawar, 1983, pp. 66–67). In short, the explanation of phenomena, not the analysis of language, is the goal of the scientist. The key to progress in all the sciences has been to abandon essentialism and to adopt operationism, our topic of inquiry in this chapter.

Operationists Link Concepts to Observable Events

Where, then, does the meaning of concepts in science come from if not from discussions about language? What are the criteria for the appropriate use of a scientific concept? To answer these questions, we must discuss operationism, an idea that is crucial to the construction of theory in science and one that is especially important for evaluating theoretical claims in psychology.

Although there are different forms of operationism, it is most useful for the consumer of scientific information to think of it in the most general way. *Operationism* is simply the idea that concepts in scientific theories must in some way be grounded in, or linked to, observable events that can be measured. Linking the concept to an observable event makes the concept public. The operational definition removes the concept from the feelings and intuitions of a particular individual and allows it to be tested by anyone who can carry out the measurable operations.

For example, defining the concept *hunger* as "that gnawing feeling I get in my stomach" is not an operational definition because it is related to the personal experience of a "gnawing feeling" and, thus, is not accessible to other observers. By contrast, definitions that involve some measurable period of food deprivation or some physiological index such as blood sugar levels are operational because they involve observable measurements that anyone can carry out. Similarly, psychologists cannot be content with a definition of *anxiety*, for example, as "that uncomfortable, tense feeling I get at times" but must define the concept by a number of operations such as questionnaires and physiological measurements. The former definition is tied to a personal interpretation of bodily states and is not replicable by others. The latter puts the concept in the public realm of science.

It is important to realize that a concept in science is defined by a *set* of operations, not by just a single behavioral event or task. Instead, several slightly different tasks and behavioral events are used to converge on a concept (we will talk more about the idea of converging operations in Chapter 8). For example, educational psychologists define a concept such as *reading ability* in terms of performance on a standardized instrument such as the Woodcock Reading Mastery Tests (Woodcock, 2011) that contains a whole *set* of tasks. The total reading ability score on the Woodcock Reading Mastery instrument comprises indicators of performance on a number of different subtests that test slightly different skills, for example, reading a passage and thinking of an appropriate word to fill in a blank in the passage, coming up with a synonym for a word, pronouncing a difficult word correctly in isolation, and several others. Collectively, performance on all of these tasks defines the concept *reading ability*.

Operational definitions force us to think carefully and empirically—in terms of observations in the real world—about how we want to define a concept. Imagine trying to define operationally something as seemingly conceptually simple as typing ability. Imagine you need to do this because you want to compare two different methods of teaching typing. Think of all the decisions you would have to make. You would want to measure typing speed, of course. But over how long a passage? A passage of only 100 words would seem too short, and a passage of 10,000 words would seem too long. But exactly how long then? How long does speed have to be sustained to match how we best conceive of the theoretical construct *typing ability?* And what kind of material has to be typed? Should it include numbers and formulas and odd spacing? And how are we going to deal with errors? It seems that both time and errors should come into play when measuring typing ability, but exactly what should the formula be that brings the two together? Do we want time and errors to be equally weighted, or is one somewhat more important than the other? The need for an operational definition would force you to think carefully about all of these things; it would make you think very thoroughly about how to conceptualize typing ability.

Consider the task of the Food and Drug Administration, which has to decide what is an "unacceptable" level of contamination for various foods as opposed to what are considered "unavoidable defects" (Levy, 2009). A federal agency such as the FDA cannot be subjective about such things. It needs strict operational definitions of its judgments with respect to contaminants in each food that it inspects. So, for example, it comes up with operational definitions of the following sort (Levy, 2009): An "unacceptable" level of contamination in tomato juice is more than 10 fly eggs per 100 grams; an "unacceptable" level of contamination in mushrooms is five or more maggots 2 millimeters or longer per 100 grams. Very gross—but commendably operational!

Reliability and Validity

Operationalizing a concept in science involves *measurement*: assigning a number to an observation via some rule. Science writer Charles Seife (2010) makes the point that once we start using numbers in measurement we suddenly start caring about them. His argument is that the nonmathematician rarely cares about the properties of numbers when they are used merely as abstract symbols. We don't care about the number five, by itself. But as soon as the number five becomes five "pounds" or five "dollars" or five "percent inflation" or five "IQ points"—then suddenly we start to care. Seife (2010) says that "a number without a unit is ethereal and abstract. With a unit, it acquires meaning—but at the same time, it loses its purity" (p. 9). What Seife means by "losing its purity" is that once we are involved with measurement—once the number has a unit attached—we are suddenly concerned that numbers have the "right" properties. What are the "right" properties for a number to have in science? The answer to this question is that, in science, the "right" properties for a number to have are the properties of reliability and validity.

For an operational definition of a concept to be useful, it must display both reliability and validity. *Reliability* refers to the consistency of a measuring instrument—whether you would arrive at the same measurement if you assessed the same concept multiple times. The scientific concept of reliability is easy to understand because it is very similar to its layperson's definition and very like one of its dictionary definitions: "an attribute of any system that consistently produces the same results."

Consider how a layperson might talk about whether something was reliable or not. Imagine a New Jersey commuter catching the bus to work in Manhattan each morning. The bus is scheduled to arrive at the commuter's stop at 7:20 A.M. One week the bus arrives at 7:20, 7:21, 7:20, 7:19, and 7:20, respectively. We would say that the bus was pretty reliable that week. If the next week the bus arrived at 7:35, 7:10, 7:45, 7:55, and 7:05, respectively, we would say that the bus was very unreliable that week.

The reliability of an operational definition in science is assessed in much the same way. If the measure of a concept yields similar numbers for multiple measurements of the same concept, we say that the measuring device displays high reliability. If we measured the same person's intelligence with different forms of an IQ test on Monday, Wednesday, and Friday of the same week and got scores of 110, 109, and, 110, we would say that that particular IQ test seems to be very reliable. By contrast, if the three scores were 89, 130, and 105, we would say that that particular IQ test does not seem to display high reliability. There are specific statistical techniques for assessing the reliability of different types of measuring instruments, and these are discussed in all standard introductory methodology textbooks.

But remember that reliability is only about consistency and nothing else. Reliability alone is not enough for an operational definition to be adequate. Reliability is necessary but not sufficient. To be a good operational definition of a concept, the operations assessed must also be a *valid* measure of that concept. The term *construct validity* refers to whether a measuring instrument (operational definition) is measuring what it is supposed to be measuring. In his methodology textbook, Professor Paul Cozby (2012) gives us a humorous example of reliability without validity. Imagine you are about to get your intelligence assessed. The examiner tells you to stick out your foot and clamps on a measuring device like those at the shoe store and reads out a number. You would, of course, think that this was a joke. But note that this measuring instrument would display many of the types of reliability that are discussed in methodology textbooks. It would give virtually the same readings on Monday, Wednesday, and Friday (what is termed *test–retest reliability*) and it would give the same reading no matter who used it (what is termed *interrater reliability*).

The problem with the shoe device as a measure of intelligence is not reliability (which it has) but validity. It is not a good measure of the concept it purports to measure (intelligence). One way we would know that it is not a valid measure of intelligence is that we would find that it does not relate to many other variables that we would expect a measure of intelligence to relate to. Measures from the shoe instrument would not relate to academic success; they would not relate to neurophysiological measures of brain functioning; they would not relate to job success; and they would not relate to measures of the efficiency of information processing developed by cognitive psychologists. By contrast, actual measures of intelligence relate to all of these things (Duncan et al., 2008; Flynn, 2007; Sternberg & Kaufman, 2011). Actual measures of intelligence in psychology have validity as well as reliability, whereas the shoe-size measure of intelligence has reliability without validity.

You might be wondering about another combination of affairs at this point, so let me recapitulate where we are. In operational definitions, we are looking for both reliability and validity, so high reliability and high validity are sought. We have just discussed the shoe-size IQ test in order to demonstrate that high reliability and low validity get us nowhere. A third case, low reliability and low validity, is so obviously useless that it is not worth discussing. But you might be wondering about the fourth and last possible combination: What if something has high validity and low reliability? The answer is that, like its converse case of low validity and high reliability (the shoe-size example), this state of affairs gets you nowhere. And, actually, it is more accurate to say that this state of affairs is impossible—because you cannot claim to be measuring validly if you cannot measure reliably.

When trying to develop valid operational definitions it is important to be precise about just what concept we are trying to measure. For example, the National Football League evaluates quarterbacks using a construct that it calls the "passer rating" (Sielski, 2010). It is important to realize that this construct is named precisely as "passer rating." That is, it is specifically *not* a quarterback rating. This is because the operational definition of "passer rating" takes into account only passing and not everything a quarterback does. Specifically, the passer rating is a mathematical formula that involves the following four things: pass completion percentage, yards per passing attempt, touchdowns per passing attempt, and interceptions per attempt. The passer rating statistic does not involve: the running yards gained by the quarterback, play-calling ability, win-loss record, sacks, fumbles, and a variety of other quantifiable quarterback variables. For this reason, another construct with a different operational definition has been developed called the "total quarterback rating."

Direct and Indirect Operational Definitions

The link between concepts and observable operations varies greatly in its degree of directness or indirectness. Few scientific concepts are defined almost entirely by observable operations in the real world. Most concepts are defined more indirectly. For example, the use of some concepts is determined by both a set of operations and the particular concept's relationship to other theoretical constructs. Finally, there are concepts that are not directly defined by observable operations but linked to other concepts that are. These are sometimes called latent constructs, and they are common in psychology.

For example, much research has been done on the so-called type A behavior pattern because it has been linked to the incidence of coronary heart disease (Chida & Hamer, 2008; Martin et al., 2011; Matthews, 2005; Suls & Bunde, 2005). We will discuss the type A behavior pattern in more detail in Chapter 8. The important point to illustrate here, however, is that the type A behavior pattern is actually defined by a set of subordinate concepts: a strong desire to compete, a potential for hostility, time-urgent behavior, an intense drive to accomplish goals, and several others. However, each one of these defining features of the type A behavior pattern (a strong desire to compete, etc.) is *itself* a concept in need of operational definition. Indeed, considerable effort has been expended in operationally defining each one. The important point for our present discussion is that the concept of the type A behavior pattern is a complex concept that is not directly defined by operations. Instead, it is linked with other concepts, which, in turn, have operational definitions.

The type A behavior pattern provides an example of a concept with an indirect operational definition. A similarly defined concept in clinical psychology is that of distress tolerance (Zvolensky, Vujanovic, Bernstein, & Leyro, 2010). This global concept is defined in terms of several simpler subconstructs more closely tied to operational measures: tolerance of uncertainty, tolerance of ambiguity, tolerance of frustration, tolerance of negative emotion, and tolerance of physical discomfort.

In short, although theoretical concepts differ in how closely they are linked to observations, all concepts acquire their meaning partially through their link to such observations.

Scientific Concepts Evolve

It is important to realize that the definition of a scientific concept is not fixed but constantly changing as the observations that apply to the concept are enriched. If the original operational definition of a concept turns out to be theoretically unfruitful, it will be abandoned in favor of an alternative set of defining operations. Thus, concepts in science are continually evolving and can increase in abstractness as the knowledge concerning them increases. For example, at one time the electron was thought of as a tiny ball of negative charge circling the nucleus of an atom. Now it is viewed as a probability density function having wavelike properties in certain experimental situations.

In psychology, the development of the concept of intelligence provides a similar example. At first, the concept had only a strict operational definition: Intelligence is what is measured by tests of mental functioning. As empirical evidence accumulated relating intelligence to scholastic achievement, learning, brain injury, neurophysiology, and other behavioral and biological variables, the concept was both enriched and refined (Deary, Penke, & Johnson, 2010; Duncan et al., 2008; Sternberg & Kaufman, 2011). It now appears that intelligence is best conceptualized as a higher order construct defined by several more specific information-processing operations. These hypothesized processes, in turn, have more direct operational definitions stated in terms of measurable performance.

The concepts in theories of human memory have likewise evolved. Psychologists now rarely use global concepts like *remembering* or *forgetting;* instead, they test the properties of more specifically defined memory subprocesses, such as short-term acoustic memory, iconic storage, semantic memory, and episodic memory. The older concepts of remembering and forgetting have been elaborated with more specifically operationalized concepts.

Thus, the usage of theoretical terms evolves from scientific activity rather than from debates about the meaning of words. This is one of the most salient differences between the operational attitude of science and the essentialist quest for absolute definition. Philosopher Paul Churchland (1988) emphasized the idea that concepts in science derive meaning not from language definitions but from observations and other concepts to which they are related:

> To fully understand the expression "electric field" is to be familiar with the network of theoretical principles in which that expression appears. Collectively, they tell us what an electric field is and what it does. This case is typical. Theoretical terms do not, in general, get their meanings from single, explicit definitions stating conditions necessary and sufficient for their application. They are implicitly defined by the network of principles that embed them. (p. 56)

As scientific concepts evolve, they often become enmeshed in several different theoretical systems and acquire alternative operational definitions. There is not necessarily anything wrong with the concept when this happens. For example, many believe that psychology is discredited by the fact that many of its important theoretical constructs, such as intelligence, are operationalized and conceptualized in more than one way. But such a situation is not unique to psychology, and it is not a matter for despair or hand-wringing. In fact, it is a relatively common occurrence in science. Heat, for example, is conceptualized in terms of thermodynamic theory and in terms of kinetic theory. Physics is not scandalized by this state of affairs. Likewise, consider the electron. Many of its properties are explained by its being conceptualized as a wave. Other properties, however, are better handled if it is viewed as a particle. The existence of these alternative conceptualizations has tempted no one to suggest that physics be abandoned.

People got a lesson in this point in 2006 when the media reported that the International Astronomical Union had recently reoperationalized the term "planet" in a way that excluded Pluto (Adler, 2006; Brown, 2010). That something as seemingly basic as the concept "planet" could be the subject of alternative views was a surprise to many in the public. But in fact it is a common occurrence in science. In this case, one group of astronomers prefers to stress the composition and geologic composition of astronomical bodies. Another group likes to emphasize their dynamical properties, for example, their orbits and gravitational effects. The operational definitions of the former group include Pluto as a planet, but the operational definitions of the latter group exclude Pluto. The differing operational definitions do not reflect badly on the field of astronomy. They merely reflect differing ways of triangulating concepts in the discipline. The same is true in psychology, where there are sometimes alternative operational definitions of concepts. Just because something is hard to define does not mean that there is not something real there to study.

Operational Definitions in Psychology

Many people understand the necessity of operationism when they think about physics or chemistry. They understand that if scientists are going to talk about a particular type of chemical reaction, or about energy, or about magnetism, they must have a way of measuring these things. Unfortunately, when people think and talk about psychology, they often fail to recognize the need for operationism. Why is it not equally obvious that psychological terms must be operationally defined, either directly or indirectly, in order to be useful explanatory constructs in scientific theories?

One reason is what has been termed the *preexisting-bias problem* in psychology. We alluded to this problem in Chapter 1. People do not come to the study of geology with emotionally held beliefs about the nature of rocks. The situation in psychology is very different. We all have intuitive theories of personality and human behavior because we have been "explaining" behavior to ourselves all our lives. All our personal psychological theories contain theoretical concepts (e.g., *smart, aggressive, anxiety*). Thus, it is only natural to ask why we have to accept some other definition. Although this attitude seems reasonable on the surface, it is a complete bar to any scientific progress in understanding human behavior and is the cause of much public confusion about psychology.

One of the greatest sources of misunderstanding and one of the biggest impediments to the accurate presentation of psychological findings in the media is the fact that many technical concepts in psychology are designated by words used in everyday language. This everyday usage opens the door to a wide range of misconceptions. The layperson seldom realizes that when psychologists use words such as *intelligence, anxiety, aggression,* and *attachment* as theoretical constructs, they do not necessarily mean the same thing that the general public does when using these words.

The nature of this difference should be apparent from the previous discussion of operationism. When terms such as *intelligence* and *anxiety* are used in psychological theories, their direct or indirect operational definitions determine their correct usage. These definitions are often highly technical, usually fairly specific, and often different from popular usage in many ways. For example, when hearing the phrase "the first principal component of the factor analysis of a large sampling of cognitive tasks," many people would not recognize it as part of the operational definition of the term *intelligence*.

Similarly, in lay usage, the word depression has come to mean something like "feeling down in the dumps." By contrast, the technical definition of major depressive disorder takes up over a dozen pages in the *Diagnostic and Statistical Manual of Mental Disorders* (American Psychiatric Association, 2000) and means something quite different from being "down in the dumps." A clinical psychologist's depression is not the same as the layperson's depression (Klein, 2010). Other sciences also have this problem, although perhaps in a less severe form than psychology. Recall the previous discussion of the concept *life*. As Medawar and Medawar (1983) pointed out, "The trouble is that 'life,' like many other technical terms in science, has been pirated from the vernacular and is used in scientific contexts far removed from those that might arise in common speech" (p. 66).

Physicist Lisa Randall (2005) discusses how this problem obscures the understanding of physics by the public. She points out that the term *relativity* in Einstein's theory has been taken by the public to imply that there are no absolutes in science because "everything is relative." In fact, Einstein's theory says just the opposite! Randall points out that actually Einstein's theory is all about invariants and absolutes. He admitted, in fact, that it might have been more apt to call it by the term "invariantentheorie" instead of relativity, but the latter had too quickly become entrenched. Randall goes on to point out that even in physics there are misunderstandings about words, because scientists sometime employ colloquial terminology, and it is often unclear to a layperson whether a word is being used in a technical or a colloquial sense. And the same is true in psychology. When the psychologist and the layperson use the same word to mean different things, they often misinterpret each other. Such confusion would be less prevalent if new words had been coined to represent psychological constructs. On occasion such words have been coined. Just as physicists have their erg and joule, psychology has its dissonance and encoding, words that are not actually coined but are uncommon enough to prevent confusion.

"But," the layperson may object, "why do psychologists inflict this on us? New jargon, highly technical definitions, uncommon uses of words. Why do we need them? Why is my idea of 'intelligence' not an acceptable idea to talk about?"

Here we see exemplified a critical misunderstanding of psychological research—a misunderstanding that is often reflected in media reports of psychological research. A national newspaper report on the 1996 meeting of the American Psychological Association (Immen, 1996) is headlined "Could You Repeat That in Klingon?" and refers to "psychologists speaking a language all their own." The article ridicules the following title of a paper delivered at the conference: "Interpreting WJ-R and KAIT Joint Factor Analyses from Gf-Gc Theory." Although the reporter states that he would "not even dare to speculate about the true meaning" of the title, almost all properly trained psychologists would recognize the title as referring to developments in intelligence test theory. And this is as it should be. Gf-Gc theory is a technical development in intelligence theory. There is no reason for the reporter to have heard of this concept—just as one would not expect the reporter to know the details of the latest elementary particle to be identified by physicists. Somehow, however, the reporter's (quite understandable) ignorance of the technical terminology is seen as reflecting negatively on modern psychology. When the topic is physics, reporters seem to know that it is their own ignorance that is preventing understanding. But when the topic is psychological, they act as if psychologists are to blame for their own lack of understanding.

We come here to the crux of the problem. The first step in resolving it is to emphasize a point from our earlier discussion: Operationism is not unique to psychology. It is characteristic of all sciences. Most of the time, we accept it readily, recognizing its obvious nature. If a scientist is investigating radioactivity, we take it for granted that he or she must have some observable way of measuring the phenomenon—a method that another investigator could use to obtain the same results. This method is what makes possible the public nature of science, one of its defining features. Two different scientists agree on the same operational definition so that it is possible for one to replicate the other's results. However, what seems obvious in other contexts is sometimes not so clear when we think about psychology. The necessity for operational definitions of concepts like *intelligence* and *anxiety* is often not recognized because we use these terms all the time, and, after all, don't we all just "know" what these things mean?

The answer is "No, we don't"—not in the sense that a scientist has to know—that is, in a public sense. A scientist must "know" what intelligence means by being able to define, precisely, how another laboratory could measure it in exactly the same way and be led to the same conclusions about the concept. This is vastly different—in terms of explicitness and precision—than the vague verbal connotations that are needed in order to achieve casual understanding in general conversation.

Operationism as a Humanizing Force

The problem with relying on what we all just "know" is the same problem that plagues all intuitive (i.e., nonempirical) systems of belief. What you "know" about something may not be quite the same as what Jim "knows" or what Jane "knows." How do we decide who is right? You may say, "Well,

I feel strongly about this, so strongly that I *know* I'm right." But what if Jim, who thinks somewhat differently, feels even more strongly than you do? And then there's Jane, who thinks differently from you or Jim, claiming that she must be right because she feels *even more* strongly than Jim does.

This simple parody is meant only to illustrate a fundamental aspect of scientific knowledge, one that has been a major humanizing force in human history: In science, the truth of a knowledge claim is not determined by the strength of belief of the individual putting forth the claim. The problem with all intuitively based systems of belief is that they have no mechanism for deciding among conflicting claims. When everyone knows intuitively, but the intuitive claims conflict, how do we decide who is right? Sadly, history shows that the result of such conflicts is usually a power struggle.

Some people mistakenly claim that an operational approach to psychology dehumanizes people and that instead we should base our views of human beings on intuition. Psychologist Donald Broadbent (1973) argued that the truly humane position is one that bases theoretical views of human beings on observable behavior rather than on the intuition of the theorizer:

> We can tell nothing of other people except by seeing what they do or say in particular circumstances.... The empirical method is a way of reconciling differences. If one rejects it, the only way of dealing with a disagreement is by emotional polemic. (p. 206)

Thus, the humanizing force in science is that of making knowledge claims public so that conflicting ideas can be tested in a way that is acceptable to all disputants. Recall the concept of replication from Chapter 1. This allows a selection among theories to take place by peaceful mechanisms that we all agree on in advance. The public nature of science rests critically on the idea of operationism. By operationally defining concepts, we put them in the public realm, where they can be criticized, tested, improved, or perhaps rejected.

Psychological concepts cannot rest on someone's personal definition, which may be uncommon, idiosyncratic, or vague. For this reason, psychology must reject all personal definitions of concepts—just as physics, for example, rejects personal definitions of energy and meteorology rejects personal definitions of what a cloud is. Psychologists instead must rely on publicly accessible concepts defined by operations that anyone with proper training and facilities can perform. In rejecting personal definitions, psychology is not shutting out the layperson but is opening up the field—as all sciences do—to the quest for a common, publicly accessible knowledge that all can share.

Such publicly accessible knowledge is available to solve human problems only when concepts have become grounded in operational definitions and are not the focus of essentialist arguments about the meaning of words. For example, Monk (1990) describes how during World War II the concept of *wound shock* had become problematic in medicine. Some physicians identified the condition based on an abnormally high concentration of red blood cells thought to be due to a leakage of plasma from the blood into tissue. Others identified wound shock on the basis of low blood pressure, skin pallor, and rapid pulse. In other words, operational definitions of the concept were inconsistent (and even idiosyncratic) and, thus, one physician by the name of Grant working for the British Medical Research Council recommended "that the very concept of 'wound shock' should be abandoned and that detailed observations of casualties should be made without using the term.... The lack of a common basis of diagnosis renders it impossible to assess the efficacy of the various methods of treatment adopted" (Monk, 1990, pp. 445–446). In other words, the concept was doing more harm than good because it did not have a definition that was common enough so that it could be considered public knowledge (i.e., generally shared and agreed upon).

Sometimes the changes in the meaning of concepts in science will put scientific understanding of a concept in conflict with the nonspecialist's understanding. Farber and Churchland (1995) discuss such a situation surrounding the concept of fire. The classical concept was used "to classify not only burning carbon-stuffs, but also activity on the sun and various stars (actually nuclear fusion), lightning (actually electrically induced incandescence), the northern lights (actually spectral emission), and the flash of fireflies (actually phosphorescence). In our modern conceptual scheme, since none of these things involves oxidation, none belongs to the same class as wood fires. Moreover, some processes that turned out to belong to the oxidation class—rusting, tarnishing, and metabolism—were not originally considered to share anything with burning, since felt heat was taken to be an essential feature of this class" (p. 1296). In short, the principle of oxidation uniting the phenomena of a campfire and rusting—and separating them from the phenomenon of lightning—may be a sign of progress to a scientist, but it can be confusing and disorienting to the layperson.

Essentialist Questions and the Misunderstanding of Psychology

Another reason many people seem to abandon the idea of operationism when they approach psychology is that they seek essentialist answers to certain human problems. Recall the questions at the beginning of this chapter: What is the real meaning of the word gravity? What is the underlying essence of it? What does it ultimately mean even to speak of gravity? Most people would recognize that these questions require knowledge of the ultimate, underlying nature of a phenomenon and that current theories in physics cannot provide answers to questions of this type. Anyone familiar with popular writing about the progress of physical science in the last few centuries will recognize that gravity is a theoretical construct of great complexity and that its conceptual and operational relationships have been in constant flux.

However, substitute the word intelligence for the word gravity in each of the preceding questions and, suddenly, a miracle occurs. Now the questions are imbued with great meaning. They seem natural and meaningful. They literally beg for an ultimate answer. When the psychologist gives the same answer as the physicist—that intelligence is a complex concept that derives meaning from the operations used to measure it and from its theoretical relationships to other constructs—he or she is belittled and accused of avoiding the real issues.

One problem facing psychology, then, is that the public demands answers to essentialist questions that it does not routinely demand of other sciences. These demands often underlie many of the attempts to disparage the progress that has been made in the field. Although these demands do not hinder the field itself—because psychologists, like other scientists, ignore demands for essentialist answers and simply go about their work—they are an obstacle to the public's understanding of psychology. The public becomes confused when an uninformed critic claims that there has been no progress in psychology. The fact that this claim so frequently goes unchallenged reflects the unfortunate truth of the major premise of this book: Public knowledge of what scientific achievement within psychology actually means is distressingly meager. When examined closely, such criticisms usually boil down to the contention that psychology has not yet provided the ultimate answer to any of its questions. To this charge, psychology readily pleads guilty—as do all the other sciences.

Some may find it discomforting to learn that no science, including psychology, can give answers to essentialist questions. Holton and Roller (1958) discussed the uneasiness that the layperson may feel when told that physicists cannot answer essentialist questions. They discuss the phenomenon of radioactive decay in which the number of atoms of a radioactive element that have decayed can be related to time via an exponential mathematical function. That function, however, does not explain *why* radioactive decay occurs. It does not answer the layperson's question of *why* it follows this function. It does not answer the question of what radioactive decay *really is*. Holton and Roller tell us that "we must try to make our peace with the limitations of modern science; it does not claim to find out 'what things really are'" (pp. 219–220). As science writer Robert Wright (1988) explained,

> There was something bothersome about Isaac Newton's theory of gravitation.... How, after all, could "action at a distance" be realized?...Newton sidestepped such questions....Ever since Newton, physics has followed his example.... Physicists make no attempt to explain why things obey laws of electromagnetism or of gravitation. (p. 61)

Likewise, those who seek essentialist answers to questions concerning human nature are destined to be disappointed if they are looking to psychology. Psychology is not a religion. It is a broad field that seeks a scientific understanding of all aspects of behavior. Therefore, psychology's current explanations are temporary theoretical constructs that account for behavior better than alternative explanations. These constructs will certainly be superseded in the future by superior theoretical conceptualizations that are closer to the truth.

The idea of an operational definition can be a very useful tool in evaluating the falsifiability of a psychological theory. The presence of concepts that are not directly or indirectly grounded in observable operations is an important clue to recognizing a nonfalsifiable theory. Thus, the presence of loose concepts—those for which the theorist cannot provide direct or indirect operational links—should be viewed with suspicion.

A principle that scientists term *parsimony* is relevant here. The principle of parsimony dictates that when two theories have the same explanatory power, the simpler theory (the one involving fewer concepts and conceptual relationships) is preferred. The reason is that the theory with fewer conceptual relationships will likely be the more falsifiable of the two in future tests.

A strong grasp of the principle of operationism will also aid in the recognition of problems or questions that are scientifically meaningless. For example, I have in my files a wire service article, from United Press International, entitled "Do Animals Think?" The article describes recent experimentation in animal behavior. There is nothing wrong with the research described in the article, but it is clear that the title is merely a teaser. The question in the title is scientifically meaningless unless some operational criteria are specified for the term *think*, and none is given in the article. A similar problem concerns the many newspaper articles that have asked, "Can computers think?" Without some operational criteria, this question is also scientifically meaningless, even though it is infinitely useful as grist for cocktail party conversation.

Summary

Operational definitions are definitions of concepts stated in terms of observable operations that can be measured. One of the main ways that we ensure that theories are falsifiable is by making certain that the key concepts in theories have operational definitions stated in terms of well-replicated behavioral observations. Operational definitions are one major mechanism that makes scientific knowledge publicly verifiable. Such definitions are in the public domain so that the theoretical concepts that they define are testable by all—unlike "intuitive," nonempirical definitions that are the special possession of particular individuals and not open to testing by everyone.

Because psychology employs terms from common discourse, such as *intelligence* and *anxiety,* and because many people have preexisting notions about what these terms mean, the necessity of operationally defining these terms is often not recognized. Psychology is like all other sciences in requiring operational definitions of its terms. However, people often demand answers to essentialist questions (questions about the absolute, underlying nature of a concept) of psychology that they do not demand of other sciences. No science provides such answers to ultimate questions. Instead, psychology, like other sciences, seeks continually to refine its operational definitions so that the concepts in theories more accurately reflect the way the world actually is.

CHAPTER **4**

Testimonials and Case Study Evidence: Placebo Effects and the Amazing Randi

Cut to the *Oprah Winfrey Show,* one of the most popular television talk shows of the last decade. Today's guest is Dr. Alfred Pontificate, director of the Oedipus Institute of Human Potential. Oprah attempts to elicit questions about the doctor's provocative new Theory of Birth Order, which is based on the idea that the course of one's life is irrevocably set by family inter-actions that are determined by birth order. The discussion inevitably turns from theoretical concerns to requests for explanations of personal events of importance to members of the audience. The doctor complies without much prodding.

For example, "Doctor, my brother is a self-destructive workaholic. He ignores his wife and family and places work-related problems above everything else. He has an ulcer and a drinking problem that he refuses to acknowledge. His family hasn't been on a real vacation in two years. He's headed for divorce and doesn't seem to care. Why has he chosen such a self-destructive course?"

To which the doctor replies, "What is his birth order, my dear?"

"Oh, he is the oldest of the children."

"Yes," the doctor says, "this is quite common. We see it often in the clinic. The underlying dynamics of a situation like this arise because parents transfer their life hopes and frustrations to their firstborn child. Through a process of unconscious wish transference, the child absorbs these hopes and frustrations, even if the parents never articulate them. Then, through the unconscious process that I call the dynamic expectation spiral, the aspira-tions of the parents become manifest as a pathological need for achievement in the child."

Although the audience members on the *Oprah* show sometimes ask hostile questions when the guest challenges their beliefs, this rarely happens when a behavioral "expert" seems to confirm conventional wisdom. Once in a while, however, the show is enlivened by an audience member who questions the evidence behind the guest's declarations. In this case, an eager, forthright questioner is in the studio. "But wait a minute, Doctor," the questioner begins. "My brother is a firstborn, too. My parents sent the bum to Harvard and told me to go to a two-year school to be a dental hygienist. So, this 'great brain' of theirs drops out after one year, goes to some mountaintop in Colorado, and the last time we saw him he was weaving baskets! I don't understand what you're saying about firstborns."

The audience tenses for the confrontation, but alas, the doctor always wins in the end: "Oh, yes, I have seen many cases like your brother. Yes, I often meet them in my practice. They are people for whom the dynamic expectation spiral has short-circuited, creating an unconscious desire to thwart wish transference. Thus, the individual's life develops in such a way as to reject conventional achievement aspirations." A hushed pause follows; then on we go to the next "case."

Of course, we are dealing with something quite familiar here. This is another example of the Benjamin Rush problem discussed in Chapter 2. This "theory" of birth order is structured so that no observation can disconfirm it. Because it is an unfalsifiable theory, the confirmations put forth to prove it are meaningless because nothing is ruled out by the theory.

However, our concern in this chapter is not with the theory itself, but with the nature of the evidence that is presented to support it. When pressed for evidence, Dr. Pontificate presents his own "clinical experience" or "case studies" as proof. This is an extremely common occurrence in the realm of media psychology. Talk shows and paperback book racks are full of psychological theories based on the clinical experience of the author. Many of the therapies presented to the public through these outlets are backed by nothing more than the testimonials of individuals who have undergone them and consider themselves improved or cured. In this chapter, we shall develop a principle of great use to consumers of psychological information: Case studies and testimonials are virtually worthless as evidence for the evaluation of psychological theories and treatments.

In this chapter, we will demonstrate why this is true, and we will also discuss the proper role of the case study in psychology.

The Place of the Case Study

A case study is an investigation that looks intensely and in detail at a single individual or very small number of individuals. The usefulness of case study information is strongly determined by how far scientific investigation has advanced in a particular area. The insights gained from case studies or clinical experience may be quite useful in the early stages of the investigation of certain problems as indicators of which variables deserve more intense study. Case studies have played a prominent role in opening up new areas of study in psychology (Martin & Hull, 2006). Well-known examples occur in the work of Jean Piaget. Piaget's investigations raised the possibility that children's thinking is not just a watered-down or degraded version of adults' thinking but has a structure of its own. Some of Piaget's conjectures about children's thinking have been confirmed, but many have not (Bjorklund, 2011; Goswami, 2008). However, what is important for our discussion here is not how many of Piaget's conjectures have been confirmed. Instead, what is important is to understand the fact that Piaget's case studies did not *prove* anything but, rather, suggested incredibly fruitful areas for developmental psychologists to investigate. It was subsequent correlational and experimental studies of the type to be described in Chapters 5 and 6 that provided the confirmatory and disconfirmatory evidence for the hypotheses that were generated by Piaget's case studies.

However, when we move from the early stages of scientific investigation, where case studies may be very useful, to the more mature stages of theory testing, the situation changes drastically. Case studies are not useful at the later stages of scientific investigation because they cannot be used as confirming or disconfirming evidence in the test of a particular theory. The reason is that case studies and testimonials are isolated events that lack the comparative information necessary to rule out alternative explanations.

One of the limitations of Freud's work was that he never took the second step of moving from interesting hypotheses based on case studies to actually *testing* those hypotheses (Dufresne, 2007). One of the leading writers about Freud's work, Frank Sulloway, has said that "science is a two-step process. The first step is the development of hypotheses. Freud had developed a set of extremely compelling, extremely plausible hypotheses for his day, but he never took that key, second procedural step in the rigorous manner that is required for true science" (Dufresne, 2007, p. 53).

Testimonials are like case studies in that they are isolated events. The problem of relying on testimonial evidence is that there are testimonials to support virtually every therapy tried. Thus, it is wrong to use them to support any *specific* remedy, because all of the competing remedies *also* have supporting testimonials. What we want to know, of course, is which remedy is *best*, and we cannot determine this by using testimonial evidence. As psychologist Ray Nickerson (1998) has said in his review of the cognitive processes we use to deceive ourselves, "Every practitioner of a form of pseudomedicine can point to a cadre of patients who will testify, in all sincerity, to having benefited from the treatment" (p. 192). For example, subliminal self-help audiotapes (tapes that use messages below hearing threshold) that are purported to raise memory performance or self-esteem generate plenty of testimonials despite the fact that controlled studies indicate that they have absolutely no effect on memory or self-esteem (Lilienfeld et al., 2010).

The idea of alternative explanations is critical to an understanding of theory testing. The goal of experimental design is to structure events so that support of one particular explanation simultaneously disconfirms other explanations. Scientific progress can occur only if the data that are collected rule out some explanations, as discussed in Chapter 2 on falsifiability. Science sets up conditions for the natural selection of ideas. Some survive empirical testing and others do not. Those that remain are closer to the truth. This is the honing process by which ideas are sifted so that those that contain the most truth are found. But there must be selection and elimination in this process: Data collected as support for a particular theory must not leave many other alternative explanations as equally viable candidates. For this reason, scientists construct control or comparison groups in their experimentation. Control groups are formed so that, when their results are compared with those from an experimental group, some alternative explanations are ruled out. How this is done will be a main topic in several later chapters.

Case studies and testimonials stand as isolated phenomena. They lack the comparative information necessary to prove that a particular theory or therapy is superior. It is thus wrong to cite a testimonial or a case study as support for a *particular* theory or therapy. Those who do so mislead the public if they do not point out that such evidence is open to a wide range of alternative explanations. In short, the isolated demonstration of a phenomenon may be highly misleading. This point can be illustrated more specifically by the example of placebo effects.

Why Testimonials Are Worthless: Placebo Effects

Virtually every therapy that has ever been devised in medicine and psychology has garnered supporters and has been able to produce individuals who will testify sincerely to its efficacy. Medical science has documented testimonials to the curative powers of swine teeth, crocodile dung, powdered Egyptian mummy, and many other even more imaginative remedies (Begley, 2008; Harrington, 2008). In fact, it has long been known that the mere suggestion that treatment is being administered is enough to make many people feel better.

The tendency of people to report that any treatment has helped them, regardless of whether it has a real therapeutic element, is known as the *placebo effect* (Begley, 2010; Benedetti, Carlino, & Pollo, 2011; Buhle, Stevens, Friedman, & Wager, 2012; Harrington, 2008; Novella, 2010). The concept of the placebo effect was well illustrated in the movie *The Wizard of Oz*. The wizard did not *actually* give the tin man a heart, the scarecrow a brain, and the lion courage, but they all felt better nevertheless. In fact, because it is only in the last hundred years or so that medical science has developed a substantial number of treatments that actually have therapeutic efficacy, it has been said that "prior to the twentieth century, the whole history of medicine was simply the history of the placebo effect" (Postman, 1988, p. 96).

We can illustrate the concept of a placebo effect by considering biomedical research, where all studies of new medical procedures must include controls for placebo effects. Typically, if a new drug is being tested on a group of patients, an equivalent group will also be formed and given a pill that does not contain the drug (a placebo). Neither group will know what it is receiving. Thus, when the two groups are compared, the placebo effect—that is, the tendency to feel better when any new treatment is introduced—is controlled for. It would not be sufficient merely to show that a percentage of patients receiving the new drug report relief from their symptoms, because in the absence of a control group it would be impossible to know what percentage is reporting relief due to a placebo effect rather than to the efficacy of the drug itself.

The placebo effect has been found to be 29 percent (of patients reporting satisfactory relief after receiving a placebo) for major depression, 36 percent for duodenal ulcer, 29 percent for migraine headache, and 27 percent for reflux esophagitis (Cho, Hotopf, & Wessely, 2005). Placebo effects can be very powerful—so powerful that there have even been reports of people who have become addicted to placebo pills (Ernst & Abbot, 1999), needing more and more to maintain their state of health! One bizarre study (see Begley, 2008) found that a group of subjects who received sham surgery (incision, but no actual procedure) reported almost as much pain relief from osteoarthritis as those actually receiving a real arthroscopy. That finding is consistent with a study that found that many people who had surgery for torn rotator-cuff tendons reported that their pain was gone even though an MRI indicated that their tendons had not healed (Kolata, 2009).

It is no doubt that examples like these account for the fact that almost 50 percent of physicians report that they deliberately prescribe placebos (Tilburt, Emanuel, Kaptchuk, Curlin, & Miller, 2008). Finally, placebo effects can be modulated by the context of expectation. Research has demonstrated (Waber, Shiv, Carmon, & Ariely, 2008) that a costly placebo provides more pain relief than a cheap placebo!

Of course, in actual research on drug therapies, the placebo control is not a pill containing nothing but instead is one containing the best currently known agent for the condition. The issue isolated by the experimental comparison is whether the new drug is superior to the best one currently available.

You are given information about placebo effects every time that you take a prescription medication. The next time you receive a prescription medication (or, if you are too healthy, take a look at your grandmother's!), examine carefully the sheet of information that comes with the drug (or look on the drug manufacturer's website) and you will find information about its placebo effects on the medical problem in question. For example, I take a medication called Imitrex (sumatriptan succinate) for relief from migraine headaches. The information sheet accompanying this drug tells me that controlled studies have demonstrated that, at a particular dosage level, 57 percent of patients taking this medication receive relief in two hours (I am one of the lucky 57 percent!). But the sheet also tells me that the same studies have shown a placebo effect of 21 percent for this type of headache—21 percent of people receive relief in two hours when their pill is filled with a neutral substance rather than sumatriptan succinate.

Placebo effects are implicated in all types of psychological therapy (Lilienfeld, 2007). Many people with psychological problems of mild to moderate severity report improvement after receiving psychotherapy. However, controlled studies have demonstrated that some proportion of this recovery rate is due to a combination of placebo effects and the mere passage of time, often termed spontaneous remission. As Dodes (1997) notes, "Even serious diseases have periods of exacerbation and remission; arthritis and multiple sclerosis are prime examples" (p. 45).

Most therapeutic treatments are some unknown combination of an active therapeutic component and a placebo effect. Dodes (1997) cautions us to realize that a positive response to a placebo does not mean that a patient's problem was imaginary and warns that, contrary to popular belief, placebos can be harmful: "Placebo responses can 'teach' chronic illness by confirming and/or reinforcing the delusion of imagined disease. Patients can become dependent on nonscientific practitioners who employ placebo therapies" (p. 45).

In studies of psychotherapy effectiveness, it is often difficult to determine exactly how to treat the placebo control group, but these complications should not concern us here. Instead, it is important to understand why researchers are concerned about separating true therapeutic effects from placebo effects and spontaneous remission. For example, research has shown that psychotherapies do have a positive effect over and above what would be expected purely as the result of a placebo (Engel, 2008; Shadish & Baldwin, 2005). But experiments using placebo controls have demonstrated that merely citing the overall percentage of people who report improvement *vastly* overestimates the degree of improvement that is uniquely due to the particular treatment. The problem here is that testimonials are just too easy to generate. Cornell University psychologist Thomas Gilovich (1991) noted that "with the body so effective in healing itself, many who seek medical assistance will experience a positive outcome even if the doctor does nothing beneficial. Thus, even a worthless treatment can appear effective when the base-rate of success is so high" (p. 128). In short, placebo effects are potentially occurring whenever a therapeutic intervention is undertaken, *regardless of the efficacy of the intervention.* The problem is that placebo effects are so potent that, no matter how ludicrous the therapy one uses, if it is administered to a large group of people a few will be willing to give a testimonial to its efficacy (the early-morning whack-on-the-head therapy—use it every day and you'll feel better! Send $10.95 for your special, medically tested rubber hammer).

But we really should not joke about such a serious matter. Unwarranted reliance on testimonials and case study evidence may have disastrous consequences. Recall from Chapter 2 that members of a research team that contributed to the modern conceptualization of Tourette syndrome as an organically based disorder pointed out that inappropriate reliance on case study evidence helped to perpetuate the unfalsifiable psychoanalytic explanations of the syndrome that impeded true scientific progress in investigating the nature of the disorder.

An editorial in the *New England Journal of Medicine* illustrates what practitioners in the medical sciences believe to be the place of the case study and the testimonial in medicine. "If, for example, the *Journal* were to receive a paper describing a patient's recovery from cancer of the pancreas after he had ingested a rhubarb diet...we might publish a case report—not to announce a remedy, but only to suggest a hypothesis that should be tested in a proper clinical trial. In contrast, anecdotes about alternative remedies (usually published in books and magazines for the public) have no such documentation and are considered insufficient in themselves as support for therapeutic claims" (Angell & Kassirer, 1998, pp. 839–840).

The "Vividness" Problem

It is fine to point out how the existence of placebo effects renders testimonials useless as evidence, but we must recognize another obstacle that prevents people from understanding that testimonials cannot be accepted as proof of a claim. Social and cognitive psychologists have studied what is termed the *vividness effect* in human memory and decision making (Li & Chapman, 2009; Slovic, 2007; Stanovich, 2009; Trout, 2008; Wang, 2009). When faced with a problem-solving or decision-making situation, people retrieve from memory the information that seems relevant to the situation at hand. Thus, they are more likely to use the facts that are more accessible to solve a problem or make a decision. One factor that strongly affects accessibility is the vividness of information.

The problem is that there is nothing more vivid or compelling than sincere personal testimony that something has occurred or that something is true. The vividness of personal testimony often overshadows other information of much higher reliability. How often have we carefully collected information on different product brands before making a purchase, only to be dissuaded from our choice at the last minute by a chance recommendation of another product by a friend or an advertisement? Car purchases are a typical example. We may have read surveys of thousands of customers in *Consumer Reports* and decided on car X. After consulting the major automotive magazines and confirming that the experts also recommend car X, we feel secure in our decision—until, that is, we meet a friend at a party who knows a friend who knows a friend who bought an X and got a real lemon, spent hundreds on repairs, and would never buy another. Obviously, this single instance should not substantially affect our opinion, which is based on a survey of thousands of owners and the judgment of several experts. Yet how many of us could resist the temptation to overweight this evidence?

Imagine that you saw the following headline one Friday morning in your newspaper: "Jumbo Jet Crash Kills 413 People." Goodness, you might think, what a horrible accident. What a terrible thing to happen. Imagine, though, that the following Thursday you got up and your newspaper said, "Another Jumbo Jet Disaster: 442 Die." Oh, no, you might think. Not another disaster! How horrible. What in the world is wrong with our air traffic system? And then imagine—please imagine as best you can—getting up the following Friday and seeing in the paper: "Third Tragic Airline Crash: 431 Dead." Not only you but also the nation would be beside itself. A federal investigation would be demanded. Flights would be grounded. Commissions would be appointed. Massive lawsuits would be filed. *Newsweek* and *Time* would run cover stories. It would be the lead item on television news programs for several days. Television documentaries would explore the issue. The uproar would be tremendous.

But this is not an imaginary problem. It is real. A jumbo jet *does* crash every week. Well, not one jet, but a lot of little jets. Well, not little jets really, but little transportation devices. These devices are called automobiles. And over 350 people die in them *each week* in the United States (over 19,000 people each year), enough to fill a jumbo jet.

A jumbo jet's worth of people die in passenger cars on our nation's highways every week, *yet we pay no attention*. This is because the "Jumbo Jet's Worth of People Who Die" are not presented to us in a vivid way by the media. Hence, the 350 people who die *each week* in passenger cars (plus the additional 85 who die *each week* on motorcycles) have no vividness for us. We don't talk about them at the dinner table as we do when a jet goes down and kills a lot of people. We do not debate the safety and necessity of car travel as we would the safety of the air traffic system if a jumbo jet crashed every week killing 350 people each time. The 350 are not on the news because they are distributed all over the country and, thus, are a statistical abstraction to most of us. The media do not vividly present to us these 350 deaths because they do not happen in the same place. Instead, the media present to us (occasionally) a number (e.g., 350 per week). This *should* be enough to get us thinking, but it is not. Driving automobiles is an extremely dangerous activity, compared to almost any other activity in our lives (Galovski, Malta, & Blanchard, 2006; Gardner, 2008; National Safety Council, 2001), yet there has never been a national debate about its risk relative to the benefits involved. Is this an acceptable toll for a suburban lifestyle that demands a lot of driving? We never ask the question because no problem is recognized. No problem is recognized because the cost is not presented to us in a vivid way, as is the cost of airline crashes.

Think of the absurdity of the following example. A friend drives you 20 miles to the airport where you are getting on a plane for a trip of about 750 miles. Your friend is likely to say, "Have a safe trip," as you part. This parting comment turns out to be sadly ironic, because your friend is *three times more likely to die in a car accident on the 20-mile trip back home than you are on your flight of 750 miles.* It is the vividness problem that accounts for the apparent irrationality of person A's wishing person B safety, when it is person A who is in more danger (Sivak & Flannagan, 2003).

These examples are not just hypothetical. Subsequent to the terrorist attacks of September 11, 2001, travel by airlines decreased because people were afraid of flying. Of course, people continued to travel. They did not just stay home. They simply took their trips by other means—in most cases by automobile. Since automobile travel is so much more dangerous than flying, it is a statistical certainty that more people died because they switched to driving. In fact, researchers have estimated that at least 300 more people died in the final months of 2001 because they took trips by car rather than flew (Gigerenzer, 2004, 2006). One group of researchers was able to come up with a vivid statistic to convey just how dangerous driving is. Sivak and Flannagan (2003) have calculated that for flying to be as dangerous as driving, an incident on the scale of September 11 would have to occur once a month!

It was for this reason that the Federal Aviation Administration, although it recommends that infants and toddlers have their own seat on airplanes (with approved child restraint), will not make it a requirement (Associated Press, 2010). The reason they will not is that the FAA worries that, if forced to buy a seat for young children, some parents would choose to drive rather than fly—thus putting the child in much, much more danger than if they were on their parents' laps in an airplane. In our workaday environment, there is no more dangerous place for a child than in a car, yet many parents simply cannot process this fact.

It is hard to avoid the effects of vividness in our judgments. Take the example of Cornell University, which has the reputation of having a high student suicide rate. We must ask the question of why it has this reputation. We have to ask the question because, statistically, it is not a high suicide school. In fact, its suicide rate is less than half of the national average (Frank, 2007). The reputation has nothing to do with the actual statistics—with the *actual* frequency of suicide at Cornell at all. It has to do with the fact that Cornell is bordered on two sides with deep glaciated gorges—gorges with dramatic bridges spanning them (Frank, 2007). Not surprisingly, the suicides that do occur often take place on these bridges, leading to traffic tie-ups as rescue teams retrieve bodies from the gorge and, most importantly, vivid television footage from the sight of the suicide. A drug overdose leads to no parallel type of media coverage. Cornell's reputation stems from vividness, not statistics.

Misleading personal judgments based on the vividness of media-presented images are widespread in other areas as well. Studies have surveyed parents to see which risks to their children worried them the most (Gardner, 2008; Radford, 2005; Skenazy, 2009). Parents turned out to be most worried about their children being abducted, an event with a probability of 1 in 600,000. By contrast, the probability of their child being killed in a car crash, which the parents worried about much less, is *dozens of times* more likely (Gardner, 2008). Likewise, children are much more likely to drown in a swimming pool than they are to be abducted and killed by a stranger (Kalb & White, 2010). Of course, the fears of abduction are mostly a media-created worry. Car crashes, accidents (including firearm accidents), childhood obesity, and suicide at older ages are much more of a threat to our children's well being than are things like abduction and shark attacks but, as science writer Dan Gardner (2008) notes, "we are vulnerable to scary scenarios" (p. 84). Such "scary scenarios" have, for example, created an annual parental fear of poisoned candy on Halloween when, in fact, there has never been a documented case of even a single child who died from poison candy on Halloween—not one (Skenazy, 2010).

Because of media-created vividness effects, our risk perception is all out of whack. For instance, developing diabetes causes less worry among most people than risks such as developing staph infections in hospitals, even though the former will affect 45 million Americans and the latter only 1,500 in a year (Fountain, 2006). This is despite the fact that, personally, we can do something about the former (by changing our diet and exercising) but not the latter.

The vividness of presentations can even affect the way we interpret scientific evidence itself. In one study, subjects were given descriptions of psychological phenomena and explanations for those phenomena (Weisberg, Keil, Goodstein, Rawson, & Gray, 2008). Some of the explanations were good ones (involving actual psychological concepts) and others were poor ones (simply redescribing the phenomenon in a circular fashion rather than explaining it). Ratings of the quality of both types of explanations (especially the poor ones) were substantially higher when the explanations were preceded by the words "brain scans indicate." Likewise, McCabe and Castel (2008) found that the conclusions of scientific experiments in cognitive neuroscience were rated as more credible if they contained a brain image summarizing the results instead of a graph depicting the identical outcome. In short, the vividness of the presentation of scientific results influences how the research is evaluated (Beck, 2010).

The Overwhelming Impact of the Single Case

A well-known example of how people respond differently to vivid anecdotal information comes from the media coverage of the Vietnam War in the mid- to late 1960s. As the war dragged on and the death toll of Americans killed continued without an end in sight, the media took to reporting the weekly number of American service personnel who had been killed that week. Week after week, the figure varied between 200 and 300, and the public, seemingly, became quite accustomed to this report. However, one week a major magazine published a spread, running on for several pages, of the individual pictures of those persons who had died in the previous week.

The public was now looking, concretely, at the approximately 250 individual lives that had been lost in a typical week. The result was a major outcry against the toll that the war was taking. The 250 pictures had an effect that the weekly numbers had not had. But we, as a society, must overcome this tendency not to believe numbers—to have to see everything. Most of the complex influences on our society are accurately captured only by numbers. Until the public learns to treat these numerical abstractions of reality as seriously as images, public opinion will be as fickle as the latest image to flicker across the screen.

History repeated itself in 2004 when the *Nightline* television program ran the names and photographs of the over 700 soldiers who had died at the time of the first anniversary of the start of the Iraq war. This was exactly the same format that the *Nightline* program had used when it ran the names and photographs of the victims of the September 11 attack on its first anniversary. Both sets of photographs were run with the permission of the families of those pictured. However, the photos of the dead soldiers drew howls of protest from supporters of the war. There were charges that the show's host, Ted Koppel, was hostile to the war, but these charges were misplaced because Koppel had not been opposed to the war (CNN.com, 2004). In fact, it was not that the number who had died had not been reported. That over 700 had died to that point was reported day after day in every newspaper in the country. But both sides in this controversy knew that the public had, in some sense, not yet "processed" that number—had not yet calculated the cost because the number was an abstraction. Both sides knew that many people would really become conscious of the costs—would really only process the information for the first time—when they had seen the pictures.

But it is not only the public that is plagued by the vividness problem. Experienced clinical practitioners in both psychology and medicine struggle all the time with the tendency to have their judgment clouded by the overwhelming impact of the single case. Writer Francine Russo (1999) describes the dilemma of Willie Anderson, an oncologist at the University of Virginia. Anderson is an advocate of controlled experimentation and routinely enrolls his patients in controlled clinical trials, but he still struggles with his own reactions to single, salient cases that have an emotional impact on his decisions. Despite his scientific orientation, he admits that "when it's real people looking you in the eye, you get wrapped up in their hopes and your hopes for their hopes, and it's *hard*" (p. 36). But Anderson knows that sometimes the best thing for his patients is to ignore the "real person looking you in the eye" and go with what the best evidence says. And the best evidence comes from a controlled clinical trial (described in Chapter 6), not from the emotional reaction to that person looking you in the eye.

In summary, the problems created by reliance on testimonial evidence are ever present. The vividness of such evidence often eclipses more reliable information and obscures understanding. Psychology instructors worry that merely pointing out the logical fallacies of reliance on testimonial evidence is not enough to provide a deep understanding of the pitfalls of these types of data. What else can be done? Is there any other way to get this concept across to people? Fortunately, there is an alternative—an alternative somewhat different from the academic approach. The essence of this approach is to fight vividness with vividness. To hoist testimonials on their own petard! To let testimonials devour themselves with their own absurdity. A practitioner of this approach is the one, the only, the indubitable Amazing Randi!

The Amazing Randi: Fighting Fire with Fire

James Randi is a magician and jack-of-all-trades who has received a MacArthur Foundation "genius" grant. For many years, he has been trying to teach the public some basic skills of critical thinking. The Amazing Randi (his stage name) has done this by exposing the fraud and charlatanism surrounding claims of "psychic" abilities. Although he has uncovered many magicians and conjurors masquerading as psychics, he is best known for exposing the trickery of Uri Geller, the psychic superstar of the 1970s. Bursting on the scene with his grand claims of psychic powers, Geller captivated the media to an extraordinary degree. He was featured in newspapers, on television shows, and in major news magazines on several continents (Geller is still around, writing books; Radford, 2006). Randi detected and exposed the common and sometimes embarrassingly simple magic tricks that Geller used to perform his psychic "feats," which included bending keys and spoons, and starting watches—mundane fare for a good magician. Since the Geller exposé, Randi has continued to use his considerable talents in the service of the public's right to know the truth in spite of itself by exposing the fallacies behind ESP, biorhythms, psychic surgery, levitation, and other pseudosciences (Randi, 1995, 2005, 2011; Sagan, 1996; Shermer, 2011).

One of Randi's minor diversions consists of demonstrating how easy it is to garner testimonial evidence for any preposterous event or vacuous claim. His technique is to let people be swallowed up in a trap set by their own testimonials. On a radio show, Randi demonstrated the basis for the popularity of another pseudoscience: biorhythms (Hines, 1998, 2003). One listener agreed to keep a day-by-day diary and compare it with a two-month biorhythm chart that had been prepared especially for her. Two months later, the woman called back to inform the audience that biorhythms should be taken very seriously because her chart was more than 90 percent accurate. Randi had to inform her of the silly mistake made by his secretary, who had sent someone else's chart to her, rather than her own. However, the woman did agree to evaluate the correct chart, which would be mailed to her right away, and to call back. A couple of days later, the woman called back, relieved. Her own chart was just as accurate—in fact, even more accurate. On the next show, however, it was discovered that, whoops, another error had been made. The woman had been sent Randi's secretary's chart rather than her own!

Randi's biorhythm scam is actually an example of a phenomenon that has been termed the "P. T. Barnum effect." (Barnum, the famous carnival and circus operator, coined the statement "There's a sucker born every minute.") This effect has been extensively studied by psychologists (Claridge, Clark, Powney, & Hassan, 2008), who have found that the vast majority of individuals will endorse generalized personality summaries as accurate and specific descriptions of themselves. Here is an example taken from Shermer (2005, p. 6):

> You can be a very considerate person, very quick to provide for others, but there are times, if you are honest, when you recognize a selfish streak in yourself.... Sometimes you are too honest about your feelings and you reveal too much of yourself. You are good at thinking things through and you like to see proof before you change your mind about anything. When you find yourself in a new situation you are very cautious until you find out what's going on, and then you begin to act with confidence.... You know how to be a good friend. You are able to discipline yourself so that you seem in control to others, but actually you sometimes feel somewhat insecure. You wish you could be a little more popular and at ease in your interpersonal relationships than you are now. You are wise in the ways of the world, a wisdom gained through hard experience rather than book learning.

Large numbers of people find this summary to be a very accurate description of their personality. But very few people spontaneously realize that most other people would also find it indicative of *themselves!* There are well-known sets of statements and phrases (like this example) that most people see as applicable to themselves. Anyone can feed them to a "client" as individualized psychological "analysis" and the client will usually be very impressed by the individualized accuracy of the "personality reading," not knowing that the same reading is being given to everyone. The Barnum effect is, of course, the basis of belief in the accuracy of palm readers and astrologists (Kelly, 1997, 1998). The Barnum effect also provides an example of how easy it is to generate testimonials and, of course, shows why they are worthless.

This is exactly what James Randi was trying to do in his little scam described previously—to teach people a lesson about the worthlessness of testimonial evidence. He consistently demonstrates how easy it is to generate testimonials in favor of just about any bogus claim. For this reason, presenting a testimonial in support of a particular claim is meaningless. Only evidence from controlled observations (to be described in Chapter 6) is sufficient to actually *test* a claim.

Testimonials Open the Door to Pseudoscience

It is sometimes claimed that pseudosciences like parapsychology, astrology, biorhythms, and fortune-telling are simply a way to have a little fun, that they really do no harm. After all, why should we care? Isn't it just a case of a few people engaging in wishful thinking and a few others making a couple of bucks out of them? In fact, a complete examination of the problem reveals that the harm done to society by the prevalence of pseudosciences is more widespread than is generally believed.

First, people tend not to think about what economists call *opportunity costs*. When you take time to do one thing, you have lost the time to do something else. You have lost the opportunity to spend your time otherwise. When you spend money on one thing you no longer have the money to do something else—you have lost the opportunity to spend otherwise. Pseudosciences have massive opportunity costs. When people spend time (and money) on pseudosciences they gain nothing and they waste time that might have been spent on more productive endeavors.

A complete examination of the problem reveals that the harm done to society by the prevalence of pseudosciences is more widespread than is generally believed. And the costs extend beyond opportunity costs. In a complex, technological society, the influence of pseudoscience can be propagated by decisions that affect thousands of other people. That is, you may be affected by pseudoscientific beliefs even if you do not share those beliefs. For example, one third of Americans are drinking unfluoridated water despite voluminous scientific evidence that fluoridation can significantly reduce tooth decay (Beck, 2008; Griffin, Regnier, Griffin, & Huntley, 2007; Singh, Spencer, & Brennan, 2007). The Centers for Disease Control estimate that for every dollar spent on fluoridation, $38 in dental treatment costs are saved (Brody, 2012). Nevertheless, millions of Americans in areas without fluoridation are suffering needless cavities because their neighbors are in the grip of pseudoscientific conspiracy theories about the harmful effects of fluoridation. Small groups of people with these pseudoscientific beliefs have pressured various communities to keep fluoridation out and have thus denied its benefits to everyone who lives near them. In short, the pseudoscientific beliefs of the few have negatively affected the many.

Consider another example of how you might be affected by pseudoscience even though you do not believe in it yourself. Major banks and several *Fortune* 500 companies employ graphologists for personnel decisions even though voluminous evidence indicates that graphology is useless for this purpose (Lilienfeld et al., 2010). To the extent that pseudodiagnostic graphological cues lead employers to ignore more valid criteria, both economic inefficiency and personal injustice are the result. How would you like to lose your chance for a job that you really want because you have a particular little "loop" in your handwriting?

Unfortunately, these examples are not rare (Shermer, 2005; Stanovich, 2009). We are all affected in numerous ways when pseudoscientific beliefs permeate society—even if we do not subscribe to the beliefs. For example, police departments hire psychics to help with investigations even though research has shown that this practice has no effectiveness (Radford, 2010; Shaffer & Jadwiszczok, 2010). There is not a single documented case of psychic information being used to successfully find a missing person (Radford, 2009).

Pseudosciences such as astrology are now large industries, involving newspaper columns, radio shows, book publishing, the Internet, magazine articles, and other means of dissemination. The leading horoscope magazines have circulations larger than that of many legitimate science magazines. The House of Representatives Select Committee on Aging has estimated that the amount wasted on medical quackery nationally reaches into the billions. In short, pseudosciences are lucrative businesses, and the incomes of thousands of individuals depend on their public acceptance.

Some associations and organizations have been more aggressive than psychology in rooting out pseudoscience. In 2007 the Federal Trade Commission (FTC) levied multimillion dollar fines against four diet-drug marketers who sold by using infomercials and celebrity endorsements. In announcing the fines, the FTC Chairwoman Deborah Platt Majoras tried to educate the public by stating that "Testimonials from individuals are not a substitute for science, and that's what Americans need to understand" (de la Cruz, 2007, p. A10). Likewise, medical associations have been more aggressive than psychology in attacking pseudoscience and dissociating legitimate medical practice from the illegitimate. Consider the guidelines published by the Arthritis Foundation and cited by the House Committee on Aging for spotting the unscrupulous promoter:

1. He may offer a "special" or "secret" formula or device for "curing" arthritis.
2. He advertises. He uses "case histories" and testimonials from satisfied "patients."
3. He may promise (or imply) a quick or easy cure.
4. He may claim to know the cause of arthritis and talk about "cleansing" your body of "poisons" and "pepping up" your health. He may say surgery, X-rays, and drugs prescribed by a physician are unnecessary.
5. He may accuse the "medical establishment" of deliberately thwarting progress, or of persecuting him...but he doesn't allow his method to be tested in tried and proven ways.

This list could also serve as a guide for spotting fraudulent psychological treatments and claims. Note, of course, point 2, which is the focus of this chapter. But also note that points 1 and 5 illustrate the importance of something discussed earlier: Science is public. In addition to putting forth testimonials as "proof," the practitioners of pseudoscience often try to circumvent the public verifiability criterion of science by charging that there is a conspiracy to suppress their "knowledge." They use this as justification for going straight to the media with their "findings" rather than submitting their work to the normal scientific publication processes.

A caution that might be added to the list above is to watch out for situations where someone seems to be offering an outcome that allows one to escape well-established tradeoffs. For example, in investing it is well known that risk is related to reward (larger investment returns require taking more risk). In dieting, it is well known that long-term weight reduction depends on long-term changes in caloric intake. Regarding educational interventions, it is well known that the more long-lasting educational gains come from intensive intervention programs of long duration. In short: investing returns and risk trade off; weight loss and caloric intake trade off; and learning gains and intensity of intervention trade off. People pushing pseudoscientific ideas in these areas will invariably claim that they can break free of these trade-offs—that you can have high returns without risk; that you can lose weight and still eat all you want; and that educational achievement can be significantly altered by short-term interventions. You can be confident that claims that such fundamental trade-offs have been avoided are bogus. For example, you can rest assured that a product called Baby Einstein can't deliver what its name implies (Bronson & Merryman, 2009; DeLoache et al., 2010).

It is important to realize that television, the Internet, and the print media will publicize virtually any outlandish claim in the area of psychology if they think there is an audience for it, no matter how much the claim is contradicted by the available evidence. The media present a mish-mosh of claims and experts—mixing together legitimate scientists with pseudoscientific charlatans. Let's go back again and consider the *Oprah Winfrey Show*—popular for two decades on television. To be fair, it must be said that the show often presented credentialed professionals who gave the audience good information on a variety of topics from breast cancer to personal finance. But mixed into the show, with often no way to tell the difference, were the most outrageous charlatans (Gardner, 2010)—often speaking on some of the same topics. For example, Oprah publicized the alternative therapies of someone who used Tarot cards to diagnose illness and who viewed women's thyroid problems as the result of "energy blockage in the throat region" that resulted from "a lifetime of swallowing words one is aching to say" (Kosova & Wingert, 2009, p. 59).

A couple of years ago, Oprah's show also gave considerable publicity to a bunch of psycho-babble called "the Secret" that had as its primary premise that "all diseases can be cured with the power of thought alone" (p. 61). But after these particular shows aired, a revealing thing happened. A woman named Kim Tinkham wrote to Oprah that she was diagnosed with breast cancer but was not going to undergo the surgery and chemotherapy that was recommended by not only her own physician but by a second and third opinion that she received. Kim told Oprah that instead of surgery, she was going to follow The Secret. Oprah was shocked by the letter, had the woman come on the show, and tried to dissuade her from foregoing surgery and chemotherapy. Kim Tinkham is dead now, but at the time Oprah pleaded with her that people had gotten the wrong idea about The Secret on her show—that "I just wanted to say it's a tool. It's not the answer to everything" (p. 62). No Oprah. It's not a tool. It's pseudoscience. And when you mixed science and pseudoscience like this on your show, even if well intended, the case of Kim Tinkham is the type of harm that can be expected.

As this tragic example shows, people can fail to take advantage of the real remedies available to them because they become involved in pseudosciences. Many sick individuals delay getting medically appropriate treatment because they waste time chasing bogus cures. Renowned computer entrepreneur Steve Jobs ignored his doctors after being told of his pancreatic cancer and delayed surgery for nine months while he pursued unproven fruit diets, consulted a psychic, and received bogus hydrotherapy (Isaacson, 2011).

Finally, consider the sad case of ten-year-old Candace Newmaker, whose discipline problems led her adoptive mother to take her to something called the Association for Treatment and Training in the Attachment of Children (Shermer, 2011). According to the bogus theory behind this treatment, certain children need "confrontation" and "restraint" to allow them to work through so-called repressed abandonment anger. Candace was covered by a sheet and pillows as adults lay on top of her so that she could be "reborn". When Candace cried out, the adults were told to press harder and Candace was called "a quitter." After forty minutes of further nonsense like this, Candace went quiet. She was dead. She had suffocated.

Society is often much too soft on the practitioners of pseudoscience who harm people. This time it was not. All of her therapists received 16-year prison sentences for reckless child abuse resulting in death. Michael Shermer (2011) notes that although the autopsy said the child died of "cerebral edema and herniation caused by hypoxic-ischemic encephalopathy, the ultimate cause was pseudoscientific quackery masquerading as psychological science.... These therapists killed Candace not because they were evil, but because they were in the grip of a pseudoscientific belief grounded in superstition and magical thinking" (p. 86).

A clear example of how we are all hurt when pseudoscientific beliefs spread is provided by the theory (first put forth in the early 1990s and continuing to this day) that autism is connected to the early vaccination of children. This theory is false (Grant, 2011; Honda, Shimizu, & Rutter, 2005; Judelsohn, 2007; Novella, 2007; Offit, 2008; Taylor, 2006), but no reader of this chapter should be surprised at how the belief arose. Many children are diagnosed with autism around the time of their first vaccinations and many begin to show clearly discernible signs of the condition (delayed language acquisition, difficulties in reciprocal social interaction, and a restricted repertoire of activities) around this time. Not surprisingly given that there are thousands of children with this condition, some parents become fully aware of their child's difficulties (either through diagnosis or increased awareness based on their own observations) shortly after the child receives a vaccination. These parents then provide the vivid and heartfelt testimonials that there must be a connection between their child's condition and the vaccination. However, many different experimental and epidemiological studies have converged (see Chapter 8) on the conclusion that no such connection exists (Deer, 2011). This pseudoscientific belief, though, had more costs than just the opportunity costs to the parents and children involved. The false belief in a connection spawned an antivaccination movement. As a result, immunization rates have decreased, many more children have been hospitalized with measles than would have been the case otherwise, and some have died (Goldacre, 2008; Grant, 2011; Judelsohn, 2007; Novella, 2007; Offit, 2008). Again, the lesson is that in an interconnected society, your neighbor's pseudoscientific belief might affect you even if you reject the belief yourself.

Political leaders, when they believe in pseudoscience, can inflict the consequences of their beliefs on thousands of people. The second postapartheid President of South Africa, Thabo Mbeki, rejected the scientific consensus that AIDS was caused by a virus (Pigliucci, 2010). The neighboring countries of Botswana and Namibia gave antiretroviral to their citizens infected with HIV, but South Africa did not. It is estimated that the rejection of the anti-retrovirals caused 365,000 South Africans to endure premature deaths (Singer, 2008).

Physicians are increasingly concerned about the spread of medical quackery on the Internet (Offit, 2008) and its real health costs. Dr. Max Coppes was prompted to write a letter to the *New England Journal of Medicine* warning of the real human costs of pseudoscience in medicine (Scott, 1999). He described the case of a nine-year-old girl who, after cancer surgery, had a 50 percent chance of three more years of life if she had undergone chemotherapy. Instead, her parents found an unproven treatment that utilized shark cartilage and opted for that instead. The young girl was dead in four months.

When I am speaking on this topic, at about this point in my lecture someone always asks a very relevant question: "Haven't you just employed vivid cases to illustrate a point—what you said shouldn't be done?" This is a good question and it allows me to elaborate on some of the subtleties involved in the argument of this chapter. The answer to the question is that yes, I *have* employed vivid cases to illustrate a point. To *illustrate* the point— but not to *prove* it. The key issue here is to distinguish two things: (1) the claim being made and (2) the communication of the claim. For each one we could ask, is its basis a vivid testimonial, yes or no? This yields four possible situations:

a. a claim based on vivid testimonials communicated by vivid testimonials
b. a claim based on vivid testimonials communicated without testimonials
c. a claim based on evidence other than testimonials communicated by vivid testimonials
d. a claim based on evidence other than testimonials communicated without testimonials

Some of the discussion in this chapter falls into category c: claims based on evidence other than testimonials communicated by vivid testimonials. For example, I cite much nontestimonial evidence throughout the chapter to establish claims such as the following: Case study evidence cannot be used to establish a causal influence, vivid examples are overweighted in people's judgments, pseudoscience is costly, and so on. I present in the citations and the reference list the public evidence for each of these claims. Nonetheless, for communicative purposes I have used some vivid cases to draw attention to these claims and to make them memorable. The key point, though, is that the claims themselves are supported by more than vivid testimonial evidence. So, for example, I have used some vivid examples to demonstrate the fact that vivid examples are overweighted in people's judgments. But the real evidence for the claim that vivid examples are overweighted in people's judgments is in the peer-reviewed scientific evidence I have cited (e.g., Li & Chapman, 2009; Obrecht, Chapman, & Gelman, 2009; Sinaceur, Heath, & Cole, 2005; Slovic, 2007; Wang, 2009).

So, to return to the main point of this section, and to summarize it: The spread of pseudoscience is quite costly. And nothing fosters the spread of pseudosciences more than confusion about what type of evidence does and does not justify belief in a claim about a phenomenon. By providing readily available support for virtually any claim and by the impact that they have when used, testimonials open the door to the development of and the belief in pseudosciences. There is no more important rule for the consumer of psychological information than to beware of them. In the next several chapters, we shall see what type of evidence *is* required to justify claims.

Summary

Case study and testimonial evidence is useful in psychology (and other sciences) in the very earliest stages of an investigation, when it is important to find interesting phenomena and important variables to examine further. As useful as case study evidence is in the early, pretheoretical, stages of scientific investigation, it is virtually useless in the later stages, when theories are being put to specific tests. This is because, as an isolated phenomenon, the outcome of a case study leaves many alternative explanations. One way to understand why case studies and testimonial evidence are useless for theory testing is to consider the placebo effect. The placebo effect is the tendency of people to report that any treatment has helped them, regardless of whether the treatment had a real therapeutic element. The existence of placebo effects makes it impossible to prove the effectiveness of a psychological (or medical) treatment by producing testimonials to its effectiveness. The reason is that the placebo effect guarantees that no matter what the treatment, it will be possible to produce testimonial evidence to its effectiveness.

Despite the uselessness of testimonial evidence in theory testing, psychological research has indicated that such evidence is often weighted quite heavily by people because of the vividness effect: People overweight evidence that is more vivid and, hence, more retrievable from memory. One thing that is particularly vivid for most people is testimonial evidence. The result is an overreliance on such evidence in the justification of specific psychological claims. In fact, testimonial and case study evidence cannot be used to justify general theoretical claims.

CHAPTER 5

Correlation and Causation: Birth Control by the Toaster Method

Many years ago, a large-scale study of the factors related to the use of contraceptive devices was conducted in Taiwan. A large research team of social scientists and physicians collected data on a wide range of behavioral and environmental variables. The researchers were interested in seeing what variables best predicted the adoption of birth control methods. After collecting the data, they found that the one variable most strongly related to contraceptive use was the number of electrical appliances (toasters, fans, etc.) in the home (Li, 1975).

This result probably does not tempt you to propose that the teenage pregnancy problem should be dealt with by passing out free toasters in high schools. But why *aren't* you tempted to think so? The correlation between appliances and contraceptive use was indeed strong, and this variable was the single best predictor among the many variables that were measured. Your reply, I hope, will be that it is not the strength but the *nature* of the relationship that is relevant. Starting a free toaster program would imply the belief that toasters *cause* people to use contraceptives. The fact that we view this suggestion as absurd means that, at least in clear-cut cases such as this, we recognize that two variables may be associated without having a causal relationship.

In this example, we can guess that the relationship exists because contraceptive use and the number of electrical appliances in the home are linked through some other variable that relates to both. Socioeconomic status (SES) would be one likely candidate for a mediating variable. We know that SES is related to contraceptive use. All we need now is the fact that families at higher socioeconomic levels tend to have more electrical appliances in their homes, and we have the linkage. Of course, other variables may mediate this correlation. However, the point is that, no matter how strong the correlation is between the number of toasters and contraceptive use, the relationship does not indicate a causal connection.

The contraceptive example makes it very easy to understand the fundamental principle of this chapter: The presence of a correlation does not necessarily imply causation. In this chapter, we will discuss the two problems that prevent the drawing of a causal inference: the third-variable problem and the directionality problem. We will also discuss how the third-variable problem often results from selection bias.

The limitations of correlational evidence are not always so easy to recognize as the toaster example. When the causal link seems obvious to us, when we have a strong preexisting bias, or when our interpretations become dominated by our theoretical orientation, it is tempting to treat correlations as evidence of causation.

The Third-Variable Problem: Goldberger and Pellagra

In the early 1900s, thousands of Americans in the South suffered and died of a disease called *pellagra*. Characterized by dizziness, lethargy, running sores, vomiting, and severe diarrhea, the disease was thought to be infectious and to be caused by a living microorganism of "unknown origin." It is not surprising, then, that many physicians of the National Association for the Study of Pellagra were impressed by evidence that the disease was linked to sanitary conditions. It seemed that homes in Spartanburg, South Carolina, that were free of pellagra invariably had inside plumbing and good sewerage. By contrast, the homes of pellagra victims often had inferior sewerage. This correlation coincided quite well with the idea of an infectious disease transmitted, because of poor sanitary conditions, via the excrement of pellagra victims.

One physician who doubted this interpretation was Joseph Goldberger, who, at the direction of the surgeon general of the United States, had conducted several investigations of pellagra. Goldberger thought that pellagra was caused by inadequate diet—in short, by the poverty common throughout the South. Many victims had lived on high-carbohydrate, extremely low-protein diets, characterized by small amounts of meat, eggs, and milk and large amounts of corn, grits, and mush. Goldberger thought that the correlation between sewage conditions and pellagra did not reflect a causal relationship in either direction (much as in the toaster–birth control example). Goldberger thought that the correlation arose because families with sanitary plumbing were likely to be economically advantaged. This economic discrepancy would also be reflected in their diets, which would contain more animal protein.

But wait a minute! Why should Goldberger get away with his causal inference? After all, both sides were just sitting there with their correlations, Goldberger with pellagra and diet and the other physicians with pellagra and sanitation. Why shouldn't the association's physicians be able to say that Goldberger's correlation was equally misleading? Why was he justi- fied in rejecting the hypothesis that an infectious organism was transmit- ted through the excrement of pellagra victims because of inadequate sewage disposal? Well, the reason Goldberger was justified has to do with one small detail that I neglected to mention: Goldberger had eaten the excrement of pellagra victims.

Why Goldberger's Evidence Was Better

Goldberger had a type of evidence (a controlled manipulation, discussed further in the next chapter) that is derived when the investigator, instead of simply observing correlations, actually manipulates the critical vari- able. This approach often involves setting up special conditions that rarely occur naturally—and to call Goldberger's special conditions unnatural is an understatement!

Confident that pellagra was not contagious and not transmitted by the bodily fluids of the victims, Goldberger had himself injected with the blood of a victim. He inserted throat and nose secretions from a victim into his own mouth. According to Bronfenbrenner and Mahoney (1975), two researchers describing Goldberger's efforts, he and his assistants even ate dough balls that contained the urine and feces of pellagra victims! Despite all of these extreme interventions, neither Goldberger nor the other volunteers came down with pellagra. In short, Goldberger had created the conditions necessary for the infectious transmission of the disease, and nothing had happened.

Goldberger had now manipulated the causal mechanism suggested by others and had shown that it was ineffective, but it was still necessary to test his own causal mechanism. Goldberger got two groups of prisoners from a Mississippi state prison farm who were free of pellagra to volunteer for his experiment. One group was given the high-carbohydrate, low-protein diet that he suspected was the cause of pellagra, while the other group received a more balanced diet. Within five months, the low-protein group was ravaged by pellagra, while the other group showed no signs of the disease. After a long struggle, during which Goldberger's ideas were opposed by those with politi- cal motives for denying the existence of poverty, his hypothesis was eventu- ally accepted because it matched the empirical evidence better than any other.

The history of pellagra illustrates the human cost of basing social and economic policy on mistaken inferences from correlational studies. This is not to say that we should never use correlational evidence. Quite the contrary. In many instances, it is all we have to work with (see Chapter 8), and in some cases, it is all we need (for instance, when prediction, rather than determina- tion of cause, is the goal). Scientists often have to use incomplete knowledge to solve problems. The important thing is that we approach correlational evi- dence with a certain skepticism. Examples such as the pellagra–sewage case occur with considerable frequency in all areas of psychology. The example illustrates what is sometimes termed the *third-variable problem*: the fact that the correlation between the two variables—in this case, pellagra incidence and sewage conditions—may not indicate a direct causal path between them but may arise because both variables are related to a third variable that has not even been measured. Pellagra incidence is related to SES (and to diet—the real causal variable) and SES is also related to sewerage quality. Correlations like that between sewage and pellagra are often called spurious correlations: correlations that arise not because a causal link exists between the two variables that are measured, but because both variables are related to a third variable.

Let's consider a more contemporary example. For decades, debates have raged over the relative efficacy of public and private schools. Some of the conclusions drawn in this debate vividly demonstrate the perils of inferring causation from correlational evidence. The question of the efficacy of private versus public schools is an empirical problem that can be attacked with the investigative methods of the social sciences. This is not to imply that it is an easy problem, only that it is a scientific problem, potentially solvable. All advocates of the superiority of private schools implicitly recognize this, because at the crux of their arguments is an empirical fact: Student achievement in private schools exceeds that in public schools. This fact is not in dispute—educational statistics are plentiful and largely consistent across various studies. The problem is the use of these achievement data to conclude that the education received in private schools *causes* the superior test scores.

The outcome of educational testing is a function of many different variables, all of which are correlated. In order to evaluate the relative efficacy of public schools and private schools, we need more complex statistics than merely the relationship between the type of school attended and school achievement. For example, educational achievement is related to many different indicators of family background, such as parental education, parental occupation, SES, the number of books in the home, and other factors. These characteristics are also related to the probability of sending a child to a private school. Thus, family background is a potential third variable that may affect the relationship between academic achievement and the type of school. In short, the relationship may have nothing to do with the effectiveness of private schools but may be the result of the fact that economically advantaged children do better academically and are more likely to attend private schools.

Fortunately, there exist complex correlational statistics such as *multiple regression*, *partial correlation*, and *path analysis* (statistics developed in part by psychologists) that were designed to deal with problems such as this one. These statistics allow the correlation between two variables to be recalculated after the influence of other variables is removed, or "factored out" or "partialed out." Using these more complex correlational techniques, researchers have analyzed a large set of educational statistics on high school students. They found that, after variables reflecting the students' home backgrounds and general mental ability were factored out, there was virtually no relationship between school achievement and the type of school attended. Their results have been confirmed by other researchers (Berliner & Biddle, 1995; Carnoy, Jacobsen, Mishel, & Rothstein, 2005; Hendrie, 2005).

Thus, it appears that advocating private schools as a means of improving educational achievement is the same as arguing for birth control by the toaster method. Academic achievement is linked to private school attendance not because of any direct causal mechanism, but because the family background and the general cognitive level of students in private schools are different from those of children in public schools.

The complex correlational statistics that allow us to partial out the effects of a third variable do not always reduce the magnitude of the original correlation. Sometimes the original correlation between two variables remains even after the partialing out of the third variable, and this result itself can be informative. Such an outcome indicates that the original correlation was not due to a spurious relationship with that particular third variable. Of course, it does not remove the possibility of a spurious relationship due to some other variable.

Another example is provided by research showing that the probability that a high school student will attend university is related to the SES of the student's family. This is an important finding that strikes at the heart of the merit-based goals of our society. It suggests that opportunities for success in life are determined by a person's economic class. However, before jumping to this conclusion, we must consider several other alternative hypotheses. That is, the correlation between university attendance and SES should be examined closely for spuriousness. One obvious candidate for a third variable is academic ability. Perhaps this is related to both university attendance and SES, and if it is partialed out, the correlation between the first two variables may disappear. However, researchers calculated the appropriate statistics and found that the correlation between university attendance and SES remained significant even after academic aptitude was partialed out (Baker & Velez, 1996; Long, 2007). Thus, the fact that children of higher economic classes are more likely to attend university is not entirely due to differences in academic aptitude. This finding, of course, does not rule out the possibility that some other variable leads to the relationship between the first two, but it is clearly important, both practically and theoretically, to be able to rule out a major alternative explanation such as academic aptitude.

Consider another example in which the technique of partial correlation was used. It turns out that the violent crime in the United States is higher in the southern states than in the northern states. Anderson and Anderson (1996) tested what has been called the *heat hypothesis*—that "uncomfortably warm temperatures produce increases in aggressive motives and (sometimes) aggressive behavior" (p. 740). Not surprisingly, they did find a correlation between the average temperature in a city and its violent crime rate. What gives the heat hypothesis more credence, however, is that they found that the correlation between temperature and violent crime remained significant even after variables such as unemployment rate, per capita income, poverty rate, education, population size, median age of population, and several other variables were statistically controlled (see also, Larrick, Timmerman, Carton, & Abrevaya, 2011).

The Directionality Problem

There is no excuse for making causal inferences on the basis of correlational evidence when it is possible to manipulate variables in a way that would legitimately justify a causal inference. Yet this is a distressingly common occurrence when psychological issues are involved, and the growing importance of psychological knowledge in the solution of social problems is making this tendency increasingly costly. A well-known example in the area of educational psychology illustrates this point quite well.

Since the beginning of the scientific study of reading about a hundred years ago, researchers have known that there is a correlation between eye movement patterns and reading ability. Poorer readers make more erratic movements, display more regressions (movements from right to left), and make more fixations (stops) per line of text. On the basis of this correlation, some educators hypothesized that deficient oculomotor skills were the cause of reading problems, and many eye movement–training programs were developed and administered to elementary school children. These programs were instituted long before it was ascertained whether the correlation really indicated that erratic eye movements *caused* poor reading.

It is now known that the eye movement–reading-ability correlation reflects a causal relationship that runs in exactly the opposite direction. Erratic eye movements do not cause reading problems. Instead, slow recognition of words and difficulties with comprehension lead to erratic eye movements. When children are taught to recognize words efficiently and to comprehend better, their eye movements become smoother. Training children's eye movements does nothing to improve their reading comprehension.

For more than a decade now, research has clearly pointed to word decoding and a language problem in phonological processing as the sources of reading problems (Snowling & Hulme, 2005; Stanovich, 2000; Wagner & Kantor, 2010). Very few cases of reading disability are due to difficulties in the area of eye movement patterns. Yet, if most school districts of at least medium size were to search diligently in their storage basements, they would find the dusty "eye movement trainers" that represent thousands of dollars of equipment money wasted because of the temptation to see a correlation as proof of a causal hypothesis.

Consider another somewhat similar example. An extremely popular hypothesis in the fields of education and counseling psychology has been that school achievement problems, drug abuse problems, teenage pregnancy, bullying, and many other problem behaviors are the result of low self-esteem. It was assumed that the causal direction of the linkage was obvious: Low self-esteem led to problem behaviors, and high self-esteem led to high educational achievement and accomplishments in other domains. This assumption of causal direction provided the motivation for many educational programs for improving self-esteem. The problem here was the same as that in the eye movement example: An assumption of causal direction was made from the mere existence of a correlation. It turns out that the relationship between self-esteem and school achievement, if it exists at all, is more likely to be in the opposite direction: Superior accomplishment in school (and in other aspects of life) leads to high self-esteem, rather than the reverse (Baumeister et al., 2003, 2005; Krueger et al., 2008).

Problems of determining the direction of causation are common in psychological research. For example, psychologist Jonathan Haidt (2006) has discussed research showing that there is a correlation between altruism and happiness. There is research showing, for instance, that people who do volunteer work are happier than those who do not. Of course, it was necessary to make sure that a third variable wasn't accounting for the link between altruism and happiness. Once third variables were eliminated, it was necessary to determine the *direction* of the linkage: Was it that happiness caused people to be altruistic or was it that acts of altruism made people happy ("it is more blessed to give than to receive")? When the proper controlled studies were done, using the logic of the true experiment to be described in Chapter 6, it was found that there was a causal relationship running in *both* directions: Being happy makes people more altruistic, and performing altruistic acts makes people happier.

Our discussion thus far has identified the two major classes of ambiguity present in a simple correlation between two variables. One is called the *directionality problem* and is illustrated by the eye movement and self-esteem examples. Before immediately concluding that a correlation between variable A and variable B is due to changes in A causing changes in B, we must first recognize that the direction of causation may be the opposite, that is, from B to A. The second problem is the third-variable problem, and it is illustrated by the pellagra example (and the toaster–birth control and private-school–achievement examples). The correlation between the two variables may not indicate a causal path in either direction but may arise because both variables are related to a third variable.

Selection Bias

There are certain situations in which the possibility of a spurious correlation is very likely. These are situations in which there is a high probability that selection bias has occurred. The term *selection bias* refers to the relationships between certain subject and environmental variables that may arise when people with different biological, behavioral, and psychological characteristics select different types of environments. Selection bias creates a spurious correlation between environmental characteristics and behavioral–biological characteristics.

Let's look at a straightforward example that illustrates the importance of selection factors in creating spurious correlations: Quickly, name a state with an above-average incidence of deaths due to respiratory illness. One answer to this question would be, of course, Arizona. What? Wait a minute! Arizona has clean air, doesn't it? Does the smog of Los Angeles spread that far? Has the suburban sprawl of Phoenix become that bad? No, it can't be. Let's slow down a minute. Maybe Arizona *does* have good air. And maybe people with respiratory illnesses tend to move there. And then they die. There you have it. A situation has arisen in which, if we're not careful, we may be led to think that Arizona's air is killing people.

However, selection factors are not always so easy to discern. They are often overlooked, particularly when there is a preexisting desire to see a certain type of causal link. Tempting correlational evidence combined with a preexisting bias may deceive even the best of minds. Let's consider some specific cases.

The importance of considering selection factors was illustrated quite well in the national debate over the quality of American education that has taken place throughout most of the last two decades. During this debate, the public was inundated with educational statistics but was not provided with corresponding guidance for avoiding the danger of inferring causal relationships from correlational data that are filled with misleading selection factors.

Throughout the continuing debate, many commentators with a political agenda repeatedly attempted to provide evidence that educational quality is not linked to teacher salary levels or class size, despite evidence that both are important (Ehrenberg, Brewer, Gamoran, & Williams, 2001). One set of findings put forth was the SAT test results for each of the 50 states. The average scores on this test, taken by high school students who intend to go to certain universities, did indeed show little relation to teacher salaries and general expenditure on education. If anything, the trends seemed to run opposite to the expected direction. Several states that had very high average teacher salaries had very low average SAT scores, and many states at the bottom of the teacher salary rankings had very high average SAT scores. A close look at the data patterns provides an excellent lesson in how easily selection factors can produce spurious correlations.

On further examination, we see that Mississippi students, for example, score higher than California students on the SAT (Grissmer, 2000; Powell & Steelman, 1996). In fact, the difference is considerable. The average Mississippi scores are over 100 points higher. Because Mississippi teachers' salaries are the lowest in the nation, this was cause for celebration among commentators arguing for cuts in teachers' salaries. But wait. Is it really true that schools are better in Mississippi than in California—that the general state of education is superior in the former? Of course not. Virtually any other objective index would show that California schools are superior. But if this is true, what about the SAT?

The answer lies in selection factors. The SAT is not taken by all high school students. Unlike much standardized testing that schools conduct, in which all children are uniformly tested, the SAT involves selection bias. Only students hoping to go to a university take the test. This factor accounts for some of the state-by-state variance in average scores on the test and also explains why some of the states with the very best educational systems have very low-average SAT scores.

Selection factors operate on the SAT scores of states in two different ways. First, some state university systems require the American College Testing (ACT) program test scores rather than the SAT scores. Thus, the only students who take the SAT in these states are students planning to go to a university out of state. It is more likely that these students will be from advantaged backgrounds and/or will have higher academic aptitude than the average student. This is what happened in the Mississippi–California example. Only 4 percent of Mississippi high school students took the SAT, whereas the figure in California was 47 percent (Powell & Steelman, 1996).

The second selection factor is a bit more subtle. In states with good educational systems, many students intend to continue their education after high school. In such states, a high proportion of students take the SAT, including a greater number with lesser abilities. States with high dropout rates and lower overall quality have a much smaller proportion of students who aspire to a university education. The group of students who eventually take the SAT in such states represents only those best qualified to go to a university. The resulting average SAT scores in these states naturally tend to be higher than those from states where larger proportions of students pursue further education.

The misuse of SAT scores also provides us with an unfortunate example of how hard it is to correct the misleading use of statistics as long as the general public lacks the simple methodological and statistical thinking skills taught in this book. Brian Powell (1993), an Indiana University professor, analyzed a column written by political columnist George Will in which Will argued against public expenditures on education because states with high SATs do not have high expenditures on education. Powell pointed out that the states that Will singled out as having particularly high scores—Iowa, North Dakota, South Dakota, Utah, and Minnesota—have SAT participation rates of only 5 percent, 6 percent, 7 percent, 4 percent, and 10 percent, respectively, whereas more than 40 percent of all high school seniors in the United States take the SAT. The reason is that in these states, the test required for admission to public institutions is the ACT test. Only students planning on studying out of state, "often at prestigious private schools" (Powell, 1993, p. 352), take the SAT. By contrast, in New Jersey, which Will used as an example of a state with low SAT scores and high expenditures, 76 percent of high school seniors take the test. Obviously the students in North and South Dakota who take the SAT are a more select group than those in New Jersey, where three-quarters of all students take the test.

Jumping to conclusions when selection effects are present can lead us to make bad real-world choices. Many women were once encouraged to take hormone replacement therapy (HRT) after menopause because of reports that it lowered the probability of heart disease. But the early studies that had indicated this had simply compared groups of women who had chosen to take HRT (i.e., who self-selected the treatment) with those who had not chosen to take HRT. However, true experiments (using random assignment, see Chapter 6) conducted later on found that HRT actually did not reduce the likelihood of heart disease at all (Bluming & Tavris, 2009; Seethaler, 2009). The earlier studies involving self-selected samples had *seemed* to indicate that it did because women who chose to have HRT were more physically active, less obese, and less likely to smoke than women who did not choose HRT.

An example from clinical psychology demonstrates how tricky and "perverse" the selection bias problem can be. It has sometimes been demonstrated that the cure rate for various addictive-appetite problems such as obesity, heroin use, and cigarette smoking is lower for those who have had psychotherapy than for those who have not. The reason, you will be glad to know, is not that psychotherapy makes addictive behavior more resistant to change. It is that, among those who seek psychotherapy, the disorder is more intractable, and self-cures have been ineffective. In short, "hard cases" seek psychotherapy more than "easy cases."

Wainer (1999) tells a story from World War II that reminds us of the sometimes perverse aspects of selection bias. He describes an aircraft analyst who was trying to determine where to place extra armor on an aircraft based on the pattern of bullet holes in the returning planes. His decision was to put the extra armor in the places that were free of bullet holes on the returning aircraft that he analyzed. He did *not* put the extra armor in the places where there were a lot of bullet holes. His reasoning was that the planes had probably been pretty uniformly hit with bullets. Where he found the bullet holes on the returning aircraft told him that, in those places, the plane could be hit and still return. Those areas that were free of bullet holes on returning planes had probably been hit—but planes hit there did not return. Hence, it was the places on the returning planes *without* bullet holes that needed more armor!

It is easy to use selection effects to "set up" people to make a causal inference. How about this one: Republicans enjoy sex more than Democrats. It's an absolute fact. Statistics show that the average Republican voter is more satisfied with their sex lives than the average Democratic voter (Blastland & Dilnot, 2009). What is it about Republicanism that makes people sexier?

OK, you guessed it. That's not right. Politics doesn't change anyone's sex life. What accounts for the data, then? Two things. First, men vote Republican more than women. Second, surveys show that men report more satisfaction with their sex lives than women. Republicanism doesn't change anyone's sex life; it's just that a demographic group (men) who have higher satisfaction levels are more prone to vote Republican.

Examples such as the "sexy Republican" show us how careful we have to be when selection effects might be operating. Economist Steven Landsburg (2007) shows us how that much of the data showing productivity tied to the use of technology might be over interpreted as causal when in fact it is only correlational data containing selection effects. Within corporations, it is often the most productive employees who are given the most advanced technology. Thus, when a correlation is calculated, productivity will be correlated with technology use. But it is not that the technology improved the performance of these employees, because they were *already* more productive before they received the advanced technology.

An important real-life health issue that implicates selection effects strongly is the debate about the health outcomes of alcohol consumption. Numerous studies have found that moderate drinkers have better health outcomes than not only frequent drinkers but also abstainers as well (Rabin, 2009). Aware of selection effects, neither you nor I will be tempted to tell anyone abstaining from alcohol that they would improve their health by drinking a little. This is because people self select themselves into drinking groups by deciding how much to drink. As Rabin (2009) explains, it has been found that moderate drinkers are moderate in everything they do. They exercise moderately and eat moderately. They tend to do a lot of things right. So of course the problem is that we do not know whether it is the moderate drinking itself that leads to positive health outcomes or whether it is all of the other good characteristics of the moderate drinking group (their exercise levels, diet, etc.). Because of selection effects, we cannot say that the moderate drinking itself is the cause.

In short, the consumer's rule for this chapter is simple: Be on the lookout for instances of selection bias, and avoid inferring causation when data are only correlational. It is true that complex correlational designs do exist that allow limited causal inferences. It is also true that correlational evidence is helpful in demonstrating convergence on a hypothesis (see Chapter 8). Nevertheless, it is probably better for the consumer to err on the side of skepticism than to be deceived by correlational relationships that falsely imply causation.

Summary

The central point of this chapter was to convey that the mere existence of a relationship between two variables does not guarantee that changes in one are causing changes in the other. The point is that correlation does not imply causation. Two problems in interpreting correlational relationships were discussed. In the third-variable problem, the correlation between the two variables may not indicate a direct causal path between them but instead may arise because both variables are related to a third variable that has not even been measured. If, in fact, the potential third variable has been measured, correlational statistics such as partial correlation (to be discussed again in Chapter 8) can be used to assess whether that third variable is determining the relationship.

The other thing that makes the interpretation of correlations difficult is the existence of the directionality problem: the fact that even if two variables are causally related, the direction of that relationship is not indicated by the mere presence of the correlation.

Selection bias is the reason for many spurious relationships in the behavioral sciences: the fact that people choose their own environments to some extent and thus create correlations between behavioral characteristics and environmental variables. As the example of pellagra demonstrated, and as will be illustrated extensively in the next two chapters, the only way to ensure that selection bias is not operating is to conduct a true experiment in which the key variable is manipulated.

CHAPTER 6

Getting Things Under Control: The Case of Clever Hans

This chapter starts with a quiz. Don't worry; it's not about what you read in the last chapter. In fact, it should be easy because it's about the observable motion of objects in the world, something with which we have all had much experience. There are just three questions in the quiz.

For the first, you will need a piece of paper. Imagine that a person is whirling a ball attached to a string around his or her head. Draw a circle that represents the path of the ball as viewed from above the person's head. Draw a dot somewhere on the circle and connect the dot to the center of the circle with a line. The line represents the string, and the dot represents the ball at a particular instant in time. Imagine that at exactly this instant, the string is cut. Your first task is to indicate with your pencil the subsequent flight of the ball.

For your next problem, imagine that you are a bomber pilot flying toward a target at 500 miles per hour at a height of 20,000 feet. To simplify the problem, assume that there is no air resistance. The question here is, at which location would you drop your bomb: before reaching the target, directly over the target, or when you have passed the target? Indicate a specific distance in front of the target, directly over the target, or a specific distance past the target.

Finally, imagine that you are firing a rifle from shoulder height. Assume that there is no air resistance and that the rifle is fired exactly parallel to the ground. If a bullet that is dropped from the same height as the rifle takes one-half second to hit the ground, how long will it take the bullet that is fired from the rifle to hit the ground if its initial velocity is 2,000 feet per second?

And the answers—oh, yes, the answers. They appear later on in this chapter. But, first, in order to understand what the accuracy of our knowledge about moving objects has to do with psychology, we need to explore more fully the nature of the experimental logic that scientists use. In this chapter, we will discuss principles of experimental control and manipulation.

Snow and Cholera

In his studies of pellagra, Joseph Goldberger was partially guided by his hunch that the disease was not contagious. But 70 years earlier, John Snow, in his search for the causes of cholera, bet the opposite way and also won (Johnson, 2007; Shapin, 2006). Many competing theories had been put forth to explain the repeated outbreaks of cholera in London in the 1850s. Many doctors believed that the exhalations of victims were inhaled by others who then contracted the disease. This was called the miasmal theory. By contrast, Snow hypothesized that the disease was spread by the water supply, which had become contaminated with the excrement of victims.

Snow set out to test his theory. Fortunately, there were many different sources of water supply in London, each serving different districts, so the incidence of cholera could be matched with the different water supplies, which varied in degree of contamination. Snow realized, however, that such a comparison would be subject to severe selection biases (recall the discussion in Chapter 5). The districts of London varied greatly in wealth, so any correlation between water supply and geography could just as easily be due to any of the many other economically related variables that affect health, such as diet, stress, job hazards, and quality of clothing and housing. In short, the possibility of obtaining a spurious correlation was nearly as high as in the case of the pellagra–sewage example discussed in Chapter 5. However, Snow was astute enough to notice and to exploit one particular situation that had occurred.

In one part of London, there happened to be two water companies that supplied a single neighborhood unsystematically. That is, on a particular street, a few houses were supplied by one company, then a few by the other, because in earlier days the two companies had been in competition. There were even cases in which a house had water from a company different from the one supplying the houses on either side of it. Thus, Snow had uncovered a case in which the SES of the people supplied by two water companies was virtually identical, or at least as close as it could be in a naturally occurring situation like this. Such a circumstance would still not have been of any benefit if the water from the two companies had been equally contaminated because Snow would have had no difference to associate with cholera incidence. Fortunately, this was not the case.

After the previous London cholera epidemic, one company, the Lambeth Company, had moved upstream on the Thames to escape the London sewage.

The Southwark and Vauxhall Company, however, had stayed downstream. Thus, the probability was that the water of the Lambeth Company was much less contaminated than the water of the Southwark and Vauxhall Company. Snow confirmed this by chemical testing. All that remained was to calculate the cholera death rates for the houses supplied by the two water companies. The rate for the Lambeth Company was 37 deaths per 10,000 houses, compared with a rate of 315 per 10,000 houses for the Southwark and Vauxhall Company.

In this chapter, we will discuss how the Snow and Goldberger stories both illustrate the logic of scientific thinking. Without an understanding of this logic, the things scientists do may seem mysterious, odd, or downright ridiculous.

Comparison, Control, and Manipulation

Although many large volumes have been written on the subject of scientific methodology, it is simply not necessary for the layperson, who may never actually carry out an experiment, to become familiar with all the details and intricacies of experimental design. The most important characteristics of scientific thinking are actually quite easy to grasp. Scientific thinking is based on the ideas of *comparison*, *control*, and *manipulation*. To achieve a more fundamental understanding of a phenomenon, a scientist compares conditions in the world. Without this comparison, we are left with isolated instances of observations, and the interpretation of these isolated observations is highly ambiguous, as we saw in Chapter 4 in our discussion of testimonials and case studies.

By comparing results obtained in different—but controlled—conditions, scientists rule out certain explanations and confirm others. The essential goal of experimental design is to *isolate a variable*. When a variable is successfully isolated, the outcome of the experiment will eliminate a number of alternative theories that may have been advanced as explanations. Scientists weed out the maximum number of incorrect explanations either by directly controlling the experimental situation or by observing the kinds of naturally occurring situations that allow them to test alternative explanations.

The latter situation was illustrated quite well in the cholera example. Snow did not simply pick any two water companies. He was aware that water companies might supply different geographic localities that had vastly different health-related socioeconomic characteristics. Merely observing the frequency of cholera in the various localities would leave many alternative explanations of any observed differences in cholera incidence. Highly cognizant that science advances by eliminating possible explanations (recall our discussion of falsifiability in Chapter 2), Snow looked for and found a comparison that would eliminate a large class of explanations based on health-related correlates of SES.

Snow was fortunate to find a naturally occurring situation that allowed him to eliminate alternative explanations. But it would be absurd for scientists to sit around waiting for circumstances like Snow's to occur. Instead, most scientists try to restructure the world in ways that will differentiate alternative hypotheses. To do this, they must manipulate the variable believed to be the cause (contamination of the water supply, in Snow's case) and observe whether a differential effect (cholera incidence) occurs while they keep all other relevant variables constant. The variable manipulated is called the *independent variable* and the variable upon which the independent variable is posited to have an effect is called the *dependent variable.*

Thus, the best experimental design is achieved when the scientist can manipulate the variable of interest and control all the other extraneous variables affecting the situation. Note that Snow did not do this. He was not able to manipulate the degree of water contamination himself but instead found a situation in which the contamination varied and in which other variables, mainly those having to do with SES, were—by lucky chance—controlled. However, this type of naturally occurring situation is not only less common but also less powerful than direct experimental manipulation.

Joseph Goldberger did directly manipulate the variables he hypothesized to be the causes of the particular phenomenon he was studying (pellagra). Although Goldberger observed and recorded variables that were correlated with pellagra, he also directly manipulated two other variables in his series of studies. Recall that he induced pellagra in a group of prisoners given a low-protein diet and also failed to induce it in a group of volunteers, including himself and his wife, who ingested the excrement of pellagra victims. Thus, Goldberger went beyond observing naturally occurring correlations and created a special set of circumstances designed to yield data that would allow a stronger inference by ruling out a wider set of alternative explanations than Snow's did. This is precisely the reason why scientists attempt to manipulate a variable and to hold all other variables constant: in order to eliminate alternative explanations.

Random Assignment in Conjunction with Manipulation Defines the True Experiment

We are not saying here that Snow's approach was without merit. But scientists do prefer to manipulate the experimental variables more directly because direct manipulation generates stronger inferences. Consider Snow's two groups of subjects: those whose water was supplied by the Lambeth Company and those whose water was supplied by the Southwark and Vauxhall Company. The mixed nature of the water supply system in that neighborhood probably ensured that the two groups would be of roughly equal social status. However, the drawback of the type of research design used by Snow is that the subjects themselves determined which group they would be in. They did this by signing up with one or the other of the two water companies years before. We must consider why some people signed up with one company and some with another. Did one company offer better rates? Did one advertise the medicinal properties of its water? We do not know. The critical question is, might people who respond to one or another of the advertised properties of the product differ in other, health-related ways? The answer to this question has to be, it is a possibility.

A design such as Snow's cannot rule out the possibility of spurious correlates more subtle than those that are obviously associated with SES. This is precisely the reason that scientists prefer direct manipulation of the variables they are interested in. When manipulation is combined with a procedure known as *random assignment* (in which the subjects themselves do not determine which experimental condition they will be in but, instead, are randomly assigned to one of the experimental groups), scientists can rule out alternative explanations of data patterns that depend on the particular characteristics of the subjects. Random assignment ensures that the people in the conditions compared are roughly equal on all variables because, as the sample size increases, random assignment tends to balance out chance factors. This is because the assignment of the participants is left up to an unbiased randomization device rather than the explicit choices of a human. Please note here that random *assignment* is *not* the same thing as random *sampling*. The difference will be discussed in Chapter 7.

Random assignment is a method of assigning subjects to the experimental and control groups so that each subject in the experiment has the same chance of being assigned to either of the groups. Flipping a coin is one way to decide to which group each subject will be assigned to. In actual experimentation, a computer-generated table of random numbers is most often used. By using random assignment, the investigator is attempting to equate the two groups on all behavioral and biological variables prior to the investigation—even ones that the investigator has not explicitly measured or thought about.

How well random assignment works depends on the number of subjects in the experiment. As you might expect, the more the better. That is, the more subjects there are to assign to the experimental and control groups, the closer the groups will be matched on all variables prior to the manipulation of the independent variable. Fortunately for researchers, random assignment works pretty well even with relatively small numbers (e.g., 20–25) in each of the groups.

The use of random assignment ensures that there will be no systematic bias in how the subjects are assigned to the two groups. The groups will always be matched fairly closely on any variable, but to the extent that they are not matched, random assignment removes any bias toward either the experimental or the control group. Perhaps it will be easier to understand how random assignment eliminates the problem of systematic bias if we focus on the concept of replication: the repeating of an experiment in all of its essential features to see if the same results are obtained.

Imagine an experiment conducted by a developmental psychologist who is interested in the effect of early enrichment experiences for preschool children. Children randomly assigned to the experimental group receive the enrichment activities designed by the psychologist during their preschool day-care period. Children randomly assigned to the control group participate in more traditional playgroup activities for the same period. The dependent variable is the children's school achievement, which is measured at the end of the children's first year in school to see whether children in the experimental group have outperformed those in the control group.

An experiment like this would use random assignment to ensure that the groups start out relatively closely matched on all extraneous variables that could affect the dependent variable of school achievement. These extraneous variables are sometimes called *confounding variables*. Some possible confounding variables are intelligence test scores and home environment. Random assignment will roughly equate the two groups on these variables. However, particularly when the number of subjects is small, there may still be some differences between the groups. For example, if after random assignment the intelligence test scores of children in the experimental group were 105.6 and those of children in the control group were 101.9 (this type of difference could occur even if random assignment has been properly used), we might worry that any difference in academic achievement in favor of the experimental group was due to the higher intelligence test scores of children in that group rather than to the enrichment program. Here is where the importance of replication comes in. Subsequent studies may again show IQ differences between the groups after random assignment, but the lack of systematic bias in the random assignment procedure ensures that the difference will not always be in favor of the experimental group. In fact, what the property of no systematic bias ensures is that, across a number of similar studies, any IQ differences will occur approximately half of the time in favor of the experimental group and half of the time in favor of the control group. In Chapter 8 we will discuss how multiple experiments such as these are used to converge on a conclusion.

Thus, there are really two strengths in the procedure of random assignment. One is that in any given experiment, as the sample size gets larger, random assignment ensures that the two groups are relatively matched on all extraneous variables. However, even in experiments where the matching is not perfect, the lack of systematic bias in random assignment allows us to be confident in any conclusions about cause—as long as the study can be replicated. This is because, across a *series* of such experiments, differences between the two groups on confounding variables will balance out.

The Importance of Control Groups

All sciences contain examples of mistaken conclusions drawn from studies that fell short of the full controls of the true experiment. Ross and Nisbett (1991) discuss the medical finding on the portacaval shunt, a treatment for cirrhosis of the liver that was popular years ago. The studies on the treatment were assembled in 1966, and an interesting pattern was revealed. In 96.9 percent of the studies that did not contain a control group, the physicians judged the treatment to be at least moderately effective. In the studies in which there was a control group but in which random assignment to conditions was not used (thus falling short of true experimental design), 86.7 percent of the studies were judged to have shown at least moderate effectiveness. However, in the studies in which there was a control group formed by true random assignment, only 25 percent of the studies were judged to have shown at least moderate effectiveness. Thus, the effectiveness of this particular treatment—now known to be ineffective—was vastly overestimated by studies that did not employ complete experimental controls. Ross and Nisbett (1991) note that "the positive results found using less formal procedures were the product either of 'placebo effects' or of biases resulting from nonrandom assignment" (p. 207). Ross and Nisbett discuss how selection effects (see Chapter 5) may operate to cause spurious positive effects when random assignment is not used. For example, if the patients chosen for a treatment tend to be "good candidates" or tend to be those with vocal and supportive families, there may be differences between them and the control group irrespective of the effectiveness of the treatment.

The tendency to see the necessity of acquiring comparative information before coming to a conclusion is apparently not a natural one—which is why training in all the sciences includes methodology courses that stress the importance of constructing control groups. The "nonvividness" of the control group—the group treated just like the experimental group except for the absence of a critical factor—makes it difficult to see how essential such a group is. Psychologists have done extensive research on the tendency for people to ignore essential comparative (control group) information. For example, in a much researched paradigm (Stanovich, 2010), subjects are shown a 2 × 2 matrix such as the one shown here that summarizes the data from an experiment.

	Improvement	*No Improvement*
Treatment	200	75
No Treatment	50	15

The numbers in the table represent the number of people in each cell. Specifically, 200 people received the treatment and showed improvement in the condition being treated, 75 received the treatment and showed no improvement, 50 received no treatment and showed improvement, and 15 received no treatment and showed no improvement. The subjects are asked to indicate the degree of effectiveness of the treatment. Many subjects think that the treatment in question is effective, and a considerable number of subjects think that the treatment has substantial effectiveness. They focus on the large number of cases (200) in the cell indicating people who received treatment and showed improvement. Secondarily, they focus on the fact that more people who received treatment showed improvement (200) than showed no improvement (75).

In fact, the particular treatment tested in this experiment is completely *ineffective*. In order to understand why the treatment is ineffective, it is necessary to concentrate on the two cells that represent the outcome for the control group (the no-treatment group). There we see that 50 of 65 subjects in the control group, or 76.9 percent, improved when they got *no* treatment. This contrasts with 200 of 275, or 72.7 percent, who improved when they received the treatment. Thus, the percentage of improvement is actually larger in the no-treatment group, an indication that this treatment is totally ineffective. The tendency to ignore the outcomes in the no-treatment cells and focus on the large number in the treatment/improvement cell seduces many people into viewing the treatment as effective. In short, it is relatively easy to draw people's attention away from the fact that the outcomes in the control condition are a critical piece of contextual information in interpreting the outcome in the treatment condition.

Unfortunately, drawing people's attention away from the necessity of comparative information is precisely what our media often do. Psychology professor Peter Gray (2008) describes an article in *Time* magazine titled "The Lasting Wounds of Divorce" in which many case histories were reported of people who had divorced parents. Many of these people with divorced parents were later living somewhat troubled lives. Of course, in the absence of a control group of individuals from nondivorced homes, we can conclude nothing from this. How do we know that individuals from divorced homes are *more* likely to display these negative outcomes? Only a matched control group would even begin to answer this question.

Despite examples such as this, both society and a variety of applied disciplines are becoming more aware of the necessity of comparative information when evaluating evidence. This is a fairly recent development that is still underway in the medical field for instance (Gawande, 2010; Redberg, 2011). Neurologist Robert Burton (2008) describes well the path that medicine has taken—from intuitive knowledge that hurt people to treatment based on truly useful knowledge obtained from comparative investigations: "For many years I have wondered why some bright, well-trained doctors would perform unnecessary surgeries, recommend the unproven, and tout the dangerous.... A powerful contradiction at the heart of medical practice is that we learn from experience, but without adequate trials we cannot know if our interpretation of the value of a particular treatment is correct....But being a good doctor requires sticking with the best medical evidence, even if it contradicts your personal experience. We need to distinguish between gut feeling and testable knowledge, between hunches and empirically tested evidence" (pp. 160–161).

The intuitive "hunches" of other practical fields are increasingly being put to the test of controlled comparison. For example, credit card companies often send out letters with alternative terms to see which is most enticing to customers (Ayres, 2007). For example, one group of randomly assigned households will receive one combination of interest rate, yearly fee, and rewards program. Another group of randomly assigned households will receive letters with a different interest rate, yearly fee, and rewards program. If there is a different rate of acceptance in the two groups, then the company finds out which combination of terms is superior (from the point of view of drawing more customers). The point is, the credit card company has no way of knowing if its current terms are "working" (i.e., enticing as many customers as possible) unless it engages in some experimentation in which alternative sets of terms are compared.

Not only business but governments as well have turned to controlled experimentation to find out how to optimize their policies. One governmental experiment was called the Move to Opportunity Test, and it was conducted by the Department of Housing and Urban Development of the United States (Ayres, 2007). One group of randomly assigned low-income families was given housing vouchers that could be used anywhere. Another group of randomly assigned low-income families was given vouchers that were only usable in low-poverty (i.e., more middle-class) neighborhoods. The purpose was to see if there would be differences in a variety of outcome variables—educational outcomes, criminal behavior, health outcomes, and so on—when low-income families were not surrounded by other low-income families. This type of investigation is known as a *field experiment*—where a variable is manipulated in a nonlaboratory setting.

Another example of a government-sponsored field experiment is the Progressa Program for Education, Health and Nutrition in Mexico (Ayres, 2007). This program involves a *conditional* transfer of money to poor households. Mothers are paid cash if they get prenatal care. They are paid cash when their children attend school and pass nutrition checkups. The government ran a field experiment in 506 villages testing the efficacy of the program. Half of the villages were enrolled in Progressa and half were not. This enabled the government to test the cost effectiveness of the program when, two years later, the villages were checked for outcomes such as educational achievement, nutrition, and health. Without a control group, the government would have had no knowledge of what the education and health levels would have been *without* the program.

International aid organizations are likewise turning to studies with manipulated variables (true experiments) to find out "what works" (Banerjee & Duflo, 2009). Writer Nicholas Kristof (2009) discusses the problem that aid organizations often evaluate themselves and end up claiming that everything they do works, which is implausible. Such an approach of course means that money will be misspent. In order to efficiently use aid money—that is, to save more lives—it is essential to make a judgment about which programs work better than others. Kristof describes how the Poverty Action Lab at MIT is designing studies that at least approximate true experiments in order to find out which programs work best by starting aid initiatives randomly in some areas but not in others.

It is sometimes hard for the public to understand that experiments are necessary in order to achieve something else that they want—that tax money be used efficiently, to help the most people. For example, New York City attempted an experimental test of one of its programs—Homebase—that tries to prevent people from becoming homeless (Buckley, 2010). More people are eligible (a person must be behind on rent and in danger of eviction) for this program (which includes job training, counseling, and other aid) than can be served. Thus, the city did the logical thing to test the efficacy of the program: They randomly assigned (until the money—$23 million—ran out) some people to the Homebase program and an equal number were followed up who were not included in the Homebase program. This design allowed the city to determine how many people were saved from homelessness by this expenditure of $23 million. The answer will allow the city to better allocate its funds, whatever the outcome is. If too few people are saved from homelessness for this level of expenditure, then perhaps the money should be directed elsewhere. Conversely, if a substantial number are saved from homelessness, given the social and economic costs of homelessness, this program may need to be ramped up and expanded. Either way, the people in New York are better served.

Unfortunately, many citizens and groups in New York did not see it that way. They reacted emotionally to the vivid word "experiment" and objected to this controlled study that would allow the city to spend its money better. They thought the homeless were being treated like guinea pigs or lab rats. What these critics were forgetting was that no one was being *denied* service by this experiment. The *same* number of people would receive Homebase whether they were randomly assigned or not. The only difference was that by collecting information from the control group, rather than simply ignoring those who were not in the program, the city would be able to determine whether the program *works*!

The confusions about field experiments in the Homebase example are quite common ones. People do not seem to understand that by doing actual experiments on the effects of social aid in real environments, we can maximize the number served by finding out what works best. As one international aid expert, Esther Duflo, noted, "it doesn't seem like a hugely innovative view of the world, but most people who are not economists don't get it. They don't get the idea that there are budget constraints" (Parker, 2010, p. 87). It is easy to detect a little frustration in Duflo's voice as we read this. Duflo is running up against something we will discuss many times in this book—what is obvious to a scientist is often totally missed by a layperson. It seems obvious to Duflo that, with a fixed aid budget, the number of people served from a given program is a certain number. Another program that is more efficient would serve more people for the same fixed cost. And the only way to figure out if a program is more efficient is to run a true experiment.

Perhaps a reframing would help people. One of Duflo's colleagues helping to run the experiments on aid in impoverished countries notes that she is often told that "you shouldn't be experimenting on people" and replies "OK, so you have no idea whether your program works—and *that's* not experimental?" (p. 87). She has the right idea in this response. The status quo—the original program being tested for its efficacy—could be called an experiment, just a poorly designed one! The program being run is an experiment—just one without the proper controls! That is, it's a condition without a control group! It is "experimenting on people" too! This type of framing might help to dissolve the silly resistance to objective methods for finding out what helps people the most.

The Case of Clever Hans, the Wonder Horse

The necessity of controls that allow the elimination of alternative explanations of a phenomenon by the use of experimental control is well illustrated by a story that is famous in the annals of behavioral science: that of Clever Hans, the mathematical horse. Almost 100 years ago, a German schoolteacher presented to the public a horse, Clever Hans, who supposedly knew how to solve mathematical problems. When Hans was given addition, subtraction, and multiplication problems by his trainer, he would tap out the answer to the problems with his hoof. The horse's responses were astoundingly accurate.

Many people were amazed and puzzled by Clever Hans's performance. Was the horse really demonstrating an ability thus far unknown in his species? Imagine what the public must have thought. Compelling testimonials to Hans's unique ability appeared in the German press. One Berlin newspaper reporter wrote that "this thinking horse is going to give men of science a great deal to think about for a long time to come" (Fernald, 1984, p. 30), a prediction that turned out to be correct, though not quite in the way the reporter expected. A group of "experts" observed Hans and attested to his abilities. Everyone was baffled. And bafflement was bound to remain as long as the phenomenon was merely observed in isolation—without controlled observations being carried out. The mystery was soon dispelled, however, when a psychologist, Oskar Pfungst, undertook systematic studies of the horse's ability (Spitz, 1997).

In the best traditions of experimental design, Pfungst systematically manipulated the conditions under which the animal performed, thus creating "artificial" situations (see Chapter 7) that would allow tests of alternative explanations of the horse's performance. After much careful testing, Pfungst found that the horse did have a special ability, but it was not a mathematical one. In fact, the horse was closer to being a behavioral scientist than a mathematician. You see, Hans was a very careful observer of human behavior. As it was tapping out its answer, it would watch the head of the trainer or other questioner. As Hans approached the answer, the trainer would involuntarily tilt his head slightly, and Hans would stop. Pfungst found that the horse was extremely sensitive to visual cues. It could detect extremely small head movements. Pfungst tested the horse by having the problems presented in such a way that the presenter did not know the answer to the problem or by having the trainer present the problem away from the horse's view. The animal lost its "mathematical abilities" when the questioner did not know the answer or when the trainer was out of view.

The case of Clever Hans is a good context in which to illustrate the importance of carefully distinguishing between the *description* of a phenomenon and the *explanation* of a phenomenon. That the horse tapped out the correct answers to mathematical problems presented by the trainer is not in dispute. The trainer was not lying. Many observers attested to the fact that the horse actually did tap out the correct answers to mathematical problems presented by the trainer. It is in the next step that the problem arises: making the inference that the horse was tapping out the correct answers *because* the horse had mathematical abilities. Inferring that the horse had mathematical abilities was a *hypothesized explanation* of the phenomenon. It did not follow logically—from the fact that the horse tapped out the correct answers to mathematical problems—that the horse had mathematical abilities. Positing that the horse had mathematical abilities was only one of many possible explanations of the horse's performance. It was an explanation that could be put to empirical test. When put to such a test, the explanation was falsified.

Before the intervention of Pfungst, the experts who looked at the horse had made this fundamental error: They had not seen that there might be alternative explanations of the horse's performance. They thought that, once they had observed that the trainer was not lying and that the horse actually did tap out the correct answers to mathematical problems, it necessarily followed that the horse had mathematical abilities. Pfungst was thinking more scientifically and realized that that was only one of many possible explanations of the horse's performance, and that it was necessary to set up controlled conditions in order to differentiate alternative explanations. By having the horse answer questions posed by the trainer from behind a screen, Pfungst set up conditions in which he would be able to differentiate two possible explanations: that the horse had mathematical abilities or that the horse was responding to visual cues. If the horse actually had such abilities, putting the trainer behind a screen should make no difference in its performance. On the other hand, if the horse was responding to visual cues, then putting the trainer behind a screen should disrupt its performance. When the latter happened, Pfungst was able to rule out the hypothesis that the horse had mathematical abilities (Spitz, 1997).

Note also the link here to the principle of parsimony discussed in Chapter 3—the principle that states that when two theories have the same explanatory power, the simpler theory (the one involving fewer concepts and conceptual relationships) is preferred. The two theories in contention here—that the horse had true mathematical abilities and that the horse was reading behavioral cues—are vastly different in parsimony. The latter requires no radical adjustments in prior psychological and brain theory. It simply requires us to adjust slightly our view of the potential sensitivity of horses to behavioral cues (which was already known to be high). The former theory—that horses can truly learn arithmetic—requires us to alter dozens of concepts in evolutionary science, cognitive science, comparative psychology, and brain science. It is unparsimonious in the extreme because it does not cohere with the rest of science and, thus, requires that many other concepts in science be altered if it is to be considered true (we shall discuss the so-called principle of connectivity in Chapter 8).

Clever Hans in the 1990s

The Clever Hans story is a historical example that has been used in methodology classes for many years to teach the important principle of the necessity of experimental control. No one ever thought that an *actual* Clever Hans case could happen *again*—but it did. Throughout the early 1990s, researchers the world over watched in horrified anticipation—almost as if observing cars crash in slow motion—while a modern Clever Hans case unfolded before their eyes and had tragic consequences.

Autism is a developmental disability characterized by impairment in reciprocal social interaction, delayed and often qualitatively abnormal language development, and a restricted repertoire of activities and interests (Baron-Cohen, 2005). The extremely noncommunicative nature of many autistic children, who may be normal in physical appearance, makes the disorder a particularly difficult one for parents to accept. It is, therefore, not hard to imagine the excitement of parents of autistic children when, in the late 1980s and early 1990s, they heard of a technique coming out of Australia that enabled autistic children who had previously been totally nonverbal to communicate. This technique for unlocking communicative capacity in nonverbal autistic individuals was called facilitated communication, and it was uncritically trumpeted in such highly visible media outlets as *60 Minutes, Parade* magazine, and the *Washington Post* (Lilienfeld et al., 2010; Offit, 2008; Twachtman-Cullen, 1997). The claim was made that autistic individuals and other children with developmental disabilities who had previously been nonverbal had typed highly literate messages on a keyboard when their hands and arms had been supported over the typewriter by a sympathetic "facilitator." Not surprisingly, these startlingly verbal performances on the part of autistic children who had previously shown very limited linguistic behavior spawned incredible hopes among frustrated parents of autistic children. It was also claimed that the technique worked for severely mentally retarded individuals who were nonverbal.

Although the excitement of the parents is easy to understand, the gullibility of many professionals is not so easy to accept. Unfortunately, claims for the efficacy of facilitated communication were disseminated to hopeful parents by many media outlets before any controlled studies had been conducted. Had the professionals involved had minimal training in the principles of experimental control, they should have immediately recognized the parallel to the Clever Hans case. The facilitator, almost always a sympathetic individual who was genuinely concerned that the child succeed, had numerous opportunities to consciously or unconsciously direct the child's hand to the vicinity of keys on the keyboard. That cuing by the facilitator was occurring should also have been suggested by the additional observation that the children sometimes typed out complicated messages while not even looking at the keyboard. Additionally, highly literate poetic English prose was produced by children who had not been exposed to the alphabet. For example, one child allegedly typed "Am I a slave or am I free? Am I trapped or can I be seen as an easy and rational spirit?" (Offit, 2008, p. 7).

A number of controlled studies have been reported that have tested the claims of facilitated communication by using appropriate experimental controls. Each study has unequivocally demonstrated the same thing: The autistic child's performance depended on tactile cuing by the facilitator (Jacobson, Foxx, & Mulick, 2004; Offit, 2008; Spitz, 1997; Wegner, Fuller, & Sparrow, 2003). The controls used in several of the studies resembled those of the classic Clever Hans case. A controlled situation was set up in which both the child and the facilitator were presented with a drawing of an object but in which they could not see each other's drawing. When both child and facilitator were looking at the *same* drawing, the child typed the correct name of the drawing. However, when the child and the facilitator were shown *different* drawings, the child typed the name of the facilitator's drawing, not the one at which the child was looking. Thus, the responses were determined by the facilitator rather than the child.

The conclusion that facilitated communication was a Clever Hans phenomenon and not a breakthrough therapeutic technique brought no joy to the investigators involved in conducting the studies. But this sad story gets even worse. At some centers, during facilitated sessions on the keyboard, clients allegedly reported having been sexually abused by a parent in the past (Offit, 2008). Children were removed from their parents' homes, only to be returned when the charges of abuse proved to be groundless.

As a result of the controlled studies, competent professional opinion finally began to be heard above the media din. Importantly, it is increasingly recognized that treatments that lack empirical foundation are not benignly neutral ("Oh, well, it might work, and so what if it doesn't?"). The implementation of unproven treatments has real costs. James Mulick (see Mulick, Jacobson, & Kobe, 1993), professor of pediatrics and psychology at Ohio State University, discussed the costs of this educational fad:

> The promotion of FC [facilitated communication] diverts effort and funding from more plausible long-term strategies that have empirical support. The theoretical confusion gratuitously injected into the research and professional literature

by FC proponents is damaging to accumulation of knowledge....The popular confusion of FC with other nonspeech communication systems that have been used successfully with disabled people will discourage public support....The genuine efforts of scientifically trained and compassionate professionals surpass all fad treatments, and always will. Advances in treatment and understanding come at the price of rigorous training, dedication to accuracy and scientific standards, and objective verification of all treatment claims. (pp. 278–279)

Here we have another example of the harm done by reliance on testimonial evidence and the fallacy of the idea that therapeutic fads and pseudoscience do no harm (see Chapter 4). We can also see that there is simply no substitute for the control and manipulation of the experimental method when we want to explain behavior.

Note again the link to the principle of parsimony. That the severe linguistic difficulties of autistic children could be solved by a single "magic bullet" (see Chapter 9) intervention flies in the face of decades of work on the cognitive, neuropsychological, and brain characteristics of autistic children (Baron-Cohen, 2005; Oberman & Ramachandran, 2007; Rajendran & Mitchell, 2007; Tager-Flusberg, 2007; Wellman, Fang, & Peterson, 2011). It would require that too much else that we know about cognition and neurology be altered. The existence of facilitated communication would show no connectivity with the rest of science (see Chapter 8).

Finally, the example of facilitated communication illustrates something discussed previously in the Clever Hans case: the importance of carefully distinguishing between the *description* of a phenomenon and the *explanation* of a phenomenon. The term "facilitated communication" is not a neutral description of what occurred between facilitator and child. Instead it posits a theoretical outcome—that communication actually occurred and had been truly enhanced by the facilitator. But that is the very thing that had to be proved! What we had here was a child tapping keys. Perhaps things would have proceeded more rationally had it originally been labeled "surprising tapping." What needed to be determined was whether the "surprising tapping" was true communication. The premature labeling of the phenomenon (key tapping) with a theory (that it represented true communication) likely made it more difficult for these practitioners to realize that further investigation was necessary to see if this theoretical label was warranted.

Other fields—not just psychology—struggle with the problem of prematurely labeling a phenomenon with a theory. The legal system still uses the term "shaken baby syndrome" when in fact the American Academy of Pediatrics has recommended that that term be discarded. The problem is exactly like the Clever Hans and facilitated communication examples we have been discussing. The term "shaken baby syndrome" is a *theory* of why a particular child has presented with head trauma. The *phenomenon* is the nature of the head trauma itself. The precise description of the trauma is what has to be *explained* by whatever theory we have of how the trauma occurred. The legal system is still working through the implications of this change in terminology that had once been standard, but that we now know to be misleading (Tuerkheimer, 2010).

Traffic safety engineers likewise feel that the term traffic "accident" carries too much theory with it. The word accident implies randomness and unpredictability and luck—pure happenstance. Safety engineers know all too well that automobile crash risk has strong statistical relationships to many behaviors, none of which are random or happenstance. The engineers have in mind cases like St. Louis Cardinals pitcher Josh Hancock who slammed his rented SUV into a truck stopped on the highway with lights flashing (Vanderbilt, 2008). Calling the crash random and unpredictable seems not at all right when we consider that Hancock was speeding (a strong risk factor), had an alcohol concentration twice the legal limit (a strong risk factor), and was on a cell phone at the time of the crash (a strong risk factor). Oh, and he had crashed another SUV just two days before (Vanderbilt, 2008). Terming this an "accident" conveys a theory of randomness and unpredictability that does not seem right when the chosen behaviors were so wantonly reckless as in this case. The *description* of what happened is—a crash. As a *theory*, accident seems not quite right.

Prying Variables Apart: Special Conditions

The Goldberger pellagra example illustrates a very important lesson that can greatly aid in dispelling some misconceptions about the scientific process, particularly as it is applied in psychology. The occurrence of any event in the world is often correlated with many other factors. In order to separate, to pry apart, the causal influence of many simultaneously occurring events, we must create situations that will never occur in the ordinary world. Scientific experimentation breaks apart the natural correlations in the world to isolate the influence of a single variable.

Psychologists operate in exactly the same manner: by isolating variables via manipulation and control. For example, cognitive psychologists interested in the reading process have studied the factors that make word perception easier or more difficult. Not surprisingly, they have found that longer words are more difficult to recognize than shorter words. At first glance, we might think that the effect of word length would be easy to measure: Simply create two sets of words, one long and one short, and measure the difference in reader recognition speed between the two. Unfortunately, it is not that easy. Long words also tend to be less frequent in language, and frequency itself also affects perception. Thus, any difference between long and short words may be due to length, frequency, or a combination of these two effects. In order to see whether word length affects perception independently of frequency, researchers must construct special word sets in which length and frequency do not vary together.

Similarly, Goldberger was able to make a strong inference about causation because he set up a special set of conditions that does not occur naturally. (Considering that one manipulation involved the ingestion of bodily discharges, this is putting it mildly!) Recall that Oskar Pfungst had to set up some special conditions for testing Clever Hans, including trials in which the questioner did not know the answer. Dozens of people who merely observed the horse answer questions under normal conditions (in which the questioner knew the answer) never detected how the horse was accomplishing its feat. Instead, they came to the erroneous conclusion that the horse had true mathematical knowledge.

Likewise, note the unusual conditions that were necessary to test the claims of facilitated communication. The stimuli presented to the facilitator and the child had to be separated in a way that neither could see the stimulus presented to the other. Such unusual conditions are necessary in order to test the alternative hypotheses for the phenomenon.

Many classic experiments in psychology involve this logic of prying apart the natural relationships that exist in the world so that it can be determined which variable is the dominant cause. Psychologist Harry Harlow's famous experiments (Harlow, 1958; Harlow & Suomi, 1970) provide a case in point. Harlow wanted to test a prevailing hypothesis about infant–mother attachment: The attachment resulted from the mother providing the infant's source of food. However, the problem was that, of course, mothers provide much more than nourishment (comfort, warmth, caressing, stimulation, etc.). Harlow examined the behavior of infant macaque monkeys in situations in which he isolated only one of the variables associated with attachment by giving the animals choices among "artificial" mothers. For example, he found that the contact comfort provided by a "mother" made of terrycloth was preferred to that provided by a "mother" made of wire mesh. After two weeks of age, the infant preferred a cold terrycloth mother to a warm wire one, a finding indicating that the contact comfort was more attractive than warmth. Finally, Harlow found that the infants preferred the terrycloth mother even when their nourishment came exclusively from a wire mother. Thus, the hypothesis that attachment was due solely to the nourishment provided by mothers was falsified. This was possible only because Harlow was able to pry apart variables that naturally covary in the real world.

Creating special conditions to test for actual causal relationships is a key tool we can use to prevent pseudoscientific beliefs from attacking us like a virus (Stanovich, 2004, 2009, 2011). Consider the case of therapeutic touch (TT)—a fad that swept the North American nursing profession in the 1990s. TT practitioners massage not the patient's body but instead the patient's so-called energy field. That is, they move their hands over the patient's body but do not actually massage it. Practitioners reported "feeling" these energy fields. Well, you guessed it. This ability to feel "energy fields" is tested properly by creating exactly the type of special conditions as in the Clever Hans and facilitated communication claims—that is, testing whether practitioners, when visually blinded, could still feel whether their hands were in proximity to a human body. Research has demonstrated the same thing as in the Clever

Hans and facilitated communication cases—when vision is occluded, this ability to feel at a distance is no greater than chance (Hines, 2003; Shermer, 2005). This example actually illustrates something that was mentioned in an earlier chapter—that the logic of the true experiment is really so straightforward that a child could understand it. This is because one of the published experiments showing that TT is ineffective was done as a school science project (Dacey, 2008).

In short, it is often necessary for scientists to create special conditions that will test a particular theory about a phenomenon. Merely observing the event in its natural state is rarely sufficient. People observed falling and moving objects for centuries without arriving at accurate principles and laws about motion and gravity. Truly explanatory laws of motion were not derived until Galileo and other scientists set up some rather artificial conditions for the observation of the behavior of moving objects. In Galileo's time, smooth bronze balls were rarely seen rolling down smooth inclined planes. Lots of motion occurred in the world, but it was rarely of this type. However, it was just such an unnatural situation, and others like it, that led to our first truly explanatory laws of motion and gravity. Speaking of laws of motion, didn't you take a little quiz at the beginning of this chapter?

Intuitive Physics

Actually, the three questions posed at the beginning of this chapter were derived from the work of Michael McCloskey, a psychologist at Johns Hopkins University. McCloskey (1983) has studied what he calls "intuitive physics," that is, people's beliefs about the motion of objects. Interestingly, these beliefs are often at striking variance from how moving objects actually behave (Bloom & Weisberg, 2007; Riener, Proffitt, & Salthouse, 2005).

For example, in the first problem, once the string on the circling ball is cut, the ball will fly in a straight line at a 90-degree angle to the string (tangent to the circle). McCloskey found that one-third of the college students who were given this problem thought, incorrectly, that the ball would fly in a curved trajectory. About half of McCloskey's subjects, when given problems similar to the bomber pilot example, thought that the bomb should be dropped directly over the target, thus displaying a lack of understanding of the role of an object's initial motion in determining its trajectory. The bomb should actually be dropped *five miles* before the plane reaches the target. The subjects' errors were not caused by the imaginary nature of the problem. When subjects were asked to walk across a room and, while moving, drop a golf ball on a target on the floor, the performance of more than half of them indicated that they did not know that the ball would move forward as it fell. Finally, many people are not aware that a bullet fired from a rifle will hit the ground at the same time as a bullet dropped from the same height.

You can assess your own performance on this little quiz. Chances are that you missed at least one if you have not had a physics course recently.

"Physics course!" you might protest. "Of course I haven't had a physics class recently. This quiz is unfair!" But hold on a second. Why should you *need* a physics course? You have seen literally hundreds of falling objects in your lifetime. You have seen them fall under *naturally occurring* conditions. Moving objects surround you every day, and you are seeing them in their "real-life" state. You certainly cannot claim that you have not experienced moving and falling objects. Granted, you have never seen anything quite like the bullet example. But most of us have seen children let go of whirling objects, and many of us have seen objects fall out of planes. And besides, it seems a little lame to protest that you have not seen these exact situations. Given your years of experience with moving and falling objects, why can not you accurately predict what will happen in a situation only slightly out of the ordinary?

McCloskey's work demonstrates something of fundamental importance in understanding why scientists behave as they do. Despite extensive experience with moving and falling objects, people's intuitive theories of motion are remarkably inaccurate. It is critical to understand that the layperson's beliefs are inaccurate precisely *because* his or her observations are "natural," rather than controlled in the manner of the scientist's. Thus, if you missed a question on the little quiz at the beginning of the chapter, don't feel ignorant or inadequate. Simply remember that some of the world's greatest minds observed falling objects for centuries without formulating a physics of motion any more accurate than that of the modern high school sophomore. In an article in *Scientific American,* McCloskey (1983) observed that many of his subjects held an incorrect theory about motion that was very similar to one held to be true some three centuries before Newton. McCloskey's modern subjects and medieval philosophers had something in common: Both groups had had much exposure to the motion of objects in the ordinary world, but none under the artificially created conditions of scientific manipulation, control, and comparison.

Intuitive Psychology

Philosopher Paul Churchland (1988) has argued that, if our intuitive (or "folk") theories about objects in motion are inaccurate, it is hard to believe that our folk theories in the more complex domain of human behavior could be correct:

> Our early folk theories of motion were profoundly confused, and were eventually displaced entirely by more sophisticated theories. Our early folk theories of the structure and activity of the heavens were wildly off the mark, and survive only as historical lessons in how wrong we can be. Our folk theories of the nature of fire, and the nature of life, were similarly cockeyed. And one could go on, since the vast majority of our past folk conceptions have been similarly exploded.... But the phenomenon of conscious intelligence is surely a more complex and difficult phenomenon than any of those just listed. So far as accurate understanding is concerned, it would be a miracle if we had got that one right the very first time, when we fell down so badly on all the others. (p. 46)

When we look at the actual literature on people's theories of behavior, we find that Churchland's speculation turns out to be right. The research literature serves to warn us that personal experience is no guarantee against incorrect beliefs about human psychology. Behavioral economist Dan Ariely (2008) tells the story of suffering burns over 70 percent of his body as the result of an accident when he was 18 years old. He describes many months of subsequent treatment in which bandages that were removed quickly caused him great pain. The theory held by the nurses was that a quick removal (which caused a sharp pain) was preferable to slow removal which would cause a longer—although less intense—pain. After leaving the hospital and beginning his career as a psychology student, Ariely conducted experiments to test the nurses' belief. To his surprise, Ariely found that the slower procedure—lower pain intensity over a longer period—would have reduced the pain perception in such situations. He says that "by the time I had finished, I realized that the nurses in the burn unit were kind and generous individuals with a lot of experience in soaking and removing bandages, but they still didn't have the right theory about what would minimize their patients' pain. How could they be so wrong, I wondered, considering their vast experience?" (p. xvi). Much research indicates that intuitive judgments of pain intensity in other people are quite bad, even among physicians with much clinical experience (Tait, Chibnall, & Kalauokalani, 2009).

As discussed in Chapter 4, reliance on testimonials, case study evidence, and "common practice" can often obscure the need for a control group to check the veracity of a conclusion derived from informal observation. For example, Dingfelder (2006) describes how many medical professionals believe that they should not advise individuals with Tourette's syndrome (described in Chapter 2) to suppress their tics (involuntary vocal expressions). The physicians believed that this caused a so-called rebound effect—a higher rate of tics occurring after the suppression. This belief, though, is based on informal observation rather than controlled experimentation. When the proper experimentation was done—observing the number of tics systematically by comparing a period of suppression to a period of nonsuppression—it appeared that there was no "rebound" effect at all following tic suppression.

In Chapter 1, we illustrated that a number of commonsense (or folk) beliefs about human behavior are wrong, and this was just a small sample. For example, it turns out that there is no strong evidence indicating that highly religious people are more altruistic than less religious people (Paloutzian & Park, 2005). Studies have indicated that there is no simple relationship between degree of religiosity and the tendency to engage in charitable acts, to aid other people in distress, or to abstain from cheating other people.

Incorrect intuitive theories are not limited to psychology. For example, they are rampant in the world of sport and physical fitness. For example, quantitative analyses have indicated that in football (at all levels, from high school to professional) most coaches increase their probability of winning by going for it on fourth down when their teams are at midfield (Moskowitz & Wertheim, 2011). Similar analyses have shown that, overall, coaches should punt less and on-side kick more. Statistics prove that if coaches reoriented their strategies in these respects, they would win more games (Moskowitz & Wertheim, 2011). Now, coaches might have a variety of reasons for ignoring this statistical advice (fear of being second-guessed, for example), but these reasons do not apply to the fans. Nevertheless, fans have the incorrect intuitive theory that the coaches are right.

Similarly, in the area of physical fitness, there are many folk beliefs that are uncorroborated by evidence. Most athletes and fitness buffs grew up thinking that stretching prior to exercise prevents injury, but the evidence for that belief is simply not there (Bernstein, 2009). Similarly, most runners know the 10% rule: When adding distance to workouts, injuries will be prevented by making sure the increase in distance is no more than 10 percent a week. The problem is the "10% rule" is unverified by research (Kolata, 2011). Finally, many baseball players put weighted doughnuts around their bats while they take their practice swings in the on-deck circle. Research shows that these weights hurt rather than help—but players cannot be convinced not to use them (Wolff, 2011).

Incorrect beliefs about human behavior can have very practical consequences. Keith and Beins (2008) mention that among their students, typical views about cell phones and driving are captured by statements such as "Talking doesn't impair my driving" and "I talk on the phone to keep myself from falling asleep." The students seem completely oblivious to the fact that driving while using a cell phone (even a hands-free phone) seriously impairs concentration and attention (Kunar, Carter, Cohen, & Horowitz, 2008; Strayer & Drews, 2007) and is a cause of accidents and deaths (Conkle & West, 2008; McEvoy et al., 2005; Novotny, 2009; Parker-Pope, 2009).

The list of popular beliefs that are incorrect is long. For example, many people believe that a full moon affects human behavior. It doesn't (Foster & Roenneberg, 2008; Lilienfeld et al., 2010). Some people believe that "opposites attract." They don't (Gaunt, 2006; Hitsch, Hortacsu, & Ariely, 2010; Reis, Maniaci, Caprariello, Eastwick, & Finkel, 2011). Some people believe that you shouldn't change an answer on a multiple choice test. They're wrong (Kruger et al., 2005). Some people believe that prayers can affect health. They can't (Benson et al., 2006). Some people believe that "familiarity breeds contempt." It doesn't (Claypool, Hall, Mackie, & Garcia-Marques, 2008; Zebrowitz, White, & Wieneke, 2008). And the list goes on and on and on (see Lilienfeld et al., 2010).

The many inadequacies in people's intuitive theories of behavior illustrate why we need the controlled experimentation of psychology: so that we can progress beyond our flat-earth conceptions of human behavior to a more accurate scientific conceptualization.

Summary

The heart of the experimental method involves manipulation and control. This is why an experiment allows stronger causal inferences than a correlational study. In a correlational study, the investigator simply observes whether the natural fluctuation in two variables displays a relationship. By contrast, in a true experiment the investigator manipulates the variable hypothesized to be the cause and looks for an effect on the variable hypothesized to be the effect while holding all other variables constant by control and randomization. This method removes the third-variable problem present in correlational studies. The third-variable problem arises because, in the natural world, many different things are related. The experimental method may be viewed as a way of prying apart these naturally occurring relationships. It does so because it isolates one particular variable (the hypothesized cause) by manipulating it and holding everything else constant. However, in order to pry apart naturally occurring relationships, scientists often have to create special conditions that are unknown in the natural world.

CHAPTER 7

"But It's Not Real Life!": The "Artificiality" Criticism and Psychology

Having covered the basics of experimental logic in the previous two chapters, we are now in a position to consider some often-heard criticisms of the field of psychology. In particular, we will discuss at length the criticism that scientific experiments are useless because they are artificial and not like "real life." Understanding why this is not a valid criticism will aid in thinking straight about psychology because the criticism is often aimed at psychological experimentation.

Why Natural Isn't Always Necessary

From the discussion in Chapter 6, it should already be fairly clear why this criticism is invalid. As was illustrated in that chapter, the artificiality of scientific experimentation is not a weakness but actually the very thing that gives the scientific method its unique power to yield explanations about the nature of the world. Contrary to common belief, the artificiality of scientific experiments is not an accidental oversight. It is intentionally sought. Scientists *deliberately* set up conditions that are unlike those that occur naturally because this is the only way to separate the many inherently correlated variables that determine events in the world. To use a phrase from Chapter 6, scientists set up special conditions in order to *pry variables apart*.

Sometimes the necessary conditions already exist naturally, as in the example of Snow and cholera. More often, this is not the case. The scientist must manipulate events in new and sometimes strange ways, as in the example of Goldberger and pellagra. In many instances, these manipulations cannot be accomplished in natural environments, and the scientist finds

107

it necessary to bring the phenomenon into the laboratory, where more precise control is possible. Early studies of gravity and motion used specially constructed objects that were designed for no other reason than to create a set of special conditions for the observation of moving objects. It is often necessary to create increasingly *unreal* and extreme conditions in order to separate the many potential causes of a phenomenon.

Indeed, some phenomena would be completely impossible to discover if scientists were restricted totally to observing "natural" conditions. Physicists probing the most fundamental characteristics of matter build gigantic mile-long accelerators that induce collisions between elementary particles. Some of the by-products of these collisions are new particles that exist for less than a billionth of a second. The properties of these new particles, however, have implications for theories of atomic structure. Many of these new particles would not ordinarily exist on earth, and even if they did, there certainly would be no chance of observing them naturally. Yet few people doubt that this is how physicists should conduct their research—that probing nature in unusual and sometimes bizarre ways is a legitimate means of coming to a deeper understanding of the universe. Somehow, though, practices that seem reasonable for physicists are often viewed as invalid when used by psychologists.

Many psychologists who have presented experimental evidence on behavior to an audience of laypersons have heard the lament "But it's not real life!" The remark reflects the belief that studying human psychology in the laboratory is somehow strange. This objection also contains the assumption that knowledge cannot be obtained unless natural conditions are studied.

It is not commonly recognized that many of the techniques used by the psychologist that are viewed as strange by the public are in no way unique to psychology; instead, they are manifestations of the scientific method as applied to behavior. Restriction to real-life situations would prevent us from discovering many things. For example, biofeedback techniques are now used in a variety of areas such as migraine and tension headache control, hypertension treatment, and relaxation training (deCharms et al., 2005; Maizels, 2005). These techniques developed out of research indicating that humans could learn partial control of their internal physiological processes if they could monitor the ongoing processes via visual or auditory feedback. Of course, because humans are not equipped to monitor their physiological functions via external feedback, the ability to control such processes does not become apparent *except* under special conditions. Observations under natural conditions would never have uncovered the ability.

The "Random Sample" Confusion

Sometimes, however, the "it's not real life" complaint arises from a different type of confusion about the purposes of psychological experimentation, one that is actually quite understandable. Through media exposure, many people are familiar with survey research, particularly in the form of election and public opinion polling. There is now a growing awareness of some of the important characteristics of election polling. In particular, the media have given more attention to the importance of a random, or representative, sample for the accuracy of public opinion polls. This attention has led many people to believe, mistakenly, that random samples and representative conditions are an essential requirement of all psychological investigations. Because psychological research seldom uses random samples of subjects, the application of the random sample criterion by the layperson seems to undermine most psychological investigations and to reinforce the criticism that the research is invalid because it doesn't reflect real life.

Again, a moment's thought about the nature of other sciences should go a long way toward exposing the fallaciousness of this belief. Chemists make no attempt to draw random samples of compounds. Biologists do not experiment on random samples of cells or organisms. The rats and monkeys in a medical research facility are not at all representative of their species. The organisms in such laboratories are often studied under conditions that are vastly different from their natural environments. Indeed, these conditions are often utterly unique. Yet they yield insights that help shed great light on human biology. The same is true of most psychological investigations. This is because it is actually *not* necessary for every psychological investigation to employ a random sample of participants. And this is a good time to stress an important point: random sampling and random assignment (discussed in Chapter 6) are not the same thing.

The Random Assignment Versus Random Sample Distinction

Because they both have the term "random" in them, many people come to think that random assignment and random sampling refer to the same thing. Actually they are very different concepts—similar only in that they make use of the properties of random number generation. But they are used for very different purposes.

Random sampling refers to how subjects are chosen to be part of a study. As noted previously, random sampling is not a requirement for all research, but when it does become necessary (in survey research, consumer research, or election polling, for example), it refers to drawing a sample from the population in a manner that ensures that each member of the population has an equal chance of being chosen for the sample. The sample that is drawn then becomes the subject of the investigation. And it is important to understand that the investigation could be either a correlational study or a true experiment. It is not a true experiment unless random assignment is *also* used.

Random assignment is a requirement of a true experiment in which an experimental group and a control group are formed by the experimenter. Random assignment is achieved when each subject is just as likely to be assigned to the control group as to the experimental group. This is why a randomizing device such as a coin flip (more often, a specially prepared table of random numbers) is employed—because it displays no bias in assigning the subjects to groups.

The best way to keep in mind that random assignment and random sampling are not the same thing is always to be clear that any of the four combinations can occur: nonrandom sampling without random assignment, nonrandom sampling with random assignment, random sampling without random assignment, and random sampling with random assignment. Most psychological research does not employ random sampling because it is not necessary. The research involves theory testing, as we will see in the next section, and a convenience sample is all that is necessary. If random assignment is employed in the study, then it becomes a true experiment. If random assignment is not employed, then the study is a correlational investigation. Many studies that do use random sampling do not employ random assignment because they are surveys and are only looking for associations—that is, they are correlational investigations.

Theory-Driven Research Versus Direct Applications

Douglas Mook (1983, 1989, 2001), a psychologist at the University of Virginia, discusses the different types of goals that characterize different types of investigation. In many kinds of applied research, the goal is to relate the results of the study directly to a particular situation. Election polling is an example of directly applied research. The goal is to predict a specific behavior in a very specific setting—in this case, voting on election day. Here, where the nature of the application is direct, questions of the randomness of the sample and the representativeness of the conditions are important because the findings of the study are going to be applied directly.

However, it would be a mistake to view this class of research as typical. The vast majority of research studies in psychology (or any other science, for that matter) are conducted with a very different purpose in mind. Their purpose is to advance theory. The findings of most research are applied only *indirectly* through modifications in a theory that, in conjunction with other scientific laws, is then applied to some practical problem. In short, most theory-driven research seeks to test theories of psychological processes rather than to generalize the findings to a particular real-world situation.

Research that focuses primarily on theory testing is often termed *basic research*. Whereas in applied research the purpose of the investigation is to go from data directly to a real-world application, basic research focuses on theory testing. However, it is probably a mistake to view the basic-versus-applied distinction solely in terms of whether a study has practical applications, because this difference often simply boils down to a matter of time. Applied findings are of use immediately. However, there is nothing so practical as a general and accurate theory. The history of science is filled with examples of theories or findings that eventually solved a host of real-world problems even though the scientists who developed the theories and/or findings did not intend to solve a specific practical problem.

Time and time again, attempts to control the direction of science (by trying to tell scientists to solve a particular practical problem) turn out to impede rather than facilitate progress. Ironically, the urge to have scientists solve only practical problems and not bother with the "other stuff" (basic research) turns out to be wildly impractical and shortsighted because the road to many practical applications is remarkably unpredictable. For example, a group of researchers at the University of Texas Southwestern Medical Center was seeking to genetically engineer a population of rats with arthritis in order to study that inflammatory disease. Unexpectedly, their rats also developed inflammation of the intestines (Fackelman, 1996) similar to ulcerative colitis. The scientists now had an animal model of the human disease. Whether these scientists make any progress on arthritis (their original problem), it now looks as if they have made a substantial contribution to the eventual treatment of ulcerative colitis and Crohn's disease. Such indirect connections are common in science. The drug company Pfizer was looking for a new heart treatment when it discovered Viagra (Gladwell, 2010).

These indirect links between basic research and applications are often difficult to appreciate. Indeed, the seemingly remote relation between basic research and real-life concerns makes basic research easy to ridicule and mock. In the 1970s and 1980s, U.S. Senator William Proxmire made a sport of singling out odd-sounding titles of basic research studies and holding them out as examples of government waste (Benson, 2006a; Munro, 2010). But time after time, the joke turned out to be on Senator Proxmire rather than the researcher. It was repeatedly found that studies that Senator Proxmire had singled out because they sounded silly when boiled down to a single sentence ("Why Monkeys Clench Their Jaws") actually had led to important theoretical advances or practical applications. For example, the study of monkey jaw clenching helped to operationalize the concept of stress. This was helpful to government agencies who wanted to objectively assess the amount of stress present when people had to operate in close quarters for extended periods of time such as in outer space or in a submarine (Benson, 2006a).

Senator Proxmire's tradition of mocking research studies that later turned out to be of real benefit was revived in the 2008 presidential campaign when candidate John McCain mocked a study of the DNA of bears in Montana (Krauss, 2008). His running mate, Sarah Palin, criticized fruit fly research in Paris, France, as having no practical good for the public (Krauss, 2008). Referring to these studies may have successfully pandered to the public's view that research is a waste of money, but they were particularly poor choices. It turned out that the bear study was mandated by the Federal Endangered Species Act, on the recommendation of scientists from the U.S. Geological Survey, the U.S. Fish and Wildlife Service, and the Montana Fish, Wildlife and Parks service. All of these agencies saw the study as essential to preserving a threatened species by allowing researchers to pinpoint bear numbers and locations.

Palin's choice of study was even worse—indeed, ironically poor. First, the lab in France was supported by the U.S. Department of Agriculture because France had had olive fruit fly infestation for decades before this infestation hit California (Krauss, 2008). It is of immediate economic benefit to the United States to be able to control olive fruit fly infestation. Even more ironically, Palin's speech in part concerned the federal Individuals with Disabilities Education Act and she herself has a child with an intellectual disability. The fruit fly was (and continues to be) a critical organism in the field of genetics—a field of direct relevance to the diagnosis and treatment of a number of disabilities that fall under the Individuals with Disabilities Education Act.

Since that election, politicians have continued to distinguish themselves by displaying their misunderstanding of how science works. Oklahoma Senator Tom Coburn attacked social science divisions of the National Science Foundation that had funded work on behavioral economics critical to understanding the economy and that had funded Nobel Prize winners (Cohen, 2009). He singled out for criticism other scientific projects that had "funny" titles—including one project that involved efficient ways of freezing rat sperm. No doubt he got a lot of political mileage in Oklahoma by making his constituents chuckle at "rat sperm science," but the ultimate joke was on him. The director of the National Institutes of Health answered the question, "Why would anybody spend money on freezing rat semen?" at a hearing. Dr. Francis Collins explained that "We have all these incredibly valuable rat strains that represent particular models of human disease, like hypertension or heart disease....If you just freeze the sperm, you can re-create that rat when you're ready, and it saves us a huge amount of money. Knowing how to do that effectively is a pretty good investment. But, of course, nobody bothered to find out the reason for this. They just thought it sounded weird and bizarre and like a waste of money" (Boyer, 2010, p. 62). Making a scientific discovery involves bringing together findings from disparate areas of science, and the connections will often be far from obvious to a layperson.

We must recognize that, although some research is designed to predict events directly in a specific environmental situation, much scientific research is basic research designed to test theory. Researchers who conduct applied and basic research have completely different answers to the question, how do these findings apply to real life? The former answers, "Directly, provided that there is a reasonably close relationship between the experimental situation and the one to which the findings are to be applied." Thus, questions of the random sampling of subjects and the representativeness of the experimental situation are relevant to the applicability of the results. However, the investigator in a theory-testing study answers that his or her findings do not apply *directly* to real life, and that the reason for conducting the study is not to produce findings that would be applicable to some specific environmental situation. Therefore, this scientist is not concerned with questions of how similar the subjects of the study are to some other group or whether the experimental situation mirrors some real-life environment. Does this mean, then, that these findings have no implications for the real world? No. These findings apply directly not to a particular situation but to a theory. The theory may, at some later date, in conjunction with other scientific laws, be applied to a particular problem.

This type of indirect application through theory has become quite common in some areas of psychology. For example, years ago when cell phones were first introduced, many cognitive psychologists immediately began to worry about the implications for safety when people began to use them while driving automobiles. The psychologists immediately expected that cell phone use would cause additional accidents—and not just because the phone would take a hand off the wheel. Instead, what they were worried about was the attentional requirements of talking on the cell phone. What is important to realize was that the psychologists became worried about cell phone use in cars long before there was a single experimental study of actual cell phone use and its relation to accidents (see Strayer & Drews, 2007; Strayer & Johnston, 2001). The psychologists made their prediction of accident problems with cell phones through *theory*, in this case theories of limited-capacity attention that were decades old (e.g., Broadbent, 1958; Kahneman, 1973). Cell phone use in a car clearly falls within the domain of those theories, which had been established through voluminous experimentation (literally hundreds of laboratory studies). When in fact the actual studies of real cell phone use were done, they confirmed the prediction from the psychological theories of attention: Cell phone use is indeed a cause of motor vehicle accidents—and hands-free phones do not solve the attentional problem, which is the main cause of the accidents (Conkle & West, 2008; Insurance Institute for Highway Safety, 2005; Kunar et al., 2008; Levy, Pashler, & Boer, 2006; McEvoy et al., 2005; Redelmeier & Tibshirani, 2001; Strayer & Drews, 2007).

Douglas Mook (1983) discussed an example that illustrates the ideas of theory-testing experimentation and the nature of indirect application in psychology. In the 1930s, Selig Hecht published a series of studies of visual sensitivity in the *Handbook of General Experimental Psychology* (Murchison, 1934). These studies concerned the phenomenon of dark adaptation. You have probably experienced the temporary blindness that occurs when you walk into a darkened movie theater. As you wait in your seat, however, you probably notice that chairs, people, and other objects begin to become visible. If you keep concentrating on this phenomenon, you will observe that the visibility of objects in the theater continues to increase for several minutes.

This phenomenon is called *dark adaptation*, and it occurs in two phases: a rather quick but fairly small increase in visual sensitivity on entering a darkened room, followed by a delayed but much larger increase in sensitivity. Hecht linked this two-part adaptation curve to the two different types of receptor cells in the retina of the eye. The cones are receptor cells that are densely packed in the center of the fovea (the part of the retina where incoming light is focused) and are very sensitive to red light. The rods are located outside the foveal area, are much less densely packed, and are not very sensitive to red light. Hecht used these facts to establish that the initial phase of dark adaptation (a small, rapid increase in visual sensitivity) is due to the adaptation of the cones and that the second phase (a larger increase in sensitivity taking place over a longer period of time) is due to rod adaptation.

Mook (1983) urged us to consider the complete unnaturalness of Hecht's experimental situation. Subjects (who were not randomly chosen) were in a dark room responding, "Yes, I see it" or "No, I don't," depending on whether or not they detected a tiny red light that was flashed at them. We normally do not respond to little red lights in this way in everyday life. Hecht, however, was not concerned about generalizing his findings to individuals in dark rooms responding "yes" or "no" to tiny red lights, so whether such a situation ever actually occurs is irrelevant. Hecht was interested in establishing facts and testing theories about the basic processes that characterize the visual system, such as dark adaptation. He was not concerned about whether his experimental situation was realistic but about whether it adequately isolated the specific visual process he was interested in studying.

Hecht's findings gain generalizability not through the nature of the setting in which they occurred, but by their ability to establish a theory of basic visual processes that are implicated in many tasks. His research uncovered the basic functional relationships that characterize the human visual system, precisely because his situation was controlled and artificial. If the theoretical model for the relationships is correct, then it should have wide applicability and should account for performance in a variety of situations much different from the one in which it was derived. In fact, the basic understanding of the visual system promoted by Hecht's findings has helped in the treatment of night blindness and in the problem of reading X-rays (Leibowitz, 1996; Mook, 1982). And more dramatically, while awaiting the night raids of Hitler's bombers during the blitz in World War II, the British fighter pilots who were to engage the German planes wore red goggles (so that the rods—not being sensitive to red light—would stay dark adapted; see Mook, 1982). The leap from subjects judging little red dots in a laboratory to the dangerous sky over London was made through *theory*, not through a redesign of Hecht's lab to resemble a Spitfire airplane.

The Hecht example shows that applications of psychological findings have been occurring for decades. There were many others during World War II. For example, at the beginning of the War, the Allied Navy found that Navy personnel were too slow at identifying planes and ships as friend or foe (Joyce, 2010). They turned to Samuel Renshaw, an experimental psychologist at Ohio State University, and asked him to determine whether a holistic identification method could be found that was faster than their WEFT (wing, engine, fuselage, tail) identification system. Renshaw came up with a holistic method that tested better in the lab. It was successful in the field too, and Renshaw has been credited with saving hundreds of lives (Joyce, 2010).

Applications of Psychological Theory

Once we understand that the purpose of most research is to develop theory rather than to predict events in a specific environment and that the findings of most research are applied indirectly, through theory, rather than directly in a specific environmental situation, we can legitimately ask how much application through theory has been accomplished in psychology. That is, have psychology's theories been put to this test of generality?

On this point, we must admit that the record is mixed. But it is wise to keep psychology's diversity in mind here. It is true that some areas of research have made only modest progress along these lines. However, other areas have quite impressive records of experimentally derived principles of considerable explanatory and predictive power.

Consider the basic behavioral principles of classical and operant conditioning. These principles and their elaborating laws were developed almost entirely from experimentation on nonhuman subjects, such as pigeons and rats, in highly artificial laboratory settings. Yet these principles have been successfully applied to a wide variety of human problems, including the treatment of autistic children, the teaching of large amounts of factual material, the treatment of alcoholism and obesity, the management of residents in psychiatric hospitals, and the treatment of phobias, to name just a few.

The principles from which these applications were derived were identified precisely because the laboratory experimentation allowed researchers to specify the relationships between environmental stimuli and behavior with an accuracy not possible in a natural situation, in which many behavioral relationships may operate simultaneously. As for the use of nonhuman subjects, in many cases theories and laws derived from their performance have provided good first approximations to human behavior (Vazire & Gosling, 2003). When humans were examined, their behavior often followed laws that were very similar to those derived from other animals. Findings such as these should hardly surprise anyone today, when just about every medical advance in the treatment of human illness has involved data from animal studies. For example, research with animals has contributed to developments in behavioral medicine; stress reduction; psychotherapy; rehabilitation of injured and handicapped individuals; studying the effects of aging on memory; methods to help people overcome neuromuscular disorders; understanding drug effects on fetal development; traffic safety; and the treatment of chronic pain (Gosling, 2001; Kalat, 2007; Michaels, 2008; Zimbardo, 2004). Recent research with monkeys has led to some real advances in understanding the underlying basis of phobias and anxiety disorders (Mineka & Zinbarg, 2006).

In fact, the it's-not-real-life argument has been used misleadingly to denigrate the results of animal research—often for political reasons. For example, lobbyists for polluting companies often put forth the argument that the evaluation of the human risk of cancer-causing agents is invalid if based on animal studies. However, in a 1988 study of 23 carcinogenic agents (benzene, asbestos, etc.) by a team of scientists, it was found that estimated death rates from animal studies were quite close to estimates from epidemiological studies of humans (Finkel, 1996).

Psychologists studying perceptual processes have made impressive theoretical progress, and the laws and theories they have derived have been applied to problems as diverse as radar monitoring, street lighting, and airplane cockpit design (Durso, Nickerson, Dumais, Lewandowsky, & Perfect, 2007; Swets, Dawes, & Monahan, 2000; Wickens, Lee, Liu, & Gordon-Becker, 2003). Much is now known about the cognitive effects of aging (Salthouse, 2012), and this new knowledge has direct implications for efforts to design systems that will help people to compensate for cognitive loss (Schaie & Willis, 2010).

Psychological studies of judgment and decision making have had implications for medical decision making, educational decision making, and economic decision making (Adler, 2009; Gigerenzer, Gaissmaier, Kurz-Milcke, Schwartz, & Woloshin, 2007; Kahneman, 2011; Stanovich, 2011; Tetlock, 2005; Thaler & Sunstein, 2008; Zweig, 2008). The famous obedience to authority studies of Stanley Milgram were used in officer training schools of the military (Blass, 2004; Cohen, 2008). An exciting new development is the increasing involvement of cognitive psychologists in the legal system, in which problems of memory in information collection, evidence evaluation, and decision making present opportunities to test the applicability of cognitive theories (Spellman & Busey, 2010; Wargo, 2011; Wells, Memon, & Penrod, 2006). In recent decades, theory and practice in the teaching of reading have been affected by research in cognitive psychology (Hulme & Snowling, 2011; Pressley, 2005; Snowling & Hulme, 2005; Stanovich, 2000).

In short, psychology has been applied to "real life" in a large number of ways, but little of this is known to the public. Research psychologists have found ways of getting people to save more for their retirement and to increase their organ donations (Thaler & Sunstein, 2008), discovered how to influence people to get their flu shots (Price, 2009), invented behavioral programs that would reduce energy use (Attari, DeKay, Davidson, & Bruine de Bruin, 2010; Todd, 2010), discovered ways to facilitate onscreen reading (Chamberlin, 2010), helped the government increase tax compliance (Hill, 2010), found ways to reduce health costs (Deangelis, 2010), found the answer to the age-old question of why children hate school (Willingham, 2009), and increased voter turnout (Bryan, Walton, Rogers, & Dweck, 2011).

Psychologists have played an important role in providing scientific evidence to inform the public debate about the status of children's testimony in legal proceedings (Bruck & Ceci, 2004) and about the validity of "recovered" memories of child abuse (Brainerd & Reyna, 2005; McNally & Geraerts, 2009; Moore & Zoellner, 2007). Cognitive psychologist Barbara Tversky studies spatial cognition, and spinoffs from her work have been used in the design of computer map route generators and in writing the instructions for do-it-yourself furniture (Benson, 2006b). The potential applications of psychology are well illustrated in the career of Judi See, who received her doctoral degree in perception and experimental psychology and works on applying psychology to the problems of the military (See, 2006). In a varied and fascinating career, she has assessed the quality of surveillance in Global Hawk unmanned aerial vehicles, evaluated eyeglass inserts for Air Force gas masks, helped B-2 pilots schedule sleep and wake periods to counter fatigue during missions, evaluated the use of handheld translation devices in Iraq, and applied signal detection theory to the neutralization of explosive devices (See, 2006).

The Association for Psychological Science maintains a website where you can read about many more of the practical applications of psychological knowledge. The website is called "We're Only Human" and it is written by Wray Herbert and discusses many applications of psychological research (see http://www.psychologicalscience.org/onlyhuman/). The magazine *Scientific American Mind* also reports on many applications of psychology.

The "College Sophomore" Problem

The concerns of many people who question the "representativeness" of psychological findings focus on the subjects of the research rather than on the intricacies of the experimental design. We are confronting here what is sometimes called the *college sophomore problem*; that is, the worry that, because college sophomores are the subjects in an extremely large number of psychological investigations, the generality of the results is in question. Psychologists are concerned about the college sophomore issue because it is a real problem in certain areas of research. Nevertheless, it is important to consider the problem in perspective and to understand that psychologists have several legitimate responses to this criticism. Here are three responses:

1. The college sophomore criticism does not *invalidate* past results, but simply calls for *more* findings that will allow assessment of the theory's generality. Adjustments in theory necessitated by contrary data from other groups can be made accurately only because we have the college sophomore data. The worst case, a failure to replicate, will mean that theories developed on the basis of college sophomore data are not necessarily wrong but merely incomplete.
2. In many areas of psychology, the college sophomore issue is simply not a problem because the processes investigated are so basic (the visual system, for example) that virtually no one would worry that their fundamental organization depends on the demographics of the subject sample. The basic information-processing operations, the functional organization of the brain, and the nature of the visual systems of people in Montana tend to be very similar to those of people in Florida (or Argentina, for that matter). In addition, these characteristics of humans also depend very little on whether one's parents are tinkers, tailors, or professors.

3. Replication of findings ensures a large degree of geographic generality and, to a lesser extent, generality across socioeconomic factors, family variables, and early educational experience. As opposed to studies conducted 50 years ago, when the sample of university subjects participating would have come from an extremely elite group, research now goes on in universities that serve populations from a great variety of backgrounds.

It would be remiss, however, not to admit that the college sophomore issue is a real problem in certain areas of research in psychology. Nevertheless, psychologists are now making greater efforts to correct the problem. For example, developmental psychologists are almost inherently concerned about this issue. Each year hundreds of researchers in this area test dozens of findings and theories that were developed from studies of college subjects by performing the same research on subjects of different ages.

The results from subject groups of different ages do not always replicate those from college students. Developmental psychology would be starkly boring if they did. But this sizable group of psychologists is busy building an age component into psychological theories, demonstrating the importance of this factor, and ensuring that the discipline will not end up with a large theoretical superstructure founded on a thin database derived from college students.

Developmental psychologists also conduct cross-cultural research in order to assess the generality of the developmental processes uncovered by researchers working only with North American children. There are many instances in which cross-cultural comparisons have shown similar trends across cultures (e.g., Demetriou et al., 2005; McBride-Chang & Kail, 2002), but there are others in which cross-cultural research does not replicate the trends displayed by American college sophomores (e.g., Buchtel & Norenzayan, 2009; Henrich, Heine, & Norenzayan, 2010). However, when these discrepancies occur, they provide important information about the contextual dependence of theories and outcomes (Buchtel & Norenzayan, 2009; Henrich et al., 2010; Medin & Atran, 2004).

As previously mentioned, findings in cognitive psychology have met the basic test of replicability. Many of the fundamental laws of information processing have been observed in dozens of laboratories all over the world. It is often not realized that if a psychologist at the University of Michigan obtains a finding of true importance, similar experiments will almost immediately be attempted at Stanford, Minnesota, Ohio State, Cambridge, Yale, Toronto, and elsewhere. Through this testing, we will soon know whether the finding is due to the peculiarities of the Michigan subjects or the study's experimental setting.

The college sophomore problem and criticisms of representativeness are most often aimed at social psychology, which makes frequent use of college subjects in laboratory paradigms in an attempt to develop theories of social interaction, group behavior, and information processing in social situations (Myers, 2006). However, even in this area of psychology, evidence has indicated that the laboratory-derived relationships and theories do in fact predict behavior in a variety of other situations involving different types of individuals.

For example, several years ago, Leonard Berkowitz, a psychologist at the University of Wisconsin, demonstrated the so-called weapons effect—the fact that the mere presence of a weapon in a person's environment increases the probability of an aggressive response. This finding originated in the laboratory and is a perfect example of an unrepresentative situation. The results were strongly criticized as misleading because they were products of a contrived situation. Yet the fact remains that the finding has been replicated in experiments using different measures of aggression, has been obtained in Europe as well as the United States, has been found to hold for children as well as adults, and has been found outside the laboratory in field studies in which the subjects did not know they were part of an experiment (Berkowitz & Donnerstein, 1982). Researchers have even isolated the cognitive mechanism behind the weapons effect. It is a process of automatic priming in semantic memory (see Meier, Robinson, & Wilkowski, 2007; Wilkowski & Robinson, 2008).

Cognitive, social, and clinical psychologists have also studied various human decision making strategies. Most of the original studies in this research area were done in laboratories, used college students as subjects, and employed extremely artificial tasks. However, the principles of decision making behavior derived from these studies have been observed in a variety of nonlaboratory situations, including the prediction of closing stock prices by bankers, actual casino betting, prediction of patient behavior by psychiatrists, economic markets, military intelligence analysis, betting on NFL football games, estimation of repair time by engineers, estimation of house prices by realtors, business decision making, and diagnoses by physicians—and these principles are also now being applied in the very practical domain of personal financial counseling (Adler, 2009; Ariely, 2008; Hilton, 2003; Kahneman, 2011; Stanovich, 2009; Thaler & Sunstein, 2008; Zweig, 2008).

Birnbaum (1999, 2004) has demonstrated that the Internet provides a way for psychology to deal with the college sophomore problem. He ran a series of decision making experiments in the laboratory and by recruiting participants over the Internet. The laboratory findings all replicated on the Internet sample even though the latter was vastly more diverse—including 1,224 participants from 44 different countries (see also Jaffe, 2005; Skitka & Sargis, 2006). Gosling, Simine, Srivastava, and John (2004) studied a large Internet sample of participants (361,703 people) and compared them with the participants in 510 traditional samples in published studies. They found that the Internet sample was more diverse with respect to gender, socioeconomic status, geographic region, and age. Importantly, they found that findings in many areas of psychology, such as personality theory, were similar on the Internet when compared to traditional methods.

Of course, not all psychological findings replicate. On the contrary, replication failures do happen, and they are often more instructive than confirmations. However, in cognitive psychology, replication failures are rarely due to the peculiarities of the subjects. Instead, most are due to subtle differences in experimental stimuli and methods. By closely examining exactly what experimental conditions are necessary for the demonstration of a phenomenon, scientists come to a more precise understanding of the phenomenon and lay the foundation for a more precise theory about its occurrence.

But how can any psychological findings be applied if replication failures sometimes occur? How can applications be justified if knowledge and theories are not established with certainty, when there is not complete agreement among scientists on all the details? This particular worry about the application of psychological findings is common because people do not realize that findings and theories in other sciences are regularly applied before they are firmly established. Of course, Chapter 2 should have made it clear that all scientific theories are subject to revision. If we must have absolutely certain knowledge before we can apply the results of scientific investigations, then no applications will ever take place. Applied scientists in all fields do their best to use the most accurate information available, realizing at the same time that the information is fallible.

Many nonscientists view medicine as much more scientific than psychology. But the uncertainty in the practice of medicine is no less than that in the practice of psychology. For example, key treatment-related findings in medicine fail to replicate with a frequency just as high as in psychology (Lehrer, 2010), diagnosis is often more a function of the physician than the disease (Welch, Schwartz, & Woloshin, 2012), and new technologies often result in overtreatment that does not increase cure rates (Saul, 2010). Knowledge in psychology is probabilistic and uncertain—but the same is true in most other biosocial sciences.

The Real-Life and College Sophomore Problems in Perspective

Several issues have been raised in this chapter, and it is important to be clear about what has, and what has not, been said. We have illustrated that the frequent complaint about the artificiality of psychological research arises from a basic misunderstanding not only of psychology but also of basic principles that govern all sciences. Artificial conditions are not a drawback of experimental research. They are *deliberately* created so that we can pry variables apart.

We have also seen why people are concerned that psychologists do not use random samples in all their research and also why this worry is often unfounded. Finally, we have seen that a legitimate concern, the college sophomore problem, is sometimes overstated, particularly by those who are unfamiliar with the full range of activities and the diverse types of research that go on in psychology.

Nevertheless, psychologists should always be concerned that their experimental conclusions not rely too heavily on any one method or particular subject population. The next chapter deals with this very point. Indeed, some areas of psychology *are* plagued by a college sophomore problem (Jaffe, 2005). Cross-cultural psychology, an antidote to the college sophomore problem, is a very underdeveloped field. However, there is reason for optimism because self-criticism is valued highly by research psychologists (see Chapter 12; Baumeister, Vohs, & Funder, 2007; Funder, 2009; Lilienfeld, 2010, 2012; Mischel, 2008; Peterson, 2009; Rozin, 2006, 2007, 2009; Simmons, Nelson, & Simonsohn, 2011). Not a year goes by without many articles in scientific journals warning psychologists of flaws in their methods and pointing out the college sophomore problem. The latter has been an issue of great concern within psychology, and no psychologist is unaware of it. So, although we should not ignore the issue, we must also keep it in perspective.

Summary

Some psychological research is applied work in which the goal is to relate the results of the study directly to a particular situation. In such applied research, in which the results are intended to be extrapolated directly to a naturalistic situation, questions of the randomness of the sample and the representativeness of the conditions are important because the findings of the study are going to be applied directly. However, most psychological research is not of this type. It is basic research designed to test theories of the underlying mechanisms that influence behavior. In most basic research, the findings are applied only indirectly through modifications in a theory that will at some later point be applied to some practical problem. In basic research of this type, random sampling of subjects and representative situations are not an issue because the emphasis is on testing the universal prediction of a theory. In fact, artificial situations are deliberately constructed in theory-testing basic research because (as described in the previous chapter) they help to isolate the critical variable for study and to control extraneous variables. Thus, the fact that psychology experiments are "not like real life" is a strength rather than a weakness.

CHAPTER 8

Avoiding the Einstein Syndrome: The Importance of Converging Evidence

"Biological Experiment Reveals the Key to Life," "New Breakthrough in Mind Control," "California Scientist Discovers How to Postpone Death"— as you can see, it is not difficult to parody the "breakthrough" headlines of the media. Because such headlines regularly come from the most irresponsible quarters of the media, it should not be surprising that most scientists recommend that they be approached with skepticism. The purpose of this chapter, though, is not only to warn against the spread of misinformation via exaggeration or to caution that the source must be considered when evaluating reports of scientific advances. In this chapter, we also want to develop a more complex view of the scientific process than was presented in earlier chapters. We shall do this by elaborating on the ideas of systematic empiricism and public knowledge that were introduced in Chapter 1.

The breakthrough headlines in the media obscure an understanding of psychology and other sciences in many ways. One particular misunderstanding that arises from breakthrough headlines is the implication that all problems in science are solved when a single, crucial experiment completely decides the issue, or that theoretical advance is the result of a single critical insight that overturns all previous knowledge. Such a view of scientific progress fits in nicely with the operation of the news media and the Internet, in which history is tracked by presenting separate, disconnected events in bite-sized units. It is also a convenient format for the Hollywood entertainment industry, where events must have beginnings and satisfying endings that resolve ambiguity. However, this is a gross caricature of scientific progress and, if taken too seriously, leads to misconceptions about scientific advance and impairs the ability to evaluate the extent of scientific knowledge on a given issue. In this chapter, we will discuss two principles of science—the connectivity principle and the principle of converging evidence—that describe scientific progress much more accurately than the breakthrough model.

The Connectivity Principle

In denying the validity of the "great-leap" or crucial-experiment model of all scientific progress, we do not wish to argue that such critical experiments and theoretical advances never occur. On the contrary, some of the most famous examples in the history of science represent just such occurrences. The development of the theory of relativity by Albert Einstein is by far the most well known. Here, a reconceptualization of such fundamental concepts as space, time, and matter was achieved by a series of remarkable theoretical insights.

However, the monumental nature of Einstein's achievement has made it the dominant model of scientific progress in the public's mind. This dominance is perpetuated because it fits in nicely with the implicit "script" that the media use to report most news events. More nonsense has been written about relativity theory than perhaps any other idea in all of history (no, Einstein did *not* prove that "everything is relative"). Of course, our purpose is not to deal with all of these fallacies here. There is one, however, that will throw light on our later discussions of theory evaluation in psychology.

The reconceptualization of ideas about the physical universe contained in Einstein's theories is so fundamental that popular writing often treats it as if it were similar to conceptual changes in the arts (a minor poet is reevaluated and emerges with the status of a genius; an artistic school is declared dead). Such presentations ignore a basic difference between conceptual change in the arts and in the sciences.

Conceptual change in science obeys a principle of *connectivity* that is absent or, at least, severely limited in the arts (see Bronowski, 1977; Haack, 2007). That is, a new theory in science must make contact with previously established empirical facts. To be considered an advance, it must not only explain new facts but also account for old ones. The theory may explain old facts in a way quite different from that of a previous theory, but explain them it must. This requirement ensures the cumulative progress of science. Genuine progress does not occur unless the realm of our explanatory power has been widened. If a new theory accounts for some new facts but fails to account for a host of old ones, it will not be considered an advance over the old theories and, thus, will not immediately replace them.

Despite the startling reconceptualizations in Einstein's theories (clocks in motion running slower, mass increasing with velocity, etc.), they did maintain the principle of connectivity. In rendering Newtonian mechanics obsolete, Einstein's theories did not negate or render meaningless the facts about motion on which Newton's ideas were based. On the contrary, at low velocities the two theories make essentially the same predictions. Einstein's conceptualization is superior because it accounts for a wide variety of new, sometimes surprising, phenomena that Newtonian mechanics cannot accommodate. Thus, even Einstein's theories, some of the most startlingly new and fundamental reconceptualizations in the history of science, maintain the principle of connectivity.

A Consumer's Rule: Beware of Violations of Connectivity

The breakthrough model of scientific progress—what we might call the Einstein syndrome—leads us astray by implying that new discoveries violate the principle of connectivity. This implication is dangerous because, when the principle of connectivity is abandoned, the main beneficiaries are the purveyors of pseudoscience and bogus theories. Such theories derive part of their appeal and much of their publicity from the fact that they are said to be startlingly new. "After all, wasn't relativity new in its day?" is usually the tactic used to justify novelty as a virtue. Of course, the data previously accumulated in the field that the pseudoscientists wish to enter would seem to be a major obstacle. Actually, however, it presents only a minor inconvenience because two powerful strategies are available to dispose of it. One strategy that we have already discussed (see Chapter 2) is to explain the previous data by making the theory unfalsifiable and, hence, useless.

The second strategy is to dismiss previous data by declaring them irrelevant. This dismissal is usually accomplished by emphasizing what a radical departure the new theory represents. The phrases "new conception of reality" and "radical new departure" are frequently used. The real sleight of hand, though, occurs in the next step of the process. The new theory is deemed so radical that experimental evidence derived from the testing of other theories is declared irrelevant. Only data that can be conceptualized within the framework of the new theory are to be considered; that is, the principle of connectivity is explicitly broken. Obviously, because the theory is so new, such data are said not yet to exist. And there you have it: a rich environment for the growth of pseudoscience. The old, "irrelevant" data are gone, and the new, relevant data do not exist. The scam is easily perpetrated because the Einstein syndrome obscures the principle of connectivity, the importance of which is ironically illustrated by Einstein's theories themselves.

Philosopher Michael Ruse (1999) illustrates an example of Darwin himself using the connectivity principle and abandoning an idea when it failed to display the necessary continuity with the rest of science. The example concerns Darwin's search for a mechanism of heredity to go with his theory of natural selection. Darwin tried to formulate a theory of so-called pangenesis, "in which little gemmules, given off by all of the body parts, circulate around the body and eventually collect in the sex organs, from where they are ready to start the next generation" (p. 64). One problem was that this theory did not cohere with cell theory. Second, Darwin could not explain how the gemmules were transported because transfusion experiments had already proven that it could not be via the blood. For these and other reasons pangenesis faded from science "because it did not cohere with the rest of biology" (p. 64).

It is likewise with psychology. A new theory that denied the existence of classical and operant conditioning would never develop in psychology because it would not connect with what else is known in behavioral science. Recall the discussion of facilitated communication in Chapter 6. It is suspected as a "cure" for the language problems of autism because it breaks the principle of connectivity—if that treatment worked, it would require that we overturn basic knowledge in fields as diverse as neurology, genetics, and cognitive psychology. This hypothesized cure shows no connectivity with the rest of science.

Consider an example from psychology. Imagine two treatments have been developed to remediate the problems of children with extreme reading difficulties. No direct empirical tests of efficacy have been carried out using either treatment. The first, Treatment A, is a training program to facilitate the awareness of the segmental nature of language at the phonological level. The second, Treatment B, involves giving children training in vestibular sensitivity by having them walk on balance beams while blindfolded. Treatments A and B are equal in one respect—neither has had a direct empirical test of its efficacy, which reflects badly on both. Nevertheless, one of the treatments has the edge when it comes to the principle of connectivity. Treatment A makes contact with a broad consensus in the research literature that children with reading difficulties are hampered because of insufficiently developed awareness of the segmental structure of language (Snowling & Hulme, 2005; Wagner & Kantor, 2010). Treatment B is not connected to any corresponding research literature consensus. This difference in connectivity dictates that Treatment A is a better choice, even though neither has been directly tested.

The "Great-Leap" Model Versus the Gradual-Synthesis Model

The tendency to view the Einsteinian revolution as typical of what science is tempts us to think that all scientific advances occur in giant leaps. The problem is that people tend to generalize such examples into a view of the way all scientific progress *should* take place. In fact, many areas in science have advanced not by single, sudden breakthroughs but by series of fits and starts that are less easy to characterize.

There is a degree of fuzziness in the scientific endeavor that most of the public is unaware of. Experiments rarely completely decide a given issue, supporting one theory and ruling out all others. New theories are rarely clearly superior to all previously existing competing conceptualizations. Issues are most often decided not by a critical experiment, as movies about science imply, but when the community of scientists gradually begins to agree that the preponderance of evidence supports one alternative theory rather than another. The evidence that scientists evaluate is not the data from a single experiment that has finally been designed in the perfect way. Instead, scientists most often must evaluate data from literally dozens of experiments, each containing some flaws but each providing a small part of the answer. This alternative model of scientific progress has been obscured because the Einstein syndrome creates in the public a tendency to think of all science by reference to physics, to which the great-leap model of scientific progress is perhaps most applicable.

Consider the rapid advances in genetics and molecular biology that have occurred in the last hundred years. These advances have occurred not because one giant, Einstein, came onto the scene at the key moment to set everything straight. Instead, dozens of different insights based on hundreds of experiments have contributed to the modern synthesis in biology. These advances occurred not by the instantaneous recognition of a major conceptual innovation, but by long, drawn-out haggling over alternative explanations, each of which had partial support. It took over ten years of inconclusive experimentation, along with much theoretical speculation, argument, and criticism, for scientists to change their view about whether genes were made of protein or nucleic acid. The consensus of opinion changed, but not in one great leap.

Ernest Rutherford, discoverer of the atom's nucleus, stressed that "scientists are not dependent on the ideas of a single person, but on the combined wisdom of thousands" (Holton & Roller, 1958, p. 166). Rutherford's point emphasizes another consumer rule for separating scientific from pseudoscientific claims. Science—a cumulative endeavor that respects the principle of connectivity—is characterized by the participation of many individuals, whose contributions are judged by the extent to which they further our understanding of nature. No single individual can dominate discourse simply by virtue of his or her status. Science rejects claims of "special knowledge" available to only a few select individuals. This rejection, of course, follows from our discussion of the public nature of science in Chapter 1. By contrast, pseudosciences often claim that certain authorities or investigators have a "special" access to the truth.

We have presented two ideas here that provide a useful context for understanding the discipline of psychology. First, no experiment in science is perfectly designed. There is a degree of ambiguity in the interpretation of the data from any one experiment. Scientists often evaluate theories not by waiting for the ideal or crucial experiment to appear, but by assessing the overall trends in a large number of experiments—each with different limitations. Second, many sciences have progressed even though they are without an Einstein. Their progress has occurred by fits and starts, rather than by discrete stages of grand Einsteinian syntheses. Also like psychology, many other sciences are characterized instead by growing mosaics of knowledge that lack a single integrating theme.

Converging Evidence: Progress Despite Flaws

The previous discussion has led to a principle of evidence evaluation of much importance in psychology. This idea is sometimes called the *principle of converging evidence* (or *converging operations*). Scientists and those who apply scientific knowledge must often make a judgment about where the preponderance of evidence points. When this is the case, the principle of converging evidence is an important tool. The principle of converging evidence is also a very useful tool for the lay consumer of scientific information and is particularly useful in evaluating psychological claims. Although a full technical discussion of the idea of converging evidence would soon take us far afield, the aspects most useful in the practical application of the concept are actually easy to understand. We will explore two ways of expressing the principle, one in terms of experiments with limitations and the other in terms of theory testing.

There are always a number of ways in which an experiment can go wrong (or become *confounded*, to use the technical term). However, a scientist with much experience in working on a particular problem usually has a good idea of what the most likely confounding factors are. Thus, when surveying the research evidence, scientists are usually aware of the critical flaws in each experiment. The idea of converging evidence, then, tells us to examine the pattern of flaws running through the research literature because the nature of this pattern can either support or undermine the conclusions that we wish to draw.

For example, suppose the findings from a number of different experiments were largely consistent in supporting a particular conclusion. Given the imperfect nature of experiments, we would go on to evaluate the extent and nature of the limitations in these studies. If all the experiments were limited in a similar way, this circumstance would undermine confidence in the conclusions drawn from them because the consistency of the outcome may simply have resulted from a particular flaw that all the experiments shared. On the other hand, if all the experiments were limited in *different* ways, our confidence in the conclusions would be increased because it is less likely that the consistency in the results was due to a contaminating factor that confounded all the experiments. As Anderson and Anderson (1996) noted, "Different methods are likely to involve different assumptions. When a conceptual hypothesis survives many potential falsifications based on different sets of assumptions, we have a robust effect" (p. 742).

Each experiment helps to correct errors in the design of other experiments, and when evidence from a wide range of experiments points in a similar direction, then the evidence has converged. A reasonably strong conclusion is justified even though no one experiment was perfectly designed. Thus, the principle of converging evidence urges us to base conclusions on data that arise from a number of slightly different experimental sources. The principle allows us to draw stronger conclusions because consistency that has been demonstrated in such a context is less likely to have arisen from the peculiarities of a single type of experimental procedure.

The principle of converging evidence can also be stated in terms of theory testing. Research is highly convergent when a series of experiments consistently supports a given theory while collectively eliminating the most important competing theory. Although no single experiment can rule out all alternative explanations, taken collectively a series of partially diagnostic experiments can lead, if the data patterns line up in a certain way, to a strong conclusion.

For example, suppose that five different theoretical accounts (call them A, B, C, D, and E) of a given set of phenomena exist at one time and are investigated in a series of experiments. Suppose that one experiment represents a strong test of theories A, B, and C, and that the data largely refute theories A and B and support C. Imagine also that another experiment is a particularly strong test of theories C, D, and E, and that the data largely refute theories D and E and support C. In such a situation, we would have strong converging evidence for theory C. Not only do we have data supportive of theory C, but we have data that contradict its major competitors. Note that no one experiment tests all the theories, but taken together, the entire set of experiments allows a strong inference. The situation might be depicted like the following:

	Theory A	Theory B	Theory C	Theory D	Theory E
Experiment 1	refuted	refuted	supported	untested	untested
Experiment 2	untested	untested	supported	refuted	refuted

	Theory A	Theory B	Theory C	Theory D	Theory E
Conclusion	refuted	refuted	supported	refuted	refuted

By contrast, if *both* experiments represented strong tests of B, C, and E, and the data of both experiments strongly supported C and refuted B and E, the overall support for theory C would be less strong than in our previous example. The reason is that, although data supporting theory C have been generated, there is no strong evidence ruling out two viable alternative theories (A and D). The situation would be something like the following:

	Theory A	Theory B	Theory C	Theory D	Theory E
Experiment 1	untested	refuted	supported	untested	refuted
Experiment 2	untested	refuted	supported	untested	refuted

	Theory A	Theory B	Theory C	Theory D	Theory E
Conclusion	untested	refuted	supported	untested	refuted

Thus, research is highly convergent when a series of experiments consistently supports a given theory while collectively eliminating the most important competing explanations. Although no single experiment can rule out all alternative explanations, taken collectively a series of partially diagnostic experiments can lead to a strong conclusion if the data converge in the manner of our first example.

Finally, the introduction of the idea of converging evidence allows us to dispel a misconception that may have been fostered by our oversimplified discussion of falsifiability in Chapter 2. That discussion may have seemed to imply that a theory is falsified when the first piece of evidence that disconfirms it comes along. This is not the case, however. Just as theories are confirmed by converging evidence, they are also disconfirmed by converging results.

Converging Evidence in Psychology

The reason for stressing the importance of convergence is that conclusions in psychology are often based on the principle of converging evidence. There is certainly nothing unique or unusual about this fact (conclusions in many other sciences rest not on single, definitive experimental proofs, but on the confluence of dozens of fuzzy experiments). But there are reasons that this might be especially true of psychology. Experiments in psychology are usually of fairly low diagnosticity. That is, the data that support a given theory usually rule out only a small set of alternative explanations, leaving many additional theories as viable candidates. As a result, strong conclusions are usually possible only after data from a very large number of studies have been collected and compared.

It should not be surprising that experiments in psychology have a high fuzzy factor, given the enormous complexity of the problems concerning behavior. Better public understanding will come about if psychologists openly acknowledge this fact and then take pains to explain just what follows from it. Psychologists should admit that, although a science of psychology exists and is progressing, progress is slow, and our conclusions come only after a sometimes excruciatingly long period of research amalgamation and debate. Media claims of breakthroughs should always engender skepticism, but this is especially true of psychological claims.

In psychology we have to walk a very fine line. For example, we must resist the temptation to regard a particular psychological hypothesis as "proven" when the evidence surrounding it is still ambiguous. This skeptical attitude has been reinforced in several chapters of this book. The cautions against inferring causation from correlation and against accepting testimonial evidence have served as examples. At the same time, we should not overreact to the incompleteness of knowledge and the tentativeness of conclusions by doubting whether firm conclusions in psychology will ever be reached. Nor should we be tempted by the irrational claim that psychology cannot be a science. From this standpoint, the principle of converging evidence can be viewed as a counterweight to the warnings against overinterpreting tentative knowledge. Convergence allows us to reach many reasonably strong conclusions despite the flaws in all psychological research.

The best way to see the power of the principle of converging evidence is to examine some areas in psychology where conclusions have been reached by an application of the principle. Let's consider an example. A research problem that illustrates the importance of the principle of converging evidence is the question of whether exposure to violent television programming increases children's tendencies toward aggressive behavior. There is now a scientific consensus on this issue: The viewing of violent programming (on television, in movies, or in streaming video) does appear to increase the probability that children will engage in aggressive behavior. The effect is not extremely large, but it is real. Again, the confidence that scientists have in this conclusion derives not from a single definitive study, but from the convergence of the results of dozens of different investigations (Anderson & Huesmann, 2005; Carnagey, Anderson, & Bartholow, 2007; Feshbach & Tangney, 2008; Fischer, Greitemeyer, Kastenmüller, Vogrincic, & Sauer, 2011b). This research conclusion holds for violent video games as well as television and movies (Carnagey et al., 2007; Sheese & Graziano, 2005). The general research designs, subject populations, and specific techniques used in these investigations differed widely, and as should now be clear, these differences are a strength of the research in this area, not a weakness.

Television network executives and video game industry executives, naturally resistant to hard evidence of the negative effects of their industry on children, have carried on a campaign of misinformation that capitalizes on the public's failure to realize that research conclusions are based on the convergence of many studies rather than on a single critical demonstration that decides the issue (Seethaler, 2009). The television networks and video game makers continually single out individual studies for criticism and imply that the general conclusion is undermined by the fact that each study has demonstrated flaws. Although social science researchers may contest particular criticisms of a specific study, it is not commonly recognized that researchers often candidly admit the flaws in a given study. The critical difference is that researchers reject the implication that admitting a flaw in a given study undermines the general scientific consensus on the effects of televised violence on aggressive behavior. The reason is that the general conclusion derives from a convergence. Research without the specific flaws of the study in question has produced results pointing in the same direction. This research may itself have problems, but other studies have corrected for these and have also produced similar results.

For example, very early in the investigation of this issue, evidence of the correlation between the amount of violent programming viewed and aggressive behavior in children was uncovered. It was correctly pointed out that this correlational evidence did not justify a causal conclusion. Perhaps a third variable was responsible for the association, or perhaps more aggressive children chose to watch more violent programming (the directionality problem).

But the conclusion of the scientific community is not based on this correlational evidence alone. There are more complex correlational techniques than the simple measurement of the association between two variables, and these correlational techniques allow some tentative conclusions about causality (one, that of partial correlation, was mentioned in Chapter 5). One of these techniques involves the use of a longitudinal design in which measurements of the same two variables—here, television violence and aggression—are taken at two different times. Certain correlational patterns suggest causal connections. Studies of this type have been conducted, and the pattern of results suggested that viewing violent programming did tend to increase the probability of engaging in aggressive behavior later in life.

Again, it is not unreasonable to counter that these longitudinal correlational techniques are controversial, because they are. The important point is that the conclusion of a causal connection between televised violence and aggressive behavior does not depend entirely on correlational evidence, either simple or complex, because numerous laboratory studies have been conducted in which the amount of televised violence was manipulated rather than merely assessed. In Chapter 6, we discussed how the manipulation of a variable, used in conjunction with other experimental controls such as random assignment, prevents the interpretation problems that surround most correlational studies. If two groups of children, experimentally equated on all other variables, show different levels of aggressive behavior, and if the only difference between the two is that one group viewed violent programming and one did not, then we are correct in inferring that the manipulated variable (televised violence—the independent variable) caused the changes in the outcome variable (aggressive behavior—the dependent variable). This result has occurred in the majority of studies.

These studies have prompted some to raise the "it's-not-real-life" argument discussed in the previous chapter and to use the argument in the fallacious way discussed in that chapter. In any case, the results on the effects of television violence are not peculiar to a certain group of children because these results have been replicated in different regions of the United States and in several countries around the world. The specific laboratory setup and the specific programs used as stimuli have varied from investigation to investigation, yet the results have held up.

Importantly, the same conclusions have been drawn from studies conducted in the field rather than in the laboratory. A design known as the *field experiment* has been used to investigate the televised-violence/aggressive-behavior issue. The existence of this type of design reminds us to avoid assuming a necessary link between experimental design and experimental setting. People sometimes think that studies that manipulate variables are conducted only in laboratories and that correlational studies are conducted only in the field. This assumption is incorrect. Correlational studies are often conducted in laboratories, and variables are often manipulated in nonlaboratory settings. Although they sometimes require considerable ingenuity to design, field experiments (several of which were mentioned in Chapter 6), in which variables are manipulated in nonlaboratory settings, are becoming more common in psychology.

For example, a field experiment was used to test the so-called broken windows theory of crime incidence (Keizer, Lindenberg, & Steg, 2008). The theory posits that seemingly incidental indicators of social disorder (broken windows, graffiti, etc.) can actually increase crime by sending signals that transgressions are the norm in a particular area. Kees Keizer and colleagues created two conditions in alleys where bikes were parked. In the control condition, a sign prohibiting graffiti was put in an alley with no graffiti. In the experimental condition, a sign prohibiting graffiti was put in an alley with lots of graffiti on the walls. A paper flyer was put on the handlebars of each bike in the alley. Keizer and colleagues found that 69 percent of the subjects in the experimental group littered with their flyer (threw it on the ground) compared with only 33 percent in the control group.

Of course, field experiments themselves have weaknesses, but many of these weaknesses are the strengths of other types of investigation. In summary, the evidence linking the viewing of televised violence to increased probabilities of aggressive behavior in children does not rest only on the outcome of one particular study or even one generic type of study.

The situation is analogous to the relationship between smoking and lung cancer. Smokers are 15 times more likely to die from lung cancer than nonsmokers (Gigerenzer et al., 2007). Cigarette company executives often attempted to mislead the public by implying that the conclusion that smoking causes lung cancer rested on some specific study, which they would then go on to criticize (Offit, 2008). Instead, the conclusion is strongly supported by a wealth of converging evidence. The convergence of data from several different types of research is quite strong and will not be changed substantially by the criticism of one study.

Actually it is appropriate to discuss here a medical problem like the causes of lung cancer. Most issues in medical diagnosis and treatment are decided by an amalgamation of converging evidence from many different types of investigations. For example, medical science is confident of a conclusion when the results of epidemiological studies (field studies of humans in which disease incidence is correlated with many environmental and demographic factors), highly controlled laboratory studies using animals, and clinical trials with human patients all converge. When the results of all these types of investigation point to a similar conclusion, medical science feels assured of the conclusion, and physicians feel confident in basing their treatment on the evidence.

However, each of the three different types of investigation has its drawbacks. Epidemiological studies are always correlational, and the possibility of spurious links between variables is high. Laboratory studies can be highly controlled, but the subjects are often animals rather than humans. Clinical trials in a hospital setting use human subjects in a real treatment context, but there are many problems of control because of placebo effects and the expectations of the medical treatment team that deals with the patients. Despite the problems in each type of investigation, medical researchers are justified in drawing strong conclusions when the data from all the different methods converge strongly, as in the case of smoking and lung cancer. Just such a convergence also justifies the conclusions that psychologists draw from the study of a behavioral problem like the effect of televised violence on aggressive behavior.

The principle of converging evidence is often a difficult one for the public to understand, however. For example, David Michaels (2008), an epidemiologist at George Washington University, describes a court case involving harm from toxic substances, *General Electric v. Joiner*, in which the judge found a flaw in each piece of scientific evidence presented and then proceeded to throw out the entire package of evidence. Michaels reminds us that "in the real world, scientists do not operate this way. They consider the strengths and weaknesses of each piece of evidence. It is entirely possible to draw a sound conclusion despite flaws or limitations in each and every test and study that constitute the evidence for that conclusion. This happens all the time" (p. 163).

Sometimes the principle of converging evidence is unknown to people. Other times it seems to be consciously ignored in order to advance a political agenda or an agenda of financial advancement. Certainly the cigarette company experts and senior executives who tried to confuse the public's understanding of the converging evidence that smoking caused lung cancer probably were aware of the convergence principle and wished to obscure it from the public. An example similar to the smoking/lung cancer case is occurring right at the present time. There is a strong convergence in science indicating that talking on a cell phone while driving (as well as the distraction from electronic dashboard devices while driving) is extremely dangerous and an important cause of car crashes. Yet cell phone companies and auto companies—like the cigarette companies before them—are attempting to obscure from the public the fact that the science surrounding this conclusion is highly convergent (Conkle & West, 2008; Insurance Institute for Highway Safety, 2005; Kunar, Carter, Cohen, & Horowitz, 2008; Levy, Pashler, & Boer, 2006; McEvoy et al., 2005; Redelmeier & Tibshirani, 2001; Strayer & Drews, 2007; Strayer & Johnston, 2001).

Scientific Consensus

The problem of assessing the impact of televised violence is typical of how data finally accumulate to answer questions in psychology. Particularly in areas of pressing social concern, it is wise to remember that the answers to these problems emerge only slowly, after the amalgamation of the results from many different experiments. To put things in the form of a simple rule, when evaluating empirical evidence in the field of psychology, think in terms of *scientific consensus* rather than *breakthrough*—in terms of *gradual synthesis* rather than *great leap*.

The failure to appreciate the "consensus rather than breakthrough" rule has impeded the public's understanding of the evidence that human activity is a contributor to global warming (Grant, 2011; Jordan, 2007; Nijhuis, 2008). Many political groups did not like the evidence that human energy consumption, gasoline usage, and carbon emission in the economy was having negative environmental effects. The evidence ran counter to their political agendas. Many of these groups would then attack individual studies and conduct a media campaign that gave their attacks wide publicity. They wished to create the impression that because a single study was in dispute, there was a great scientific controversy about the role of human activity in global warming (Grant, 2011; Manjoo, 2008; Michaels, 2008; Nijhuis, 2008; Pigliucci, 2010). In fact, there was no great controversy, because the conclusion did not rest on a single study. There were over 900 global climate-change papers published between 1993 and 2003, and they overwhelmingly converged on the conclusion that human activity was involved in global warming (Oreskes, 2004; Oreskes & Conway, 2011). No single study was definitive in establishing the conclusion so, obviously, undermining a single study would not change the conclusion at all. Nevertheless, the political groups wished to create doubt among the public—and in this they were successful. Surveys show that about 50 percent of the public think that scientists are still debating the conclusion when in fact a strong convergence has been achieved (Frazier, 2009).

Unfortunately, the media, with their "he-said, she-said" orientation, played right into the hands of the global-warming deniers, because the media's "one-side, otherside" reporting suggested that there was great controversy when there was not (Oreskes & Conway, 2011). Late in the day, several media outlets stepped in to stop political groups from exploiting the public's failure to understand that scientific conclusions derive from convergence and consensus. On the cover of its August 13, 2007 issue, *Newsweek* magazine printed the large title "Global Warming is a Hoax" with an asterisk. In the lower left part of the cover, the asterisk explained that the title was a joke! The lead article in the issue was instead all about how well-funded political groups were trying to convince the public that there was controversy about the existence of human-caused climate change. The magazine contained a large feature article on what was termed "the denial machine"— the political groups who had successfully convinced the public that there was doubt about global warming because a single study was flawed (Oreskes & Conway, 2011). The article described how the political groups had exploited public misunderstanding—specifically, the public's mistaken belief that this issue must rest on a single crucial study.

Science writers Barbara Kantrowitz and Claudia Kalb (2006) warn that the proliferation of media reports of medical studies is good in one sense but may have the potential to backfire and result in *less* public understanding if the public is not schooled in the convergence principle. They point out that in medicine, science advances in small steps and is a brick-by-brick process rather than a breakthrough process. The media tends to portray things in just the opposite manner.

Methods and the Convergence Principle

The convergence principle also implies that we should expect many different methods to be used in all psychological research areas. A relative balance among the methodologies used to arrive at a given conclusion is desirable because the various classes of research techniques have different strengths and weaknesses. Psychology has long been criticized for relying too heavily on laboratory-based experimental techniques. The validity of this criticism depends on the specific research area that is the focus of discussion. Nevertheless, an unmistakable trend in recent years has been to expand the variety of methods used in all areas of psychology. For example, social psychologists, who have perhaps received the most criticism for overreliance on laboratory techniques, have turned to increasingly imaginative field designs in search of converging evidence to support their theories.

As an example, consider the voluminous research done on what has been called the unresponsive bystander phenomenon, that is, the failure of some people to respond with help when observing another individual in an emergency situation (Fischer et al., 2011a). Probability of helping can sometimes go down the more potential helpers that are present. The early investigators of this phenomenon were well aware that their conclusions would be tenuous if they were based only on the responses of individuals who witnessed emergencies after reporting to a laboratory to participate in an experiment. Therefore, in an early famous study of this effect, researchers found a cooperative liquor store that agreed to have fake robberies occur in the store 96 different times. While the cashier was in the back of the store getting some beer for a "customer," who was actually an accomplice of the experimenter, the "customer" walked out the front door with a case of beer. This was done in the view of either one or two real customers who were at the checkout counter. The cashier then came back and asked the customers, "Hey, what happened to that man who was in here? Did you see him leave?" thus giving the customers a chance to report the theft. Consistent with the laboratory results, the presence of another individual inhibited the tendency to report the theft.

Many of the principles of probabilistic decision making to be discussed in Chapter 10 originated in the laboratory but have also been tested in the field. For example, researchers have used the laboratory-derived principles to explain the way that physicians, stockbrokers, jurors, economists, and gamblers reason probabilistically in their environments (Adler, 2009; Hilton, 2003; Kahneman, 2011; Stanovich, 2011; Thaler & Sunstein, 2008; Zweig, 2008). The convergence of laboratory and nonlaboratory results has also characterized several areas of educational psychology. For example, both laboratory studies and field studies of different curricula have indicated that early phonics instruction facilitates the acquisition of reading skill (Ehri, Nunes, Stahl, & Willows, 2001; Pressley, 2005; Snowling & Hulme, 2005; Vellutino, Fletcher, Snowling, & Scanlon, 2004).

It should be remembered that research convergence is not always positive, in the sense of supporting the original hypothesis. Sometimes research converges on a negative conclusion—that the hypothesis that was originally posited cannot be supported. This has been the case with the study of learning styles in educational psychology. It has long been thought there was a way for teachers to measure each child's "learning style." Now I won't mention a specific style here, because different writers have different lists of what the "styles" are (which turns out to be part of the problem). In any case, teachers are then supposed to be able to "teach to" these styles—resulting in higher achievement for all. (It is sometimes also claimed that students will all achieve much more equally if this is done.) The problem is that after hundreds of studies on this idea, research has not confirmed it (Lilienfeld et al., 2010; Pashler, McDaniel, Rohrer, & Bjork, 2009; Stahl & Kuhn, 1995). There is no replicable evidence that teachers can "match" instruction to these styles in ways that lead to greater learning.

The Progression to More Powerful Methods

Research on a particular problem often proceeds from weaker methods to ones that allow more powerful conclusions to be drawn. For example, interest in a particular hypothesis may originally stem from a particular case study of unusual interest. As we discussed in Chapter 4, this is the proper role of case studies: to suggest hypotheses for further study with more powerful techniques and to motivate scientists to apply more rigorous methods to a research problem. Thus, following the case studies, researchers undertake correlational investigations to verify whether the link between variables is real rather than the result of the peculiarities of a few case studies. If the correlational studies support the relationship between relevant variables, researchers will attempt experiments in which variables are manipulated in order to isolate a causal relationship between the variables. The progression, then, is from case studies, to correlational studies, to experiments with manipulated variables.

Discussing the idea of the progression through the more powerful research methods provides us with a chance to deal with a misconception that some readers may have derived from Chapter 5—that is, that correlational studies are not useful in science. It is true that, when a causal hypothesis is at issue, studies with true experimental manipulation are preferred. However, this does not mean that correlational studies cannot contribute to knowledge (West, 2009). First, many scientific hypotheses are stated in terms of correlation or lack of correlation, so that such studies are directly relevant to these hypotheses. Second, although correlation does not imply causation, causation does imply correlation. That is, although a correlational study cannot definitively prove a causal hypothesis, it may rule one out. Third, correlational studies are more useful than they may seem, because some of the recently developed complex correlational designs allow for some very limited causal inferences. We discussed in Chapter 5 the complex correlational technique of partial correlation, in which it is possible to test whether a particular third variable is accounting for a relationship.

Perhaps most important, however, some variables simply cannot be manipulated for ethical reasons (for instance, human malnutrition or physical disabilities). Other variables, such as birth order, sex, and age, are inherently correlational because they cannot be manipulated, and, therefore, the scientific knowledge concerning them must be based on correlational evidence. This circumstance, again, is not unique to psychology. Astronomers obviously cannot manipulate all the variables affecting the objects they study, yet they are able to arrive at conclusions.

An example of the evolution of research methods in health psychology is the work concerning the link between the type A behavior pattern and coronary heart disease (Chida & Hamer, 2008; Martin et al., 2011; Matthews, 2005; Suls & Bunde, 2005). The original observations that led to the development of the concept of the type A behavior pattern occurred when two cardiologists thought they noticed a pattern in the behavior of some of their coronary patients that included a sense of time urgency, free-floating hostility, and extremely competitive striving for achievement. Thus, the idea of the type A personality originated in a few case studies made by some observant physicians. These case studies suggested the concept, but they were not taken as definitive proof of the hypothesis that a particular type of behavior pattern is a partial cause of coronary heart disease. Proving the idea required more than just the existence of a few case studies. It involved decades of work by teams of cardiologists and psychologists.

The research quickly moved from merely accumulating case studies, which could never establish the truth of the hypothesis, to more powerful methods of investigation. Researchers developed and tested operational definitions of the type A concept. Large-scale epidemiological studies established a correlation between the presence of type A behavior and the incidence of coronary heart disease. The correlational work then became more sophisticated. Researchers used complex correlational techniques to track down potential third variables. The relation between type A behavior and heart attacks could have been spurious because the behavior pattern was also correlated with one of the other traditional risk factors (such as smoking, obesity, or serum cholesterol level). However, results showed that type A behavior was a significant independent predictor of heart attacks. When other variables were statistically partialed out, there was still a link between the type A behavior pattern and coronary heart disease.

Finally, researchers undertook experimental studies with manipulated variables to establish whether a causal relationship could be demonstrated. Some of the studies attempted to test models of the physiological mechanisms that affected the relationship and used animals as subjects—what some might call "not real life." Another experimental study used human subjects who had had a heart attack. These subjects were randomly assigned to one of two groups. One group received counseling designed to help them avoid traditional risky behavior such as smoking and eating fatty foods. The other group received this counseling and were also given a program designed to help them reduce their type A behavior. Three years later, there had been significantly fewer recurrent heart attacks among the patients given the type A behavior counseling.

In short, the evidence converged to support the hypothesis of the type A behavior pattern as a significant causal factor in coronary heart disease. The investigation of this problem provides a good example of how research gradually moves from interesting case studies, to correlational techniques, to more complex correlational techniques, and finally to studies in which variables are manipulated.

A final lesson we can draw from this example is that scientific concepts evolve, an issue first raised in Chapter 3 when we discussed operational definitions. Recent research seems to indicate that it is oversimplifying to talk about the connection between heart attacks and the type A behavior pattern *as a whole*. The reason is that only certain components of the pattern (particularly antagonistic hostility) appear to be linked to coronary heart disease (Chida & Hamer, 2008; Matthews, 2005; Suls & Bunde, 2005). Thus, we have an example of how science uncovers increasingly specific relationships as it progresses and how theoretical concepts become elaborated.

A Counsel Against Despair

One final implication of the convergence principle is that we should not despair when the initial results of studies on a problem appear to be contradictory. The process of evidence amalgamation in science is like a projector slowly bringing an unknown slide into focus. At first, the blur on the screen could represent just about anything. Then, as the slide is focused a bit more, many alternative hypotheses may be ruled out even though the image cannot be identified unambiguously. Finally, an identification can be made with great confidence. The early stages of the evidence amalgamation process are like the beginning of the focusing process. The ambiguous blur of the slide corresponds to contradictory data or to data that support many alternative hypotheses.

Thus, contradictory data obtained at the beginning of an investigation should not drive us to despair of ever finding the truth. Nor is such a situation unique to psychology. It also occurs in more mature sciences. Indeed, the public is usually unaware that contradictory data are obtained often in science. Such contradictory data are simply the result of our current inadequate understanding of the problem. The contradictions may be simply chance occurrences (something we will discuss at length in Chapter 11), or they may be due to subtle methodological differences between experiments.

Many other sciences have endured confusing periods of uncertainty before a consensus was achieved (Ioannidis, 2004; Lehrer, 2010; Simonton, 2004). Medical science certainly displays this pattern all the time. For example, research has confirmed that taking a daily baby aspirin helps prevent cardiovascular disease. However, research into aspirin's role as a cancer preventative has been extremely confusing, uncertain, and nonconverging. Aspirin fights inflammation by inhibiting substances known as cyclooxygenase, or COX, enzymes. Because COX enzymes also are involved in the formation of some cancerous tumors, it was thought that daily aspirin might also inhibit this effect. But actual research on this speculation has produced inconsistent results. Some researchers think that the inconsistency has to do with the fact that the optimal dosage level has not yet been found. Regardless of how this issue is finally resolved, it is illustrative of the uncertainty that often precedes the resolution of a scientific problem. Dr. Michael Thun, of the American Cancer Society, acknowledged the feeling of frustration that the public might have if they do not understand how science works and how conclusions only gradually emerge from a slow-developing convergence (Associated Press, 2007). He admitted that it must be difficult for the public to understand why we cannot find out all of the effects of a very common medicine like aspirin. But this example just illustrates how very hard it is to come to a causal conclusion. Arriving at causal conclusions is not easy, as we have seen throughout this book. Psychology is not alone in having long periods of uncertainty that precede a firm conclusion.

Writer Malcolm Gladwell (2004), in an article titled "The Picture Problem," discusses how people have difficulty understanding why the medical profession still has disagreements about the degree of benefit derived from mammograms. This is because a mammography picture seems so "concrete" to most people that they think it should be determinative. They fail to understand that human judgment is necessarily involved, and that mammography assessment and disease prediction are inherently probabilistic (Gigerenzer et al., 2007). Gladwell notes that "the picture promises certainty, and it cannot deliver on that promise. Even after forty years of research, there remains widespread disagreement over how much benefit women in the critical fifty-to-sixty-nine age bracket receive from breast X-rays, and further disagreement about whether there is enough evidence to justify regular mammography in women under fifty and over seventy" (p. 81). However, Gladwell, goes on to note that in this area of medicine—just as in psychology—knowledge can be useful even when it is not certain: "The answer is that mammograms do not have to be infallible to save lives....Mammography isn't as a good as we'd like it to be. But we are still better off than we would be without it" (p. 81).

In psychology and many other sciences, the combining of evidence from disparate studies to form a conclusion is now being done more formally by the use of the statistical technique termed *meta-analysis* (Borenstein, Hedges, Higgins, & Rothstein, 2009; Card, 2011). In a meta-analysis, the results of several studies that address the same research hypothesis are combined statistically. The effects obtained when one experimental group is compared with another are expressed in a common statistical metric that allows comparison of effects across studies. The findings are then statistically amalgamated in some standard ways and a conclusion about differential effects is reached if the amalgamation process passes certain statistical criteria. In some cases, of course, no conclusion can be drawn with confidence, and the result of the meta-analysis is inconclusive.

More and more commentators are calling for a greater emphasis on meta-analysis as a way of dampening the contentious disputes about conflicting studies in the behavioral sciences. The method is useful for ending disputes that seem to be nothing more than a "he-said, she-said" debate. An emphasis on meta-analysis has often revealed that we actually have more stable and useful findings than is apparent from a perusal of the conflicts in our journals.

The National Reading Panel (2000; Ehri et al., 2001) found just this in their meta-analysis of the evidence surrounding several issues in reading education. For example, they concluded that the results of a meta-analysis of the results of 38 different studies indicated "solid support for the conclusion that systematic phonics instruction makes a bigger contribution to children's growth in reading than alternative programs providing unsystematic or no phonics instruction" (p. 84). In another section of their report, the National Reading Panel reported that a meta-analysis of 52 studies of phonemic awareness training indicated that "teaching children to manipulate the sounds in language helps them learn to read. Across the various conditions of teaching, testing, and participant characteristics, the effect sizes were all significantly greater than chance and ranged from large to small, with the majority in the moderate range" (p. 5).

It is likewise in the domain of health psychology. Chida and Hamer (2008) meta-analyzed data from a whopping 281 studies relating the hostility and aggression aspects of the Type A behavior pattern to cardiovascular reactivity (heart rate and blood pressure) in order to establish that there was indeed a relationship. As another example, Currier, Neimeyer, and Berman (2008) meta-analyzed 61 controlled studies of psychotherapeutic interventions for bereaved persons. Their meta-analysis had a disappointing outcome, however. Psychotherapeutic intervention had an immediate effect after bereavement, but had no positive effect at follow-up.

The follow-up outcome from this meta-analysis helps to remind us that the outcome of a meta-analysis is not always positive. That is, it does not always tell us that, from a series of widely varying studies, something is there. Just as often it tells us that, when we amalgamate the results from a large number of varying studies—nothing is there! For example, Dietrich and Kanso (2010) meta-analyzed over 70 experiments on the neurophysiological correlates of creativity. Combining the results of several studies using neuroimaging, they found no specific neural correlate of divergent thinking. Overall, they found that "creative thinking does not appear to critically depend on any single mental process or brain region, and it is not especially associated with right brains, defocused attention, low arousal, or alpha synchronization, as sometimes hypothesized" (p. 822). Our point here is that sometimes meta-analyses yield negative conclusions.

The fact that meta-analyses involve synthesizing conclusions from dozens (sometimes hundreds) of studies contains the implicit message that any single study represents just a small part of a much larger endeavor. Also, when we worry that progress is slow in some area of psychology, we should remember that this "low yield" is characteristic of medicine and many other scientific research areas.

In closing, a statement by a task force of the American Psychological Association (Wilkinson, 1999) on statistical methods in psychology journals provides an apt summary for this section. The task force stated that investigators should not "interpret a single study's results as having importance independent of the effects reported elsewhere in the relevant literature" (p. 602). Science progresses by convergence upon conclusions. The outcomes of one study can only be interpreted in the context of the present state of the convergence on the particular issue in question.

Summary

In this chapter, we have seen how the breakthrough model of scientific advance is a bad model for psychology and why the gradual-synthesis model provides a better framework for understanding how conclusions are reached in psychology. The principle of converging operations describes how research results are synthesized in psychology: No one experiment is definitive, but each helps us to rule out at least some alternative explanations and, thus, aids in the process of homing in on the truth. The use of a variety of different methods makes psychologists more confident that their conclusions rest on a solid empirical foundation. Finally, when conceptual change occurs, it adheres to the principle of connectivity: New theories not only must account for new scientific data but must also provide an explanation of the previously existing database.

CHAPTER 9

The Misguided Search for the "Magic Bullet": The Issue of Multiple Causation

In Chapter 8, we focused on the importance of converging operations and the need to progress to more powerful research methods in order to establish a connection between variables. In this chapter, we go beyond a simple connection between two variables to highlight an important point: Behavior is multiply determined.

Any particular behavior is caused not by one variable but by a large number of different variables. To conclude that there is a significant causal connection between variable A and behavior B does not mean that variable A is the *only* cause of behavior B. For example, researchers have found a negative relationship between amount of television viewing and academic achievement, but they do not claim that the amount of television viewed is the *only* thing that determines academic achievement. That, of course, would be silly, because academic achievement is partially determined by a host of other variables (home environment, quality of schooling, and the like). In fact, television viewing is only a minor determinant of academic achievement when compared with these other factors. Similarly, the amount of television violence viewed by children is not the only reason that they may display aggressive behavior. It is one of many contributing factors.

But often people forget that behavior is multiply determined. They seem to want to find the so-called magic bullet—the *one* cause of the behavioral outcome that interests them. Psychologist Theodore Wachs (2000) uses as an example the way that people tried to explain the wave of school shootings that took place in the United States in 1998 and 1999. He points out that people argued that the causes involved were the easy availability of guns, low parental involvement with their children, information on the Internet, violence on television and the movies, peer influences, and mental illness. Wachs noted that "rarely was the possibility considered that the increase in school shootings was the result of a convergence among a number of the above factors, and that any solution must go beyond dealing with a single potential cause" (p. x).

Like so many of the other principles discussed in this book, it is important to put the idea of multiple causes in perspective. On the one hand, this idea warns us not to overinterpret a single causal connection. The world is complicated, and the determinants of behavior are many and complex. Just because we have demonstrated a cause of behavior does not mean that we have uncovered the only cause or even the most important cause. To provide a thorough explanation of a particular behavior, researchers must study the influence of many different variables and amalgamate the results of these studies to give a complete picture of all the causal connections.

On the other hand, to say that a variable is only one of many determinants and that it explains only a small portion of the variability in a given behavior is not to say that the variable is unimportant. First, the relationship may have far-reaching theoretical implications. Second, the relationship may have practical applications, particularly if the variable can be controlled, as is the case with television violence, for example. Few would argue that a variable that could reduce the number of acts of physical violence by as much as 1 percent annually is not of enormous importance. In short, if the behavior in question is of great importance, then knowing how to control only a small proportion of it can be extremely useful.

There have been medical studies in which a treatment accounted for less than 1 percent of the variability in the outcome, yet the results were considered so startlingly positive that the study was terminated prematurely for ethical considerations—that is, the outcome of the experiment was considered so strong that it was deemed unethical to withhold the treatment from the placebo group (Ferguson, 2009; Rosenthal, 1990). Likewise, any factor that could cut motor vehicle deaths by just 1 percent would be immensely important—it would save over 400 lives each year. Reducing the homicide rate by just 1 percent would save over 170 lives each year. In short, the fact that an outcome is determined by many different variables does not reduce the importance of any one variable that is causally related to the outcome—even if the variable accounts for only a small portion of the outcome.

The Concept of Interaction

The idea of multiple causation leads to an important concept that is often discussed at length in methodology texts, although we can only mention it here: A factor that influences behavior may have different effects depending on the presence or absence of other factors. This is called the concept of *interaction:* The magnitude of the effect that one variable has may depend on the level of another variable.

Consider an example. Researchers examined the academic grade point averages of a group of adolescents as a function of life changes (school transition, pubertal development, early dating behavior, residential mobility, and family disruption). They found that the combination of life changes was the critical factor in cases of negative outcome. No single factor had a huge effect, but when several of the factors were conjoined together, there was a sizeable effect (see Simmons, Burgeson, Carlton-Ford, & Blyth, 1987).

A similar example occurs in Michael Rutter's (1979) review of the factors related to psychiatric disorders in children, in which he stated:

> The first very striking finding is that single isolated chronic stresses carry no appreciable psychiatric risk....None of these risk factors, when they occurred in isolation, was associated with disorder in the children; the risk was no higher than that for children without any family stresses. However, when any two stresses occurred together, the risk went up no less than fourfold. With three and four concurrent stresses, the risk went up several times further still. It is clear that the combination of chronic stresses provided very much more than an additive effect. There was an interactive effect such that the risk which attended several concurrent stresses was much more than the sum of the effects of the stresses considered individually. (p. 295)

To understand the logic of what is happening when an interaction occurs such as that described by Rutter, imagine a risk scale where a score of 80–110 represents low risk, 110–125 moderate risk, and 125–150 high risk. Imagine that we had found an average risk score of 82 for children with no stressors, an average risk score of 84 for children with stress factor A, and an average risk score of 86 for children with stress factor B. An interaction effect would be apparent if, when studying children with both risk factor A *and* risk factor B, we found an average risk score of 126. That is, the joint risk when two risk factors were conjoined was much greater than what would be predicted from studying each risk factor separately.

Developmental psychology contains many examples like the one described by Rutter. Researchers Bonnie Breitmeyer and Craig Ramey studied two groups of infants, one of a nonoptimal perinatal status and the other of normal status. One-half of the members of each group were randomly assigned at birth either to a day-care program designed to prevent mild mental retardation or to a control group that did not receive special treatment. The results indicated that when the children reached four years of age, the children who were at risk perinatally and the normal children were at the same level of cognitive maturity when *both* were given the day-care program. However, when *neither* group was given the day-care program, the children with nonoptimal perinatal scores showed slower cognitive development. Thus, biology interacted with environment in this situation to illustrate that a complex outcome (cognitive development) is determined by a multitude of factors. A negative cognitive outcome occurred only when nonoptimal perinatal status was combined with the absence of a day-care program. The researchers concluded, "The results provide support for a framework stressing initial biological vulnerability and subsequent environmental insufficiency as cumulative risk factors in the development of children from low SES [socioeconomic status] families" (Breitmeyer & Ramey, 1986, p. 1151).

Many negative behavioral and cognitive outcomes have a similar logic to them—including many situations where biological and environmental variables have been found to be in interactive relationships. For example, variations in the so-called *5-HTT* gene have been found to be related to major depression in humans (Hariri & Holmes, 2006). People with one variant (the S allele) are more likely to suffer from major depression than people with the other variant of the gene (the L allele). However, this greater risk for those with the S allele is *only* true for those who have *also* suffered multiple traumatic life events, such as child abuse or neglect, job loss, and/or divorce. Such gene-environment interactions are common in the field of developmental psychopathology (Dodge & Rutter, 2011).

For example, it is likewise with the variants of the monoamine oxidase A (*MAOA*) gene and antisocial behavior. One variant of the gene increases the probability of antisocial behavior, but only if other risk factors are present such as child abuse, birth complications, or negative home environments (Raine, 2008). A final example is provided by research on the link between rumination and depression. The tendency to ruminate does predict the duration of depressive symptoms, but it interacts with cognitive styles—rumination predicts lengthened periods of depressive symptoms only when conjoined with negative cognitive styles (Nolen-Hoeksema, Wisco, & Lyubomirsky, 2008).

Positive outcomes also have the characteristic that they are explained by multiple, interactive factors. In a study of prosocial behavior on the part of six- to nine-year-old children, Knight, Johnson, Carlo, and Eisenberg (1994) examined the psychological factors that were associated with children's tendency to help other children (which was operationalized as donating money to children in need). They found that certain variables, such as levels of sympathy, affective reasoning, and knowledge about money—when taken alone—were only weakly related to prosocial behavior. However, in combination, these variables were much more potent predictors of prosocial behavior. For example, children high in sympathy, affective reasoning, and knowledge about money donated four times as much as the children low in all of these variables.

Developmental psychologist Dan Keating (2007) has reviewed the literature on the consequences of states' Graduated Driver Licensing programs on teen driver safety. These programs work—they lower the rate of teen auto crashes and teen auto fatalities. However, the programs are all different from state to state, each state having somewhat different subsets of several basic components: required driver education, passenger restrictions, night driving restrictions, extended legal age, minimum practice driving requirements, and extended learner's permit time. Thus, the question becomes whether each of these components is causally effective and whether they have any interactive effects. Research indicates that no *one* of the components lowers teen crash or fatality rates. However, in *combination* they can lower the number of teen fatalities by over 20 percent.

Thus, the concept of multiple causes involves even more complexities than you might have thought at first. Not only is it necessary to track down and measure the many factors that may influence the behavior in question, but it is also necessary to investigate how these factors operate together.

Clinical psychologist Scott Lilienfeld (2006) discusses the continuum of causal influence for variables—from strong to weak. Only at the very strongest end of the continuum does a variable act in isolation. The strongest form of causal influence is one where a variable is necessary *and* sufficient for producing an effect on dependent variable. The variable must be present for the effect to occur (it is necessary) and when it is, by itself, it is sufficient to produce the effect. Weaker forms of causation, however, all involve the contextualization of a variable's effect by other variables. A causal variable might be necessary (it must be there for the dependent variable to display an effect) but not sufficient (it depends on the presence of another variable for its effect). Finally, a weak causal variable might be *neither* necessary nor sufficient—its presence just increases the overall statistical probability of the effect.

The Temptation of the Single-Cause Explanation

It seems that the basic idea that complex events in the world are multiply determined should be an easy one to grasp. In fact, the concept *is* easy to grasp and to apply when the issues are not controversial. However, when our old nemesis, preexisting bias (see Chapter 3), rears its head, people have a tendency to ignore the principle of multiple causation. How many times do we hear people arguing about such emotionally charged issues as the causes of crime, the distribution of wealth, the causes of terrorism, the treatment of women and minorities, the causes of poverty, the effect of capital punishment, and the level of taxation in a way that implies that these issues are simple and unidimensional and that outcomes in these areas have a single cause? These examples make it clear that people will sometimes acknowledge the existence of multiple causes if asked *directly* about multiple causes; but seldom will they *spontaneously* offer many different causes as an explanation for something they care about. Most often, people adopt a "zero sum" attitude toward potential causes—that all causes compete with one another and that emphasizing one necessarily reduces the emphasis on another. This "zero sum" view of causes is incorrect.

A zero-sum game—in which one person's gain is another's loss—often characterizes our discussions of emotionally charged issues. Under emotional influence, we tend to forget the principle of multiple causation. For example, consider discussions of crime by people on opposite ends of the political spectrum. Liberals may argue that people of low-socioeconomic status who commit crimes may themselves be victims of their circumstances (e.g., joblessness, poor housing, poor education, and lack of hope about the future). Conservatives may reply that a lot of poor people do not commit crimes; therefore, economic conditions are not the cause. Instead, the conservative may argue, it is personal values and personal character that determine criminal behavior. Neither side in the debate ever seems to acknowledge that *both* individual factors and environmental factors contribute to criminal behavior. There is no one explanation of crime. Criminal behavior is determined by a multitude of factors, some of which are environmental and some of which are characteristics of the individual.

Consider also discussions of the causes of complex economic outcomes. These outcomes are hard to predict precisely because they are multiply determined. For example, economic debate has focused on a problem of the last several decades with important social implications: the growing inequality of wealth in the United States (Bartels, 2008; Bilmes & Stiglitz, 2009; Brooks, 2008; Gelman, 2008; Madrick, 2006; Surowiecki, 2010). Here, the facts are not in dispute—it is the *explanation* of the facts that is the subject of contentious argument. The facts are these. Since 1979, the real (i.e., adjusted for inflation) income of all male workers in the United States has been quite stagnant. That is, middle-income Americans and lower-income Americans have barely been holding their own in income. In contrast, the incomes of the top 1 percent of the population have gone up over 100 percent in the same period (in real terms, adjusted for inflation). Another way to put this is that over 80 percent of all of the income gains in America from 1980 to 2005 went to the richest 1 percent of taxpayers (Bartels, 2008). In 1977, the richest 20 percent of the population earned four times what the poorest 20 percent earned. By 2006, they earned over ten times as much.

The social consequences of this massive transfer of wealth from one class of citizens to another have set off a contentious political debate about its cause. The debate has been notable for its focus on single causes. Each side in the political debate picks a single cause and then tries to denigrate all others. In fact, quantitative economic studies (Bartels, 2008; Bilmes & Stiglitz, 2009; Gelman, 2008; Madrick, 2006) have focused on four variables (many more than four have been proposed, but these four have been the most extensively studied). One factor discussed is that the rising immigration of unskilled workers into the United States puts downward pressure on the wages of the lower-paid workers because it creates an oversupply of unskilled labor. A second argument is that globalization increases income disparity because corporations can outsource labor to countries with lower wage rates, thus putting downward pressure on wages in the United States. A third factor is the declining power of labor unions and the increasing power of large corporations. A fourth factor is that tax cuts enacted in the 1980s and in 2001 disproportionately eased the tax burden on the rich.

What have economic studies found with respect to these four variables? You guessed it. All four are factors contributing to the rising inequality in our society. This example also illustrates the concept of interaction mentioned previously. Virtually all of the studies of the matter have indicated that these factors interacted and reinforced each other. Greater global competition gave corporations increased leverage in fighting unions. Likewise, immigrants pushing down unskilled labor rates have the additional effect of making it even harder for existing unions to bargain.

Like economic problems, virtually all of the complex problems that psychologists investigate are multiply determined. Take the problem of learning disabilities, for example, which educational psychologists, cognitive psychologists, and developmental psychologists have investigated extensively. Research has revealed that there are brain anomalies associated with learning disabilities (Shaywitz & Shaywitz, 2004; Snowling & Hulme, 2005; Tanaka et al., 2011; Wolf, 2007). Studies have also indicated that there is a genetic component in learning disabilities (Olson, 2004; Pennington & Olson, 2005). These two findings may seem to suggest the conclusion that learning disabilities are solely biological-brain problems. This conclusion would be wrong. The reason it would be wrong is that research has also revealed that learning disabilities are caused partly by the lack of certain instructional experiences in early schooling (Pressley, 2005) and by poor home environments (Dickinson & Neuman, 2005; Senechal, 2006). There is no single cause of learning disabilities; instead, there is a confluence of biological predispositions and environmental causes.

A similar situation characterizes the causes and treatment of depression. Depression is multiply determined by genetic propensities and environmental risk factors. Likewise, a multiplicity of treatments combined—medication plus psychotherapy—seems to result in the best therapeutic outcome (Engel, 2008).

Once the multiple causes of a complex phenomenon are found, if the phenomenon is a problem, this necessarily means that the solution to the problem will require multiple interventions. Decades ago we had a major health problem—an epidemic of smoking, a habit linked to many diseases. In recent decades, various interventions have reduced the level of smoking in our society: Tobacco advertising was banned, tobacco taxes were raised, the nicotine patch became available, smoking was banned in public places, and many more interventions were instituted (Brody, 2011). Slowly, over decades, the rate of smoking went down because of these multiple interventions targeted at its many causes.

Just as it took many different interventions to reduce smoking years ago, it will take multiple societal interventions to halt and reverse our *current* national epidemic of obesity (Chernev, 2011; Herman & Polivy, 2005). The reason is that our current obesity epidemic started a couple of decades ago because of many different trends coinciding: Suburban living decreased walking; fewer meals were prepared at home when more women entered the workforce; the fast-food industry exploded in size; food advertising became ubiquitous; electronic entertainment made children sedentary; and many other factors (Brody, 2008, 2011). The solution to this national problem will have to be correspondingly multifaceted.

As a final example, consider that psychologists have been recruited to add their knowledge to the understanding of the causes of Islamic terrorism (Kruglanski, Crenshaw, Post, & Victoroff, 2007). Because the causes are multiple, the solution will be multiply determined too. For example, psychologists helping to deradicalize captured terrorists have recommended a variety of interventions, including working with their families; programs to encourage marriage; vocational training; the use of scholars who are experts in religious dialogue; and others (Kruglanski, Gelfand, & Gunaratna, 2010).

Summary

The single lesson of this chapter is an easy but important one. When thinking about the causes of behavior, think in terms of multiple causes. Do not fall into the trap of thinking that a particular behavior must have a single cause. Most behaviors of any complexity are multiply determined. A variety of factors act to cause their occurrence. Sometimes these factors interact when in combination. That is, the effect of the variables acting together is different than what one would have expected from simply studying them in isolation.

CHAPTER 10

The Achilles' Heel of Human Cognition: Probabilistic Reasoning

Question:
Men are taller than women, right?

Answer:
"Right."

Question:
All men are taller than all women, right?

Answer:
"Wrong."

Correct. Believe it or not, we are going to devote part of this chapter to something that you just demonstrated you knew by answering the previous two questions. But don't skip the chapter just yet, because there are some surprises waiting in the explanation of what seems like a very simple principle.

You answered affirmatively to the first question because you did not interpret "Men are taller than women" to mean what the second statement said: "All men are taller than all women." You correctly took the first statement to mean *"There is a tendency for* men to be taller than women," because everyone knows that not all men are taller than all women. You correctly interpreted the statement as reflecting a probabilistic trend rather than a fact that holds in every single instance. By *probabilistic trend*, we simply mean that it is more likely than not but does not hold true in all cases. That is, the relationship between sex and height is stated in terms of likelihoods and probabilities rather than certainties. Many other relationships in nature are probabilistic: It tends to be warmer near the equator. Families tend to have fewer than eight children. Most parts of the earth tend to have more insects than humans. These are all statistically demonstrable trends, yet there are exceptions to every one of them. They are probabilistic trends and laws, not relationships that hold true in every single case.

Americans received a sad lesson in the probabilistic nature of medical knowledge in the summer of 2008 when much-loved political broadcaster Tim Russert died of a heart attack at age 58. Russert took cholesterol pills and aspirin, rode an exercise bike, and had yearly stress tests, yet he still died early of a heart attack (Grady, 2008). The fact that he had been fairly vigilant toward his health led many readers of the *New York Times* to write in saying that the doctors must have missed something. These readers did not understand that medical knowledge is probabilistic. Every failure to predict is not a mistake. In fact, his doctors missed nothing. They applied their probabilistic knowledge as best they could—but this does not mean that they could predict individual cases of heart attack. Science writer Denise Grady (2008) tells us that, based on his stress test and many other state-of-the-art diagnostics that Mr. Russert was given in his last exam, the doctors estimated—from a widely used formula—that Mr. Russert's probability of a heart attack in the next ten years was 5 percent. This means that 95 out of 100 people with Mr. Russert's medical profile should not have a heart attack in the next ten years. Mr. Russert was just one of the unlucky five—and medical science, being probabilistic, cannot tell us in advance who those unlucky five will be.

The Tim Russert example provides an opportunity to emphasize that probabilistic prediction is, indeed, real prediction. Here is what we mean by this. Because probabilistic prediction is numerical, and therefore abstract, people sometimes have a hard time viewing it as real. Because the 5 out of 100 can't be specifically *named* in advance, somehow people feel that the prediction is not as real as it should be. But after they are dead, those five people most definitely *do* have names. For example, Tim Russert turned out to be one of the five. He is no less dead than he would be if we could have named him in advance. We must get over this feeling that, because of its numerical abstraction, probabilistic prediction is not real.

Scientists are indeed talking about *real people* when they make these probabilistic predictions. Recall from Chapter 8 the point that, because of cell phone talking and texting in cars, hundreds of Americans will die unnecessarily in crashes in the upcoming year. Because this is a probabilistic prediction, I cannot tell you who these hundreds will be. However, the prediction is no less real just because it is probabilistic. Perhaps I should put it in a more vivid way. Someone who reads this passage will have their lives changed this year because of a car crash caused by a distracted driver on a smartphone.

People have a hard time accepting the reality of probabilistic prediction—that they do not live in a world of certainties. Science writer Natalie Angier

(2007) discusses how some people think that seismologists really *can* predict individual earthquakes, but that they do not make these predictions public so as "not to create a panic." One seismologist received a letter from a woman asking him to tell her if he ever sent his children to see out-of-town relatives. From this example, Angier notes that people seem to prefer to believe that authorities are engaged in monstrous lying than to simply admit that there is uncertainty in science. A formal study by Gigerenzer and colleagues (Gigerenzer et al., 2007) confirms Angier's fears. Gigerenzer et al. found that 44 percent of a sample of German citizens thought (wrongly) that mammography tests give an "absolutely certain" result and 63 percent thought (wrongly) that fingerprinting gave an "absolutely certain" result.

Virtually all the facts and relationships that have been uncovered by the science of psychology are stated in terms of probabilities. There is nothing unique about this. Many of the laws and relationships in other sciences are stated in probabilities rather than certainties. The entire subdiscipline of population genetics, for example, is based on probabilistic relationships. Physicists tell us that the distribution of the electron's charge in an atom is described by a probabilistic function. Thus, the fact that behavioral relationships are stated in probabilistic form does not distinguish them from those in other sciences.

Many writers have made the point that "people seem to be in a land of sometimes and perhaps, and they had hoped to go on living with always and with certainty" (Bronowski, 1978a, p. 94). In this chapter, we will try to make you more comfortable in the "land of sometimes and perhaps," because to understand psychology one must be comfortable with the subject of this chapter: probabilistic reasoning.

"Person-Who" Statistics

Most of the public is aware that many of the conclusions of medical science are statements of probabilistic trends and are not predictions of absolute certainty. Smoking causes lung cancer and a host of other health problems. Voluminous medical evidence documents this fact (Gigerenzer et al., 2007). Yet will everyone who smokes get lung cancer, and will everyone who refrains from smoking be free of lung cancer? Most people know that these implications do not follow. The relationship is probabilistic. Smoking vastly increases the probability of contracting lung cancer but does not make it a certainty. Medical science can tell us with great confidence that more people in a group of smokers will die of lung cancer than in an equivalent group of nonsmokers. It cannot tell us which ones will die, though. The relationship is probabilistic; it does not hold in every case. We are all aware of this—or are we? How often have we seen a nonsmoker trying to convince a smoker to stop by citing the smoking—lung-cancer statistics, only to have the smoker come back with "Oh, get outta here! Look at old Joe Ferguson down at the store. Three packs of Camels a day since he was sixteen! Eighty-one years old and he looks great!" The obvious inference that one is supposed to draw is that this single case somehow invalidates the relationship.

It is surprising and distressing how often this ploy works. Too frequently, a crowd of people will begin to nod their heads in assent when a single case is cited to invalidate a probabilistic trend. This agreement reflects a failure to understand the nature of statistical laws. If people think a single example can invalidate a law, they must feel the law should hold in every case. In short, they have failed to understand the law's probabilistic nature. There will always be a "person who" goes against even the strongest of trends. Consider our smoking example. Only 5 percent of men who live to the age of 85 are smokers (University of California, Berkeley, 1991). Or to put it another way, 95 percent of men who live to age 85 are either nonsmokers or have smoked for a period and then quit. Continuous smoking without quitting markedly shortens lives. Yet a few smokers do make it to 85.

Psychologists call instances like the "old Joe Ferguson" story examples of the use of "person-who" statistics: situations in which well-established statistical trends are questioned because someone knows a "person who" went against the trend. For example, "You say job opportunities are expanding in service industries and contracting in heavy industry? No way. I know a man who got a job in a steel mill just last Thursday"; "You say families are having fewer children than they did 30 years ago? You're crazy! The young couple next door already has three and they're both under 30"; "You say children tend to adopt the religious beliefs of their parents? Well, I know a man at work whose son converted to another religion just the other day."

The ubiquitous "person who" is usually trotted out when we are confronted with hard statistical evidence that contradicts a previously held belief. Thus, it could be argued that people actually know better and simply use the "person who" as a technique to invalidate facts that go against their opinions. However, the work of psychologists who have studied human decision making and reasoning suggests that the tendency to use the "person who" comes not simply from its usefulness as a debating strategy. Instead, it appears that this fallacious argument is used so frequently because people experience great difficulty in dealing with probabilistic information. Much research into the nature of human thinking has indicated that probabilistic reasoning may well be the Achilles' heel of human cognition.

Probabilistic Reasoning and the Misunderstanding of Psychology

The findings of psychology are often misunderstood because of the problems people have in dealing with probabilistic information. We all understand "men are taller than women" as a statement of probabilistic tendency. We realize that it is not invalidated by a single exception (one man who is shorter than a woman). Most people understand the statement "smoking causes lung cancer" in the same way (although old "Joe Ferguson" can be convincing to some smokers who do not want to believe that their habit may be killing them!). However, very similar probabilistic statements about behavioral trends cause widespread disbelief and are often dismissed by many people with the first appearance of a single "person who." Most psychology instructors have witnessed a very common reaction when they discuss the evidence on certain behavioral relationships. For example, the instructor may present the fact that children's scholastic achievement is related to the socioeconomic status of their households and to the educational level of their parents. This statement often prompts at least one student to object that he has a friend who is a National Merit Scholar and whose father finished only eighth grade. Even those who understood the smoking—lung-cancer example tend to waver at this point.

People who would never think of using "person-who" arguments to refute the findings of medicine and physics routinely use them to refute psychological research. Most people understand that many treatments, theories, and facts developed by medical science are probabilistic. They understand that, for example, a majority of patients, but not all of them, will respond to a certain drug. Medical science, however, often cannot tell in advance which patients will respond. Often all that can be said is that if 100 patients take treatment A and 100 patients do not, after a certain period the 100 patients who took treatment A will *collectively* be better off. I mentioned in an earlier chapter that I take a medication called Imitrex (sumatriptan succinate) for relief from migraine headaches. The information sheet accompanying this drug tells me that controlled studies have demonstrated that, at a particular dosage level, 57 percent of patients taking this medication receive relief in two hours. I am one of the lucky 57 percent—but neither the drug company nor my physician could give me a guarantee that I would not be one of unlucky 43 percent. The drug does not work in every case.

No one would doubt the worth of medical knowledge just because it is probabilistic and does not apply in every case. Yet this is exactly what happens in the case of many psychological findings and treatments. The fact that a finding or treatment does not apply in every case often engenders profound disappointment and denigration of psychology's progress. When the issues are psychological, people tend to forget the fundamental principle that knowledge does not have to be certain to be useful—that even though individual cases cannot be predicted, the ability to forecast *group* trends accurately is often very informative. The prediction of outcomes based on group characteristics is often called *aggregate* or *actuarial prediction* (we will discuss actuarial prediction in more detail in the next chapter).

Consider an unhealthy person going to a physician. The person is told that unless he or she exercises and changes diet, he or she has a high risk of heart attack. We are not tempted to say that the doctor has no useful knowledge because he or she cannot tell the person that without a change of diet he or she will have a heart attack on September 18, 2014. We tend to understand that the physician's predictions are probabilistic and cannot be given with that level of precision. It is likewise when geologists tell us that there is an 80 percent probability of a magnitude 8.0 or greater earthquake in a certain area in the next 30 years. We do not denigrate their knowledge because they cannot say that there will be an earthquake exactly *here* on July 5, 2016. Science writer Elizabeth Kolbert (2005) describes how a group of prominent climatologists posted an essay on their website titled, "Could New Orleans be the first major U.S. city ravaged by human-caused climate change?" In an attempt to educate the public, they pointed out that this is entirely the wrong question to ask. Their point was that "the science of global warming has nothing to say about any particular hurricane (or drought or heat wave or flood), only about the larger statistical pattern" (p. 36).

When a school psychologist recommends a program for a child with learning disabilities, of course he or she is making a probabilistic prediction—that the child has a higher probability of good academic achievement if in a certain program. It is likewise when a clinical psychologist recommends a program for a child with self-injurious behavior. The psychologist judges that there is a higher probability of a good outcome if a certain approach is followed. But unlike the heart attack and earthquake examples, the psychologist is often confronted with questions like "but *when* will my child be reading at grade level?" or "exactly how long will he have to be in this program?" These are unanswerable questions—in the same way that the questions about exactly when the earthquake or the heart attack will occur are also unanswerable questions. They are unanswerable because in all these cases—the heart attack, the learning disabled child, the earthquake, the child with self-injurious behavior—the prediction being made is probabilistic.

For these reasons, a thorough understanding of probabilistic reasoning is critical to an understanding of psychology. There is a profound irony here. Psychology probably suffers the most from the general public's inability to think statistically. Yet, of all the disciplines, the most research into the nature of probabilistic reasoning abilities has been done in psychology.

Psychological Research on Probabilistic Reasoning

In the past three decades, the research of psychologists such as Daniel Kahneman of Princeton University (winner of the Nobel Prize in 2002) and the late Amos Tversky has revolutionized the way we think about people's reasoning abilities. In the course of their studies, these investigators have uncovered some fundamental principles of probabilistic reasoning that are absent or, more commonly, insufficiently developed in many people. As has often been pointed out, it should not be surprising that they are insufficiently developed. As a branch of mathematics, probability theory is a very recent development. The key initial developments did not occur until the sixteenth and seventeenth centuries (Mazur, 2010) and many essential developments date not much past the last century.

The dates of the initial developments in probability theory highlight a significant fact: Games of chance existed centuries before the fundamental laws of probability were discovered. Here is another example of how personal experience does not seem to be sufficient to lead to a fundamental understanding of the world (see Chapter 7). It took formal study of the laws of probability to reveal how games of chance work. Thousands of gamblers and their "personal experiences" were insufficient to uncover the underlying nature of games of chance.

The problem is that as society becomes more complex, the need for probabilistic thinking becomes greater for everyone. If ordinary citizens are to have a basic understanding of the society in which they live, they must possess at least a rudimentary ability to think statistically.

"Why did they raise my insurance rate," you might wonder, "and why is John's rate higher than Bill's? Is Social Security going broke? Is our state lottery crooked? Is crime increasing or decreasing? Why do doctors order all those tests? Why can people be treated with certain rare drugs in Europe and not in the United States? Do women really make less than men in comparable jobs? Do international trade deals cost Americans jobs and drive down wages? Is educational achievement in Japan really higher than here? Is Canadian health care better than that in the United States and cheaper as well?" These are all good questions—concrete, practical questions about our society and how it works. To understand the answers to each of them, one must think statistically.

Clearly, a complete discussion of statistical thinking is beyond the scope of this book. We will, however, briefly discuss some of the more common pitfalls of probabilistic reasoning. A good way to start developing the skill of probabilistic thinking is to become aware of the most common fallacies that arise when people reason statistically.

Insufficient Use of Probabilistic Information

One finding that has been much replicated is that there is a tendency for concrete single-case information to overwhelm more abstract probabilistic information in people's judgments (the vividness problem discussed in Chapter 4). The tendency to give insufficient weight to probabilistic information is not limited to the scientifically unsophisticated layperson. Here is a problem (see Stanovich, 2010) that even experienced decision makers such as physicians find difficult: Imagine that the virus (HIV) that causes AIDS occurs in 1 in every 1,000 people. Imagine also that there is a test to diagnose the disease that always indicates correctly that a person who has HIV actually has it. Finally, imagine that the test has a false-positive rate of

5 percent. This means that the test wrongly indicates that HIV is present in 5 percent of the cases in which the person does not have the virus. Imagine that we choose a person randomly and administer the test and that it yields a positive result (indicates that the person is HIV-positive). What is the probability that the individual actually has the HIV virus, assuming that we know nothing else about the individual's personal or medical history?

The most common answer to this problem (even among experienced physicians) is 95 percent. The correct answer is approximately 2 percent. People vastly overestimated the probability that a positive result truly indicated the disease because of the tendency to overweight the case information and underweight the base rate information (that only 1 in 1,000 people are HIV-positive). A little logical reasoning can help to illustrate the profound effect that base rates have on probabilities. Of 1,000 people, only one will actually be HIV-positive. If the other 999 (who do not have the disease) are tested, the test will indicate incorrectly that approximately 50 of them have the virus (0.05 multiplied by 999) because of the 5 percent false-positive rate. Thus, of the 51 patients testing positive, only one (approximately 2 percent) will actually be HIV-positive. In short, the base rate is such that the vast majority of people do not have the virus (only 1 in 1,000). This fact, combined with a substantial false-positive rate, ensures that, in absolute numbers, the vast majority of positive tests will be of people who do not have the virus.

Although most people recognize the correctness of this logic, their initial tendency is to discount the base rates and overweight the clinical evidence. In short, people actually know better but are initially drawn to an incorrect conclusion. Psychologists have termed problems like these "cognitive illusions" (see Kahneman, 2011; Pohl, 2004). In *cognitive illusions*, even when people know the correct answer, they may be drawn to an incorrect conclusion by the structure of the problem.

In this problem, the case evidence (the laboratory test result) seems tangible and concrete to most people, whereas the probabilistic evidence seems, well—probabilistic. This reasoning, of course, is fallacious because case evidence itself is always probabilistic. A clinical test misidentifies the presence of a disease with a certain *probability*. The situation is one in which two probabilities—the probable diagnosticity of the case evidence and the prior probability (base rate)—must be combined if one is to arrive at a correct decision. There are right and wrong ways of combining these probabilities, and more often than not—particularly when the case evidence gives the illusion of concreteness (recall our discussion of the vividness problem in Chapter 4)—people combine the information in the wrong way.

The HIV example above also illustrates the importance of paying attention to the false-positive rate when interpreting test results. In that example, a substantial false-positive rate (5 percent) combined with a low base rate for the disease (only 1 in 1,000) resulted in the following consequence: More people with a *positive* test result did *not* have the disease than did have it. Attention to false-positives is a critical concern in all diagnostic testing, including in medicine where, despite great advances in treatment and diagnosis, most clinical tests still have substantial false-positive rates. In one study of 30,000 older men, it was found that after taking four screening tests for prostate, lung, and colorectal cancer, more than *one-third* of the men received a false-positive result—the test indicated that they had cancer when in fact they were cancer free (Croswell et al., 2009).

Failure to Use Sample-Size Information

Consider these two problems, developed by Tversky and Kahneman (1974):

1. A certain town is served by two hospitals. In the larger hospital, about 45 babies are born each day, and in the smaller hospital, about 15 babies are born each day. As you know, about 50 percent of all babies are boys. However, the exact percentage varies from day to day. Sometimes it is higher than 50 percent, sometimes lower. For a period of one year, each hospital recorded the days on which more than 60 percent of the babies born were boys. Which hospital do you think recorded more such days?
   a. The larger hospital
   b. The smaller hospital
   c. About the same
2. Imagine an urn filled with balls, two-thirds of which are of one color and one-third of which are of another. One individual has drawn 5 balls from the urn and found that 4 are red and 1 is white. Another individual has drawn 20 balls and found that 12 are red and 8 are white. Which of the two individuals should feel more confident that the urn contains two-thirds red balls and one-third white balls, rather than vice versa? What odds should each individual give?

In problem 1, the majority of people answer "about the same." People not choosing this alternative pick the larger and the smaller hospital with about equal frequency. Because the correct answer is the smaller hospital, approximately 75 percent of subjects given this problem answer incorrectly. These incorrect answers result from an inability to recognize the importance of sample size in the problem. Other things being equal, a larger sample size always more accurately estimates a population value. Thus, on any given day, the larger hospital, with its larger sample size, will tend to have a proportion of births closer to 50 percent. Conversely, a small sample size is always more likely to deviate from the population value. Thus, the smaller hospital will have more days on which the proportion of births displays a large discrepancy from the population value (60 percent boys, 40 percent boys, 80 percent boys, etc.).

In problem 2, most people feel that the sample of 5 balls provides more convincing evidence that the urn is predominantly red. Actually, the probabilities are in the opposite direction. The odds are 8 to 1 that the urn is predominantly red for the 5-ball sample, but they are 16 to 1 that the urn is predominantly red for the 20-ball sample. Even though the proportion of red balls is higher in the 5-ball sample (80 percent versus 60 percent), this is more than compensated for by the fact that the other sample is four times as large and, thus, is more likely to be an accurate estimate of the proportions in the urn. The judgment of most subjects, however, is dominated by the higher proportion of red in the 5-ball sample and does not take adequate account of the greater reliability of the 20-ball sample.

These two problems illustrate a very useful principle concerning sample size: Smaller samples will always generate more extreme values. Psychologist Daniel Kahneman (2011) shows an example of how the failure to apply this principle can send us on a wild goose chase in search of causal theories when none are needed. He pointed out that a study of 3,141 counties in the United States found that the counties in which the incidence of kidney cancer was lowest tended to be rural counties that were sparsely populated. Kahneman (2011) pointed out how easy it would be to come up with a causal theory about why this was the case: "the clean living of the rural lifestyle—no air pollution, no water pollution, access to fresh food without additives" (p. 109). The only problem with this causal theory is that it does not account for another finding from the *same* study: The counties in which the incidence of kidney cancer was *highest* tended to be rural counties that were sparsely populated! Had we been told this last fact first, we might have started to posit explanations of rural counties having more smoking, drinking, and high-fat diets. But this, and the earlier explanation for the low-incidence counties, would both have been off the mark. What we have here is the hospital problem discussed previously playing out in real life. Rural counties with sparse populations are small samples, and they are bound to produce more extreme values of *all* types—extremely high values and extremely low values.

Many people have problems recognizing that they are in situations involving sampling. That is, they have difficulty realizing that they are dealing with a sample rather than the entire entity. Failure to realize this leads them to miss the fact that a sample measurement will be subject to sampling *error*. For example, when a blood test is ordered by your physician, what is taken from you will be a *sample* and *it* will be assessed, not the state of your entire blood system. An assumption is made that the sample will be representative of your entire system; but that assumption is probabilistic and will be only more or less true. There will be some error, because the cells in the sample and their composition and properties will necessarily deviate a little bit from absolute truth because the test cannot measure your entire blood system. In short, your physician is making assumptions about your entire composition from a tiny sample.

It is likewise when a tumor is biopsied. There is some error involved, because the biopsy yields only a small sample from a larger tumor. Medical writer Tara Parker-Pope (2011), in discussing the biopsy done for suspected prostate cancer, informs us that a very common type of biopsy samples only about one three-thousandth of the prostate. She cites evidence that staging and grading mistakes occur in about 20 percent of specimens. The point to realize is that it is the same when we are measuring behavior. We often are taking a small sample to represent a much larger population of behavior.

The Gambler's Fallacy

Please answer the following two problems:

> Problem A: Imagine that we are tossing a fair coin (a coin that has a 50/50 chance of coming up heads or tails) and it has just come up heads five times in a row. For the sixth toss, do you think that
> _____ It is more likely that tails will come up than heads?
> _____ It is more likely that heads will come up than tails?
> _____ Heads and tails are equally probable on the sixth toss?
>
> Problem B: When playing slot machines, people win something one out of every 10 times. Julie, however, has just won on her first four plays. What are her chances of winning the next time she plays? _____ out of _____

These two problems probe whether a person is prone to the so-called gambler's fallacy—the tendency for people to see links between events in the past and events in the future when the two are really independent. Two outcomes are independent when the occurrence of one does not affect the probability of the other. Most games of chance that use proper equipment have this property. For example, the number that comes up on a roulette wheel is independent of the outcome that preceded it. Half the numbers on a roulette wheel are red, and half are black (for purposes of simplification, we will ignore the green zero and double zero), so the odds are even (0.50) that any given spin will come up red. Yet after five or six consecutive reds, many bettors switch to black, thinking that it is now more likely to come up. This is the gambler's fallacy: acting as if previous outcomes affect the probability of the next outcome when the events are independent. In this case, the bettors are wrong in their belief. The roulette wheel has no memory of what has happened previously. Even if 15 reds in a row come up, the probability of red coming up on the next spin is still 0.50.

In problem A, some people think that it is more likely that either heads or tails will come up after five heads, and they are displaying the gambler's fallacy by thinking so. The correct answer is that heads and tails are equally probable on the sixth toss. Likewise, for problem B any answer other than 1 out of 10 indicates the gambler's fallacy.

The gambler's fallacy is not restricted to the inexperienced. Research has shown that even habitual gamblers, who play games of chance over

20 hours a week, still display belief in the gambler's fallacy (Petry, 2005; Wagenaar, 1988). In fact, research has shown that individuals in treatment for pathological gambling problems were *more* likely to believe in the gambler's fallacy compared to control subjects (Toplak, Liu, Macpherson, Toneatto, & Stanovich, 2007).

It is important to realize that the gambler's fallacy is not restricted to games of chance. It operates in any domain in which chance plays a substantial role, that is, in almost *everything.* The genetic makeup of babies is an example. Psychologists, physicians, and marriage counselors often see couples who, after having two female children, are planning a third child because "We want a boy, and it's *bound* to be a boy this time." This, of course, is the gambler's fallacy. The probability of having a boy (approximately 50 percent) is exactly the same after having two girls as it was in the beginning. The two previous girls make it *no more likely* that the third baby will be a boy.

The gambler's fallacy stems from many mistaken beliefs about probability. One is the belief that if a process is truly random, no sequence—not even a small one (six coin flips, for instance)—should display runs or patterns. People routinely underestimate the likelihood of runs (HHHH) and patterns (HHTTHHTTHHTT) in a random sequence. For this reason, people cannot generate truly random sequences when they try to do so. The sequences that they generate tend to have too few runs and patterns. When generating such sequences, people alternate their choices too much in a mistaken effort to destroy any structure that might appear (Olivola & Oppenheimer, 2008; Scholl & Greifeneder, 2011).

Those who claim to have psychic powers can easily exploit this tendency. Consider a demonstration sometimes conducted in college psychology classes. A student is told to prepare a list of 200 numbers by randomly choosing from the numbers 1, 2, and 3 over and over again. After it is completed, the list of numbers is kept out of view of the instructor. The student is now told to concentrate on the first number on the list, and the instructor tries to guess what the number is. After the instructor guesses, the student tells the class and the instructor the correct choice. A record is kept of whether the instructor's guess matched, and the process continues until the complete record of 200 matches and nonmatches is recorded. Before the procedure begins, the instructor announces that she or he will demonstrate "psychic powers" by reading the subject's mind during the experiment. The class is asked what level of performance—that is, percentage of "hits"—would constitute empirically solid evidence of psychic powers. Usually a student who has taken a statistics course volunteers that, because a result of 33 percent hits could be expected purely on the basis of chance, the instructor would have to achieve a larger proportion than this, probably at least 40 percent, before one should believe that she or he has psychic powers. The class usually understands and agrees with this argument. The demonstration is then conducted, and a result of more than 40 percent hits is obtained, to the surprise of many.

The students then learn some lessons about randomness and about how easy it is to fake psychic powers. The instructor in this example merely takes advantage of the fact that people do not generate enough runs: They alternate too much when producing "random" numbers. In a truly random sequence of numbers, what should the probability of a 2 be after three consecutive 2s? One-third, the same as the probability of a 1 or a 3. But this is not how most people generate such numbers. After even a small run, they tend to alternate numbers in order to produce a representative sequence. Thus, on each trial in our example, the instructor merely picks one of the two numbers that the student did not pick on the previous trial. Thus, if on the previous trial the student generated a 2, the instructor picks a 1 or a 3 for the next trial. If on the previous trial the subject generated a 3, the instructor picks a 1 or a 2 on the next trial. This simple procedure usually ensures a percentage of hits greater than 33 percent—greater than chance accuracy without a hint of psychic power.

The tendency for people to believe that if a sequence is random, then it should display no runs or patterns was illustrated humorously in the controversy over the iPod's "shuffle" feature that broke out in 2005 (Levy, 2005). This feature plays the songs loaded into the iPod in a random sequence. Of course, knowing the research I have just discussed, many psychologists and statisticians chuckled to themselves when the inevitable happened—users complained that the shuffle feature could not be random because they often experienced sequences of songs from the same album or genre. Technical writer Steven Levy (2005) described how he had experienced the same thing. His iPod seemed always to have a fondness for Steely Dan in the first hour of play! But Levy was smart enough to accept what the experts told him: Truly random sequences will often not seem random to people because of our tendency to see patterns everywhere.

A Further Word About Statistics and Probability

These, then, are just a few of the shortcomings in statistical reasoning that obscure an understanding of psychology. More complete and detailed coverage is provided in the book *Heuristics and Biases: The Psychology of Intuitive Judgment* (2002), edited by Gilovich, Griffin, and Kahneman. Introductions to many of these ideas (and good places to start for those who lack extensive statistical training) are contained in Kahneman's *Thinking, Fast and Slow* (2011), Hastie and Dawes's *Rational Choice in an Uncertain World* (2010), Baron's *Thinking and Deciding* (2008), and Nickerson's *Cognition and Chance: The Psychology of Probabilistic Reasoning* (2004).

The probabilistic thinking skills discussed in this chapter are of tremendous practical significance. Because of inadequately developed probabilistic thinking abilities, physicians choose less effective medical treatments (Groopman, 2007); people fail to assess accurately the risks in their environment (Gardner, 2008); information is misused in legal proceedings

(Gigerenzer, 2002; Gigerenzer et al., 2007); animals are hunted to extinction (Baron, 1998); unnecessary surgery is performed (Gigerenzer et al., 2007; Groopman, 2007); and costly financial misjudgments are made (Zweig, 2008).

Of course, a comprehensive discussion of statistical reasoning cannot be carried out in a single chapter. Our goal was much more modest: to emphasize the importance of statistics in the study and understanding of psychology. Unfortunately, there is no simple rule to follow when confronted with statistical information. Unlike some of the other components of scientific thinking that are more easily acquired, functional reasoning skills in statistics probably require some type of formal study.

Although many scientists sincerely wish to make scientific knowledge accessible to the general public, it is intellectually irresponsible to suggest that a deep understanding of a particular subject can be obtained by the layperson when that understanding is crucially dependent on certain technical information that is available only through formal study. Such is the case with statistics and psychology. No one can be a competent contemporary psychologist without being fully conversant with statistics and probability (Evans, 2005). The president of the Association for Psychological Science, Morton Ann Gernsbacher (2007), derived a list of 10 things of intellectual value that she thinks psychological training specifically instills, and 4 of her 10 were in the domains of statistics and methodology. Ludy Benjamin, winner of a prestigious APA teaching award, discussed the most important features that he says should be in an introductory psychology class. While acknowledging that of course such a class must present the most important findings in the discipline, Benjamin went on to say that he thought that "in the long run, teaching students to evaluate data may be just as important. They are not going to remember the difference between negative reinforcement and punishment six weeks after the exam, but if they can remember the lessons about critical-thinking about data...that is what I'd really like to see as the legacy of the course" (Dingfelder, 2007, p. 26).

Our current world is awash in statistics and graphic display of numbers. In medicine, finance, advertisements, and on the news, we are presented with claims based on statistics (Lutsky, 2006). We need to learn to evaluate them, and fortunately the study of psychology has a unique ability to inculcate statistical instincts and insights. That probability and statistics are so central to so *many* sciences is apparent in a popular book on the essential discoveries in science by writer Natalie Angier (2007). Her book covered *all* of the sciences. However, at the very beginning, in the second chapter in fact, Angier introduced the importance of understanding probability and statistics.

Clearly, one of the goals of this book is to make research in the discipline of psychology more accessible to the general reader. However, the empirical methods and techniques of theory construction in psychology are so intertwined with statistics (as is the case in many other fields, such as economics, sociology, and genetics) that it would be wrong to imply that one can thoroughly understand the field without having some statistical knowledge. Thus, although this chapter has served as an extremely brief lesson in statistical thinking, its main purpose has been to highlight the existence of an area of expertise that is critical to a full understanding of psychology.

Summary

As in most sciences, the conclusions that are drawn from psychological research are probabilistic conclusions—generalizations that hold more often than not but that do not apply in every single case. The predictions derived from psychological findings and theories are still useful even though they are not 100 percent accurate (just as is the case in other sciences). One thing that prevents the understanding of much psychological research is that many people have difficulty thinking in probabilistic terms. In this chapter, we discussed several well-researched examples of how probabilistic reasoning goes astray for many people: They make insufficient use of probabilistic information when they also have vivid testimonial evidence available; they fail to take into account the fact that larger samples give more accurate estimates of population values; and, finally, they display the gambler's fallacy (the tendency to see links among events that are really independent). The gambler's fallacy derives from a more general tendency that we will discuss in the next chapter: the tendency to fail to recognize the role of chance in determining outcomes.

CHAPTER 11

The Role of Chance in Psychology

In the last chapter, we discussed the importance of probabilistic trends, probabilistic thinking, and statistical reasoning. In this chapter, we will continue that discussion with an emphasis on the difficulties of understanding the concepts of randomness and chance. We will emphasize how people often misunderstand the contribution of research to clinical practice because of a failure to appreciate how thoroughly the concept of chance is integrated within psychological theory.

The Tendency to Try to Explain Chance Events

Our brains have evolved in such a way that they engage in a relentless search for patterns in the world. We seek relationships, explanations, and meaning in the things that happen around us. Eric Wargo (2008) writes in the *APS Observer* that "the brain could be described as an 'acausal connecting organ'—an insatiable meaning maker" (p. 19).

This strong tendency to search for structure has been studied by psychologists. It is characteristic of human intelligence, and it accounts for many of the most astounding feats of human information processing and knowledge acquisition.

Nevertheless, this extremely adaptive aspect of human cognition sometimes backfires on us. The quest for conceptual understanding is maladaptive when it takes place in an environment in which there is nothing to conceptualize. What plays havoc with one of the most distinguishing features of human cognition? What confounds our quest for structure and obscures understanding? You guessed it: probability. Or, more specifically, chance and randomness.

Chance and randomness are integral parts of our environment. The mechanisms of biological evolution and genetic recombination are governed by laws of chance and randomness. Physics has taught us to explain the fundamental structure of matter by invoking statistical laws of chance. Many things that happen in nature are a complex result of systematic, explainable factors and chance. Again, recall a previous example: Smoking causes lung cancer. A systematic, explainable aspect of biology links smoking to this particular disease. But not all smokers contract lung cancer. The trend is probabilistic. Perhaps we will eventually be able to explain why some smokers do not contract cancer. However, for the time being, this variability must be ascribed to the multitude of chance factors that determine whether a person will contract a particular disease.

As this example illustrates, when we say that something is due to chance, we do not necessarily mean that it is *indeterminate,* only that it is currently *indeterminable.* A coin toss is a chance event, but not because it is in principle impossible to determine the outcome by measuring the angle of the toss, the precise composition of the coin, and many other variables. In fact, the outcome of a toss is determined by all these variables. But a coin toss is called a chance event because there is no easy way to measure all the variables in the event. The outcome of a toss is not in principle indeterminate, just currently indeterminable.

Many events in the world are not entirely explainable in terms of systematic factors, at least not currently. Often, however, when no systematic explanation of a particular phenomenon is currently available, our conceptualizing apparatus still grinds away, imposing meaningless theories on data that are inherently random. Psychologists have conducted experiments on this phenomenon. In one experimental situation, subjects view a series of stimuli that vary in many different dimensions. The subjects are told that some stimuli belong to one class and other stimuli belong to another. Their task is to guess which class each of a succession of stimuli belongs to. However, the researcher actually assigns the stimuli to classes randomly. Thus, there is no rule except randomness. The subjects, however, rarely venture randomness as a guess. Instead, they often concoct extremely elaborate and complicated theories to explain how the stimuli are being assigned.

The thinking of many financial analysts illustrates how difficult it is to acknowledge the large effect of randomness in certain domains. It is common for financial analysts to concoct elaborate explanations for every little fluctuation in stock market prices. In fact, much of this variability is simply random fluctuation (Kahneman, 2011; Taleb, 2007). What we should be hearing many nights on television is something like "The Dow Jones average gained 27 points today because of random fluctuation in a complex interacting system." You will never hear this headline, because financial analysts want to imply that they can explain *everything*—every little burp in market behavior. They continue to imply to their customers (and perhaps themselves believe) that they can "beat the market" when there is voluminous evidence that the vast majority of them can do no such thing. Throughout most of the last several decades, if you had bought all of the 500 stocks in the Standard and Poor's Index and simply held them (what we might call a no-brain strategy—a strategy you could carry out by buying a mutual fund that tracks that index), then you would have had higher returns than over two-thirds of the money managers on Wall Street (Bogle, 2010; Malkiel, 2011; Mamudi, 2009; Regnier, 2010). You would also have beaten 80 percent of the financial newsletters that subscribers buy at rates of up to $1,000 per year.

But what about the managers who *do* beat the no-brain strategy? You might be wondering whether this means that they have some special skill. We can answer that question by considering the following thought experiment. One hundred monkeys have each been given ten darts, and they are each going to throw them at a wall containing the names of each of the Standard and Poor's 500 stocks. Where the darts land will define that monkey's stock picks for the year. How will they do a year later? How many will beat the Standard and Poor's 500 Index? You guessed it. Roughly half of the monkeys. Would you be interested in paying the 50 percent of the monkeys who beat the index a commission to make your picks for you next year?

The logic by which purely random sequences seem to be the result of predictable factors is illustrated by a continuation of this example of financial predictions (Paulos, 2001). Imagine that a letter comes in the mail informing you of the existence of a stock-market-prediction newsletter. The newsletter does not ask for money but simply tells you to test it out. It tells you that IBM stock is going to go up during the next month. You put the letter away, but you do notice IBM stock does go up the next month. Having read a book like this one, however, you know better than to make anything of this result. You chalk it up to a lucky guess. Subsequently, you receive *another* newsletter from the same investment-advice company telling you that IBM stock will go down the following month. When the stock does go down, you again chalk the prediction up to a lucky guess, but you do get a bit curious. When the third letter from the same company comes and predicts that IBM will go down again the next month, you do find yourself watching the financial pages a little more closely, and you confirm for the third time that the newsletter's prediction was correct. IBM has gone down this month. When the fourth newsletter arrives from the same company and tells you that the stock will rise the next month, and it actually does move in the predicted direction for the fourth time, it becomes difficult to escape the feeling that this newsletter is for real—difficult to escape the feeling that maybe you should send in the $29.95 for a year's worth of the newsletter. Difficult to escape the feeling, that is, unless you can imagine the cheap basement office in which someone is preparing next week's batch of 1,600 newsletters to be sent to 1,600 addresses: 800 of the newsletters predict that IBM will go up during the next month, and 800 of the newsletters predict that IBM will go down during the next month. When IBM does go up, that office sends out letters to *only* the 800 addressees who got the correct prediction the month before (400 predicting that the stock will go up in the next month and 400 predicting that it will go down, of course). Then you can imagine the "boiler room"—probably with telemarketing scams purring on the phones in the background—sending the third month's predictions to only the 400 who got the correct prediction the second week (200 predicting that the stock will go up in the next month and 200 predicting that it will go down). Yes, you were one of the lucky 100 who received four correct random predictions in a row! Many of these lucky 100 (and probably very impressed) individuals will pay the $29.95 to keep the newsletters coming.

Now this seems like a horrible scam to play on people. And indeed it is. But it is no less a scam than when "respectable" financial magazines and TV shows present to you the "money manager who has beaten more than half his peers four years in a row!" Again, think back to our monkeys throwing the darts. Imagine that they were money managers making stock picks year after year. By definition, 50 percent of them will beat their peers during the first year. Half of these will again—by chance—beat their peers in the second year, making a total of 25 percent who beat their peers two years in a row. Half of these will again—by chance—beat their peers in the third year, making a total of 12.5 percent who beat their peers *three* years in a row. And finally, half of these 12.5 percent (i.e., 6.25 percent) will again beat their peers in the fourth year. Thus, about 6 of the 100 monkeys will have, as the financial shows and newspapers say, "consistently beaten other money managers for four years in a row." These 6 monkeys who beat their dartboard peers (and, as we just saw, would beat a majority of *actual* Wall Street money managers; Malkiel, 2011) certainly deserve spots on the financial television programs, don't you think?

Explaining Chance: Illusory Correlation and the Illusion of Control

The tendency to explain chance events is illustrated in a phenomenon psychologists have studied that is called *illusory correlation*. When people believe that two types of events should commonly occur together, they tend to think that they are seeing co-occurrences with great frequency, even when the two critical events are occurring randomly and, thus, do not co-occur more frequently than any other combination of events. In short, people tend to see their expected correlation even in random events. They see structure where there is none (Kahneman, 2011; Whitson & Galinsky, 2008).

Controlled studies have demonstrated that when people have a prior belief that two variables are connected, they tend to see that connection even in data in which the two variables are totally unconnected. Unfortunately, this finding generalizes to some real-world situations that adversely affect people's lives. For example, many psychological practitioners continue to believe in the efficacy of the Rorschach test. This is the famous inkblot test in which the subject responds to blotches on a white paper. Because the inkblots lack structure, the theory is that people will respond to them in the same style that they typically respond to ambiguity and, thus, reveal "hidden" psychological traits. The test is called *projective* because the subjects presumably project unconscious psychological thoughts and feelings in their responses to the inkblots. The problem with all of this is that there is no evidence that the Rorschach test provides any additional diagnostic utility when used as a projective test (Lilienfeld et al., 2010; Wood, Nezworski, Lilienfeld, & Garb, 2003). Belief in the Rorschach test arises from the phenomenon of illusory correlation. Clinicians see relationships in response patterns because they believe they are there, not because they are actually present in the pattern of responses being observed.

Many of the interpersonal encounters in our lives have a large amount of chance in them: the blind date that leads to marriage, the canceled appointment that causes the loss of a job, the missed bus that leads to a meeting with an old high school friend. It is a mistake to think that each chance event of our lives requires an elaborate explanation. But when essentially chance events lead to important consequences, it is difficult to avoid constructing complicated theories to explain them.

The tendency to try to explain chance probably derives from a deep desire to believe that we can control such events. Psychologists have studied what has been termed the "illusion of control," that is, the tendency to believe that personal skill can affect outcomes determined by chance (Matute, Yarritu, & Vadillo, 2011). Evidence of the widespread nature of this fallacy comes from the experience of states in which lotteries have been instituted. These states are descended on by purveyors of bogus books advising people how to "beat" the lottery—books that sell because people do not understand the implications of randomness. In fact, the explosion in the popularity of state lotteries in the United States did not occur until the mid-1970s, when New Jersey introduced participatory games in which players could scratch cards or pick their own numbers. These participatory games exploit the illusion of control investigated by Langer: people's mistaken belief that their behavior determines random events. This illusion is so strong in some people who like to gamble that they will pay $1,495 for a "special course" that will supposedly teach them to control the outcomes of the dice that they throw (Schwartz, 2008). Such "courses" are of course entirely bogus.

Other psychologists have studied a related phenomenon known as the *just-world hypothesis,* that is, the fact that people tend to believe that they live in a world in which people get what they deserve (Hafer & Begue, 2005). Researchers have found empirical support for one corollary of the belief in a just world: People tend to derogate the victims of chance misfortune. The tendency to seek explanations for chance events contributes to this phenomenon. People apparently find it very hard to believe that a perfectly innocent or virtuous person can suffer misfortune purely because of chance. We long to believe that good things happen to good people and that bad things happen to the bad. Chance, though, is completely unbiased—it does not operate to favor "good people."

People's misunderstanding of chance that is reflected in their belief in a just world serves to support many other incorrect folk beliefs. It leads to the tendency to see illusory correlations. We mentioned in Chapter 6, for example, the incorrect belief that blind people are "blessed" with supersensitive hearing, a folk myth probably perpetuated because people desire to see a correlation that "evens things out."

Chance and Psychology

In psychology, the tendency to try to explain everything, to have our theories account for every bit of variability rather than just the systematic nonchance components of behavior, accounts for the existence of many unfalsifiable psychological theories, both personal theories and those that are ostensibly scientific. Practitioners of "psychohistory" are often guilty of committing this error. Every minor twist and turn in a famous individual's life is explained in these psychohistories, usually via psychoanalytic principles. The problem with most psychohistories is not that they explain too little but that they explain too much. Rarely do they acknowledge the many chance factors that determine the course of a person's life.

An understanding of the role of chance is critical to the lay consumer of psychological information. Legitimate psychologists admit that their theories account for a portion of the variability in human behavior but not for all of it. They openly acknowledge the chance factor. The *Oprah Winfrey Show* guest (Chapter 4) who has an answer for every single case, for every bit of human behavior, should engender not admiration but suspicion. True scientists are not afraid to admit what they do not know. In short, another consumer rule for evaluating psychological claims is this: Before accepting a complicated explanation of an event, consider what part chance may have played in its occurrence.

Coincidence

The tendency to seek explanations for essentially chance occurrences leads to much misunderstanding regarding the nature of coincidental events. Many people think that coincidences need special explanation. They do not understand that coincidences are bound to occur even if nothing other than chance is operating. Coincidences need no special explanation.

Most dictionary definitions of the word "coincidence" interpret it to refer to an accidental remarkable occurrence of related events. Because the same dictionaries define *accidental* as "occurring by chance," there is no problem here. A coincidence is merely an occurrence of related events that is due to chance. Unfortunately, this is not how many people interpret what is meant by coincidence. The tendency to seek patterns and meanings in events, combined with the "remarkable" aspect of coincidences, leads many to overlook chance as an explanation. Instead, they seek elaborate theories in order to understand these events. How many times have you heard stories like this: "You know, the other day I was sitting around thinking about how I hadn't called old Uncle Bill down in Texas in a long time. And guess what? The next thing that happens...ring, ring. Yeah, you guessed it! It's old Uncle Bill on the phone. There must be something to this telepathy stuff after all!" This is a fairly typical example of an elaborate explanation of a coincidental event. On any given day, most of us probably think about several different distant people. How often do these people call us after we think of them? Almost never. Thus, during a year, we probably think about hundreds of people who do not call. Eventually, in the course of these hundreds of "negative trials," which we never recognize as such, someone is going to call after we think of her or him. The event is rare, but rare events do happen—purely by chance. No other explanation is necessary.

If people truly understood what coincidence meant (a remarkable occurrence that is due to chance), they would not fall prey to the fallacy of trying to develop systematic, nonchance explanations for these chance events. Yet, completely contrary to the dictionary definition, coincidence has come to imply to many people something that needs an explanation rather than something that can be explained by chance. For example, most of us have heard statements like "My goodness, what a coincidence! I wonder *why* that happened!" This reflects a fundamental error—coincidences do not *need* an explanation.

Psychologist David Marks (2001) has suggested the neutral term "oddmatch" to signify two events whose co-occurrence strikes us as odd or strange. One thing that contributes to the tendency to search for explanations of coincidental events is the mistaken idea that rare events never happen, that oddmatches are never due to chance. Our belief in this fallacy is intensified because probabilities are sometimes stated in terms of odds and because of the connotations that such statements have. Think of how we phrase the following: "Oh, goodness, that's very unlikely. The odds are 100 to 1 against that happening!" The manner in which we articulate such a statement strongly implies that it will never happen. Of course, we could say the same thing in a very different way, one that has very different connotations: "In 100 events of this type, this outcome *will* probably happen once." This alternative phrasing emphasizes that, although the event is rare, in the long run rare events do happen. In short, oddmatches do occur purely because of chance.

In fact, the laws of probability guarantee that as the number of events increases, the probability that some oddmatch will occur becomes very high. Not only do the laws of chance allow oddmatches to happen, but they virtually *guarantee* them in the long run. Consider one of Marks's (2001) examples. If you flipped 5 coins all at once and they all came up heads, you would probably consider this result an oddmatch, an unlikely event. You would be right. The probability of this happening in any one flip of 5 coins is 1/32 or 0.03. But if you flipped the 5 coins 100 times and asked how likely it is that in at least 1 of those 100 trials the coins would all come up heads, the answer would be 0.96. That is, in 100 trials, this rare event, this oddmatch, is *very likely* to happen.

In short, virtually *any* oddmatch you can think of is bound to occur if you wait long enough. In August 1913, in a casino in Monte Carlo (Kaplan & Kaplan, 2007), black came up on a roulette wheel 26 times in a row!

Since many states have instituted lotteries, in which the winning numbers are usually drawn randomly, either by a computer or by some mechanical randomizing device, many statisticians and behavioral scientists have had occasion to chuckle to themselves when the inevitable has happened—that is, when the same winning sequence of numbers are drawn twice. Such an outcome often provokes howls of protest from the public, who interpret the outcome as proof that the lottery is rigged or "crooked." The public's feeling that there is something wrong with this outcome arises from the mistaken view that something this odd or unlikely cannot happen by chance alone. Of course, the reason the statisticians are chuckling is that chance works in just the opposite way. If lotteries go on long enough, consecutive identical winning numbers are bound to be drawn eventually. For example, on June 21, 1995, in a German lottery called 6/49 (6 numbers are picked out of 49 possible) the numbers drawn were 15-25-27-30-42-48— exactly the same set of numbers that had been drawn on December 20, 1986 (Mlodinow, 2008). Many people were surprised to learn that over that time period the chance that *some* set of numbers would repeat was as high as 28 percent.

There are websites devoted to the "spooky" fact that many famous musicians died at age 27: Amy Winehouse, Kurt Cobain, Jim Morrison, Jimi Hendrix, Janis Joplin, and so on (O'Connor, 2011). Except that there is nothing "spooky" about it. It is not a fact in need of explanation. It is, instead, a random occurrence. The reason we know this is because of a statistical analysis published in the *British Medical Journal* of 1,046 musicians who had a No. 1 album on the British charts from 1956 to 2007 (Barnett, 2011). The analysis indicated that there is no tendency for star musicians to die disproportionately at age 27.

It is practically useful to know when to refrain from concocting complicated explanations for events that simply reflect the operation of chance factors. Cognitive psychologist Daniel Kahneman (2011) describes how during the Yom Kippur War in 1973 he approached by the Israeli Air Force for advice. Two squads of aircraft had gone out and one squad had lost four aircraft and one had lost none. The Air Force wanted Kahneman to investigate whether there were factors specific to the different squadrons that were correlated with the outcome. But Kahneman knew that, with a sample this small, any such factors found would most likely be spurious—the result of mere chance fluctuation. Instead of doing a study, Kahneman used the insights in this chapter and told the Israeli Air Force not to waste their time. He says, "I reasoned that luck was the most likely answer, that a random search for a nonobvious cause was hopeless, and that in the meantime the pilots in the squadron that had sustained losses did not need the extra burden of being made to feel that they and their dead friends were at fault" (p. 116).

Personal Coincidences

Oddmatches that happen in our personal lives often have special meaning to us and, thus, we are especially prone not to attribute them to chance. There are many reasons for this tendency. Some are motivational and emotional, but others are due to failures of probabilistic reasoning. We often do not recognize that oddmatches are actually just a small part of a much larger pool of "nonoddmatches." It may seem to some of us that oddmatches occur with great frequency. But do they?

Consider what an analysis of the oddmatches in your personal life would reveal. Suppose on a given day you were involved in 100 distinct events. This does not seem an overestimate, considering the complexity of life in a modern industrial society. Indeed, it is probably a gross underestimate. You watch television, talk on the telephone, meet people, negotiate the route to work or to the store, do household chores, take in information while reading, send and receive email, complete complex tasks at work, and so on. All these events contain several components that are separately memorable. One hundred, then, is probably on the low side, but we will stick with it. An oddmatch is a remarkable conjunction of two events. How many possible different pairs of events are there in the 100 events of your typical day? Using a simple formula to obtain the number of combinations, we calculate that there are 4,950 different pairings of events possible in your typical day. This is true 365 days a year.

Now, oddmatches are very memorable. You would probably remember for several years the day Uncle Bill called. Assume that you can remember all the oddmatches that happened to you in a ten-year period. Perhaps, then, you remember six or seven oddmatches (more or less, people differ in their criteria for oddness). What is the pool of nonoddmatches from which these six or seven oddmatches came? It is 4,950 pairs per day multiplied by 365 days per year multiplied by ten years, or 18,067,500. In short, six oddmatches happened to you in ten years, but 18,067,494 things that could have been oddmatches also happened. The probability of an oddmatch happening in your life is 0.00000033. It hardly seems strange that 6 out of 18 million conjunctions of events in your life should be odd. Odd things do happen. They are rare, but they do happen. Chance guarantees it (recall the example of simultaneously flipping five coins). In our example, six odd things happened to you. They were probably coincidences: remarkable occurrences of related events that were due to chance. Psychologist Daniel Kahneman (2011) has argued that our language fails us here. We have terms for past thoughts that turned out to be true (premonition, intuition), but we have no words to mark and bring to our attention past beliefs that turned out to be false. Most people would not spontaneously think to say, "I had a premonition that the marriage would not last, but I was wrong" (p. 202), because somehow that would seem strange to them. Without a word to mark the occurrence, we are not prone to mark all of our past predictions that failed to occur.

Psychologists, statisticians, and other scientists have pointed out that many oddmatches are commonly thought to be more odd than they really are. The famous "birthday problem" provides a good example of this. In a class of 23 people, what is the probability that 2 of them will have their birthday on the same day? What is the probability in a class of 35 people? Most people think that the odds are pretty low. Actually, in the class with 23 people, the odds are better than 50–50 that 2 people will have birthdays on the same day. And in the class of 35 students, the odds are very high (the probability is over 0.80). Thus, because there have been 43 presidents of the United States, it is not surprising that 2 (James Polk and Warren Harding) were born on the same day (November 2). Nor is it surprising, because 38 presidents have died, that 2 (Millard Fillmore and William Howard Taft) have died on the same day (March 8) and, furthermore, that three *more* (John Adams, Thomas Jefferson, James Monroe) have all also died on the same day. And the day that Adams, Jefferson, and Monroe all died on was July 4! Isn't that amazing? No, not amazing—probabilistic.

Accepting Error in Order to Reduce Error: Clinical Versus Actuarial Prediction

The reluctance to acknowledge the role of chance when trying to explain outcomes in the world can actually decrease our ability to predict real-world events. Acknowledging the role of chance in determining outcomes in a domain means that we must accept the fact that our predictions will never be 100 percent accurate, that we will always make some errors in our predictions. But interestingly, acknowledging that our predictions will be less than 100 percent accurate can actually help us to increase our overall predictive accuracy. It may seem paradoxical, but it is true that we must accept error in order to reduce error (Einhorn, 1986).

The concept that we must accept error in order to reduce error is illustrated by a very simple experimental task that has been studied for decades in cognitive psychology laboratories. The subject sits in front of two lights (one red and one blue) and is told that she or he is to predict which of the lights will be flashed on each trial and that there will be several dozen such trials (subjects are often paid money for correct predictions). The experimenter has actually programmed the lights to flash randomly, with the provision that the red light will flash 70 percent of the time and the blue light 30 percent of the time. Subjects do quickly pick up the fact that the red light is flashing more, and they predict that it will flash on more trials than they predict that the blue light will flash. In fact, they predict that the red light will flash approximately 70 percent of the time. However, as discussed earlier in this chapter, subjects come to believe that there is a pattern in the light flashes and almost never think that the sequence is random. Instead, they switch back and forth from red to blue, predicting the red light roughly 70 percent of the time and the blue light roughly 30 percent of the time. Subjects rarely realize that—despite the fact that the blue light is coming on 30 percent of the time—if they stopped switching back and forth and predicted the red light every time, they would actually do better! How can this be?

Let's consider the logic of the situation. How many predictions will subjects get correct if they predict the red light roughly 70 percent of the time and the blue light roughly 30 percent of the time and the lights are really coming on randomly in a ratio of 70 to 30? We will do the calculation on 100 trials in the middle of the experiment—after the subject has noticed that the red light comes on more often and is, thus, predicting the red light roughly 70 percent of the time. In 70 of the 100 trials, the red light will come on and the subject will be correct on about 70 percent of those 70 trials (because the subject predicts the red light 70 percent of the time). That is, in 49 of the 70 trials (70 times 0.70), the subject will correctly predict that the red light will come on. In 30 of the 100 trials, the blue light will come on, and the subject will be correct in 30 percent of those 30 trials (because the subject predicts the blue light 30 percent of the time). That is, in 9 of the 30 trials (30 times 0.30), the subject will correctly predict that the blue light will come on. Thus, in 100 trials, the subject is correct 58 percent of the time (49 correct predictions on red light trials and 9 correct predictions on blue light trials). But notice that this is a poorer performance than could be achieved if the subject simply noticed which light was coming on more often and then predicted it in every trial—in this case, noticing that the red light came on more often and predicting it in every trial (let's call this the 100 percent red strategy). Of the 100 trials, 70 would be red flashes, and the subject would have predicted all 70 of these correctly. Of the 30 blue flashes, the subject would have predicted none correctly but still would have a prediction accuracy of 70 percent—12 percent better than the 58 percent correct that the subject achieved by switching back and forth.

The optimal strategy does have the implication though—that you will be wrong every time a blue occurs. And since blue light stimuli are occurring on at least *some* of the trials, it just does not seem right *never* to predict them. But this is just what correct probabilistic thinking requires. It requires accepting the errors that will be made on blue trials in order to attain the higher overall hit rate that will be obtained when predicting red each time. In short, we must *accept* the blue errors in order to make *fewer* errors overall. Predicting human behavior with some accuracy often involves accepting error in order to reduce error, that is, getting better prediction by relying on general principles but acknowledging that we cannot be right in every single case.

Accepting error in order to make fewer errors is a difficult thing to do, however, as evidenced by the 60-year history of research on clinical versus actuarial prediction in psychology. The term *actuarial prediction* refers to predictions based on group trends derived from statistical records, the type of group (i.e., aggregate) predictions that we discussed at the beginning of this chapter. A simple actuarial prediction is one that predicts the same outcome for all individuals sharing a certain characteristic. So, to take an imaginary example, predicting a life span of 77.5 years for people who do not smoke and a life span of 64.3 years for individuals who smoke would be an example of an actuarial prediction. More accurate predictions can be made if we take more than one group characteristic into account (using the complex correlational techniques mentioned in Chapter 5—specifically a technique known as *multiple regression*). For example, predicting a life span of 58.2 years for people who smoke, are overweight, and do not exercise would be an example of an actuarial prediction based on a set of variables (smoking behavior, weight, and amount of exercise), and such predictions are almost always more accurate than predictions made from a single variable.

Such actuarial predictions are common in economics, human resources, criminology, business and marketing, and the medical sciences. For example, in studies published in the *Journal of the American Medical Association* and in the *Annals of Internal Medicine* the following probabilistic trends were reported: people who are obese in middle age are four times more likely than nonobese people to have heart problems after age 65; overweight (but not obese) people are twice as likely to develop kidney problems; and obese people are seven times more likely to develop kidney problems (Seppa, 2006). But probabilistic prediction admits error. Not all obese people will have health problems. Recall the case (from Chapter 10) of the political broadcaster Tim Russert who died of a heart attack at age 58. Physicians determined that Mr. Russert's probability of a heart attack in the next ten years was only 5 percent. That is, *most* people (95 out of 100) with Mr. Russert's profile would be heart-attack free for ten years. Mr. Russert was one of the unlucky 5 percent—he was an exception to the general trend.

People sometimes find it difficult to act on actuarial evidence, however, because doing so often takes mental discipline. For example, in 2003 the Food and Drug Administration issued a health-advisory warning of a potential link between a popular antidepressant drug and teen suicide. Many physicians worried that, on an actuarial basis, the warning would result in more suicides. They worried that perhaps fewer teenagers would die of suicide *because* of the drug but that *even more* children would die because of an increased hesitancy to prescribe the drug. This is indeed what happened. Treatment with this drug can put children at a temporary risk, but untreated depression is far worse. Most doctors thought that the warning would cost more lives than it would save (Dokoupil, 2007). That was the mathematics of the situation. Or, perhaps we should say: That's the calculus of actuarial prediction. But it can be a hard calculus to follow when folk wisdom is saying things like "better to be safe than sorry." But in the domain of medical treatment "better to be safe than sorry" ignores one half of the equation. It focuses our attention on those who might be hurt by the treatment, but it totally ignores those who would be hurt if the treatment were unavailable.

Knowledge in most subareas of psychology, such as cognitive psychology, developmental psychology, organizational psychology, personality psychology, and social psychology, is stated in terms of actuarial predictions. In contrast, some subgroups of clinical psychological practitioners claim to be able to go beyond group predictions and to make accurate predictions of the outcomes of particular individuals. This is called *clinical,* or *case, prediction.* When engaged in clinical prediction, as opposed to actuarial prediction,

> professional psychologists claim to be able to make predictions about individuals that transcend predictions about "people in general" or about various categories of people.... Where professional psychologists differ is in their claim to understand the single individual as unique rather than as part of a group about which statistical generalizations are possible. They claim to be able to analyze "what caused what" in an *individual's* life rather than to state what is "in general" true. (Dawes, 1994, pp. 79–80)

Clinical prediction would seem to be a very useful addition to actuarial prediction. There is just one problem, however. Clinical prediction doesn't work.

For clinical prediction to be useful, the clinician's experience with the client and her or his use of information about the client would have to result in better predictions than we can get from simply coding information about the client and submitting it to statistical procedures that optimize the process of combining quantitative data in order to derive predictions. In short, the claim is that the experience of psychological practitioners allows them to go beyond the aggregate relationships that have been uncovered by research. The claim that clinical prediction is efficacious is, thus, easily testable. Unfortunately, the claim has been tested, and it has been falsified.

Research on the issue of clinical versus actuarial prediction has been consistent. Since the publication in 1954 of Paul Meehl's classic book *Clinical Versus Statistical Prediction,* six decades of research consisting of over a hundred research studies have shown that, in just about every clinical prediction domain that has ever been examined (psychotherapy outcome, parole behavior, college graduation rates, response to electroshock therapy, criminal recidivism, length of psychiatric hospitalization, and many more), actuarial prediction has been found to be superior to clinical prediction (Kahneman, 2011; Morera & Dawes, 2006; Swets et al., 2000; Tetlock, 2005).

In a variety of clinical domains, when a clinician is given information about a client and asked to predict the client's behavior, and when the same information is quantified and processed by a statistical equation that has been developed based on actuarial relationships that research has uncovered, invariably the equation wins. That is, the actuarial prediction is more accurate than the clinician's prediction. In fact, even when the clinician has more information available than is used in the actuarial method, the latter is superior. That is, when the clinician has information from personal contact and interviews with the client, in addition to the *same* information that goes into the actuarial equation, the clinical predictions still do not achieve an accuracy as great as the actuarial method. The reason is of course that the equation integrates information accurately and consistently. This factor—consistency—can overcome any informational advantage the clinician has from information gleaned informally.

A final type of test in the clinical–actuarial prediction literature involves actually giving the clinician the predictions from the actuarial equation and asking the clinician to adjust the predictions based on his or her personal experience with the clients. When the clinician makes adjustments in the actuarial predictions, the adjustments actually *decrease* the accuracy of the predictions (see Dawes, 1994). Here we have an example of failing to "accept error in order to reduce error" that is directly analogous to the light prediction experiment previously described. Rather than relying on the actuarial information that the red light came on more often and predicting red each time (and getting 70 percent correct), the subjects tried to be correct on each trial by alternating red and blue predictions and ended up being 12 percent less accurate (they were correct on only 58 percent of the trials). Analogously the clinicians in these studies believed that their experience gave them "clinical insight" and allowed them to make better predictions than those that can be made from quantified information in the client's file. In fact, their "insight" is nonexistent and leads them to make predictions that are worse than those they would make if they relied only on the public, actuarial information. It should be noted, though, that the superiority of actuarial prediction is not confined to psychology but extends to many other clinical sciences as well—for example, to medicine (Groopman, 2007), and to fields such as financial services (Bogle, 2010; Kahneman, 2011) and athletic coaching (Moskowitz & Wertheim, 2011).

Regarding the research showing the superiority of actuarial prediction over clinical prediction, Paul Meehl (1986) said, "There is no controversy in social science which shows such a large body of qualitatively diverse studies coming out so uniformly in the same direction as this one" (pp. 373–374). Yet, embarrassingly, the field of psychology does not act on this knowledge. For example, the field continues to use personal interviews in the graduate admissions process and in the mental-health-training admissions process, even though voluminous evidence suggests that these interviews have virtually no validity. Instead, practitioners continue to use specious arguments to justify their reliance on "clinical intuition" rather than aggregate predictions that would work better. For example, Dawes, Faust, and Meehl (1989) noted,

> A common anti-actuarial argument, or misconception, is that group statistics do not apply to single individuals or events. The argument abuses basic principles of probability.... An advocate of this anti-actuarial position would have to maintain, for the sake of logical consistency, that if one is forced to play Russian roulette a single time and is allowed to select a gun with one or five bullets in the chamber, the uniqueness of the event makes the choice arbitrary. (p. 1672)

An analogy to the last point would be to ask yourself how you react to the scientific findings that the probability of a successful kind of surgery is higher for surgeons that perform many of that particular type of surgical operation (Grady, 2009; Groopman, 2007). Would you rather have your operation done by a surgeon A, who is practiced in that type of surgery and has a low failure probability, or by surgeon B, who is unpracticed in that type of surgery and has a high failure probability? If you believe that "probabilities don't apply to the single case," you shouldn't mind having your surgery done by the unpracticed surgeon.

The field of psychology has little to lose in prestige by admitting the superiority of actuarial to clinical judgment in a domain such as predicting psychotherapeutic outcome because the same is true of professionals in numerous other domains as varied as medicine, business, criminology, accounting, and livestock judging. Although the field as a whole would have little to lose, individual practitioners who engage in activities in the role of "experts" (i.e., in courtroom testimony) and imply that they have unique clinical knowledge of individual cases would, of course, lose prestige and perhaps income.

In fact, the field, and society, would benefit if we developed the habit of "accepting error in order to reduce error." In attempting to find unique explanations of every single unusual case (unique explanations that simply may not be possible given the present state of our knowledge), we often lose predictive accuracy in the more mundane cases. Recall the red–blue light experiment again. The "100 percent red strategy" makes incorrect predictions of all of the minority or unusual events (when the blue lights flash). What if we focused more on those minority events by adopting the "70-percent-red-30-percent-blue strategy"? We would now be able to predict 9 of those 30 unusual events (30 times 0.30). But the cost is that we lose our ability to predict 21 of the majority events. Instead of 70 correct predictions of red, we now have only 49 correct predictions (70 times 0.70). Predictions of behavior in the clinical domain have the same logic. In concocting complicated explanations for every case, we may indeed catch a few more unusual cases—but at the cost of losing predictive accuracy in the majority of cases, where simple actuarial prediction would work better.

Wagenaar and Keren (1986) illustrated how overconfidence in personal knowledge and the discounting of statistical information can undermine safety campaigns advocating seat belt use because people think, "I am different, I drive safely." The problem is that the vast majority of the population thinks that they are "better than the average driver" (De Craen, Twisk, Hagenzieker, Elffers, & Brookhuis, 2011)—obviously a patent absurdity.

The same fallacy of believing that "statistics don't apply to the single case" is an important factor in the thinking of individuals with chronic gambling problems. In his study of gambling behavior, Wagenaar (1988) concluded,

> From our discussions with gamblers it has become abundantly clear that gamblers are generally aware of the negative long-term result. They know that they have lost more than they have won, and that it will be the same in the future. But they fail to apply these statistical considerations to the next round, the next hour, or the next night. A rich repertoire of heuristics...gives them the suggestion that statistics do not apply in the next round, or the next hour. That they can predict the next outcome. (p. 117)

Wagenaar found that compulsive gamblers had a strong tendency not to "accept error in order to reduce error." For example, blackjack players had a tendency to reject a strategy called *basic* that is guaranteed to decrease the casino's advantage from 6 or 8 percent to less than 1 percent. Basic is a long-term statistical strategy, and the compulsive players tended to reject it because they believed that "an effective strategy ought to be effective in every single instance" (p. 110). The gamblers in Wagenaar's study "invariably said that the general prescriptions of such systems could not work, because they neglect the idiosyncrasies of each specific situation" (p. 110). Instead of using an actuarial strategy that was guaranteed to save them thousands of dollars, these gamblers were on a futile chase to find a way to make a clinical prediction based on the idiosyncrasies of each specific situation.

Another domain in which actuarial prediction often beats clinical prediction is sports. Many people saw the movie *Moneyball* in 2011, based on the book by Michael Lewis (2004). It told the story of Oakland A's manager Billy Beane, who overruled the "clinical" judgments of his baseball scouts (who tended to rely heavily on visible physical characteristics) and relied on statistics of past performance when evaluating potential team members. His teams overperformed relative to the money they spent, and the actuarial methods that he had borrowed from baseball statisticians were then copied by many other teams. Statistical methods have been shown to be superior to "coaches' judgments" in many other sports (see Moskowitz & Wertheim, 2011, for many examples).

Of course, this discussion of the literature on clinical versus actuarial prediction is not meant to imply that there is not a role for the case study in psychology. Keep in mind that we have been speaking about the specific situation of the prediction of behavior. Recall the discussion of the role of the case study in Chapter 4. Case information is highly useful in drawing attention to variables that are important and that need to be measured. What we have been saying in this section is that, once the relevant variables have been determined and we want to use them to predict behavior, measuring them and using a statistical equation to determine the predictions constitute the best procedure. First, we get more accurate predictions by using the actuarial approach. Second, the actuarial approach has an advantage over clinical prediction in that an actuarial equation is public knowledge—open for all to use, modify, criticize, or dispute. In contrast, the use of clinical prediction amounts to reliance on an authority whose assessments—precisely because these judgments are claimed to be singular and idiosyncratic—are not subject to public criticism.

Summary

The role of chance in psychology is often misunderstood by the lay public and by clinical practitioners alike. People find it difficult to recognize that part of the variability in behavioral outcomes is determined by chance factors. That is, variation in behavior is in part a function of random factors and, thus, psychologists should not claim to be able to predict behavior case by case. Instead, psychological predictions are probabilistic—predictions of aggregate trends.

The error of implying that psychological predictions can be made at the level of the individual is often made by clinical psychologists themselves, who sometimes mistakenly imply that clinical training confers an "intuitive" ability to predict an individual case. Instead, decades' worth of research has consistently indicated that actuarial prediction (prediction in terms of group statistical trends) is superior to clinical prediction in accounting for human behavior. There is no evidence of a clinical intuition that can predict whether a statistical trend will hold or not in a particular case. Thus, statistical information should never be set aside when one is predicting behavior. Statistical prediction also correctly signals that there will always be errors and uncertainties when one is predicting human behavior.

CHAPTER 12

The Rodney Dangerfield of the Sciences

Rodney Dangerfield was a popular comedian for over three decades and whose trademark was the plaintive cry, "I don't get no respect!" In a way, this is a fitting summary of psychology's status in the public mind. This chapter will touch on some of the reasons that psychology appears to be the Rodney Dangerfield of the sciences.

Although there is a great public fascination with psychological topics, most judgments about the field and its accomplishments are resoundingly negative. Psychologists are aware of this image problem, but most feel that there is little they can do about it, so they simply ignore it. This is a mistake. Ignoring psychology's image problem threatens to make it worse.

Psychology's Image Problem

Some of the reasons for psychology's image problem have already been discussed. For example, the Freud problem discussed in Chapter 1 undoubtedly contributes to the low esteem in which psychology is held. To the extent that the public knows about any psychologists at all, Freud and B. F. Skinner are those psychologists (Overskeid, 2007). Many aspects of Freudian psychoanalysis are indeed unscientific, but as described in Chapter 1, these unfalsifiable ideas play no role in modern psychological research. As for Skinner, there would appear to be little hope for a field when one of its most renowned scholars is said to have claimed that we have no minds and that we are just like rats. Of course, Skinner said no such thing (Gaynor, 2004), but distorted versions of his ideas abound, and few know that many principles of operant conditioning that he developed from work with animals *have* been shown to generalize to human behavior. However, the public is little aware of any of these facts.

Psychology and Parapsychology

The layperson's knowledge of reputable psychological research, outside of the work of Freud or Skinner, is virtually nonexistent. One way to confirm this fact is to look in your local bookstore to see what material on psychology is available to the general public. Inspection will reveal that the material generally falls into three categories. First, there will be a few classics (Freud, Skinner, Fromm, Erickson, Jung, etc.) heavily biased toward old-style psychoanalytic views that are totally unrepresentative of modern psychology. Frustratingly for psychologists, works of real worth in the field are often shelved in the science and/or biology sections of bookstores. For example, psychologist Steven Pinker's well-known and esteemed book *How the Mind Works* (1997) is often in the science section rather than the psychology section. Thus, the important work in cognitive science that he discusses becomes associated with biology, neurophysiology, or computer science rather than psychology.

The second class of material found in most stores might be called pseudoscience masquerading as psychology—that is, the seemingly never-ending list of so-called paranormal phenomena such as telepathy, clair-voyance, psychokinesis, precognition, reincarnation, biorhythms, astral projection, pyramid power, plant communication, and psychic surgery. The presence of a great body of this material in the psychology sections of bookstores undoubtedly contributes to the widespread misconception that psychologists are the people who have confirmed the existence of such phenomena. There is a bitter irony for psychology in this misconception. In fact, the relationship between psychology and the paranormal is easily stated. These phenomena are simply not an area of active research interest in modern psychology. The reason, however, is a surprise to many people.

The statement that the study of ESP and other paranormal abilities is not accepted as part of the discipline of psychology will undoubtedly provoke the ire of many readers. Surveys have consistently shown that more than 40 percent of the general public believes in the existence of such phenomena and often holds these beliefs with considerable fervor (Farha & Steward, 2006; Kida, 2006; Shermer, 2011). Historical studies and survey research have suggested why these beliefs are held so strongly (Begley, 2008; Humphrey, 1996; Park, 2008; Stanovich, 2004). Like most religions, many of the so-called paranormal phenomena seem to promise things such as life after death, and for some people, they serve the same need for transcendence. It should not be surprising, then, that the bearer of the bad tidings that research in psychology does not validate ESP is usually not greeted with enthusiasm.

The statement that psychology does not consider ESP a viable research area invariably upsets believers and often provokes charges that psychologists are dogmatic in banishing certain topics from their discipline. Psychologists do not contribute to public understanding when they throw up their hands and fail to deal seriously with these objections. Instead, psychologists should give a careful and clear explanation of why such objections are ill founded. Such an explanation would emphasize that scientists do not determine by edict which topics to investigate. No proclamation goes out declaring what can and cannot be studied. Areas of investigation arise and are expanded or terminated according to a natural selection process that operates on ideas and methods. Those that lead to fruitful theories and empirical discoveries are taken up by a large number of scientists. Those that lead to theoretical dead ends or that do not yield replicable or interesting observations are dropped. This natural selection of ideas and methods is what leads science closer to the truth.

The reason that ESP, for example, is not considered a viable topic in contemporary psychology is simply that its investigation has not proved fruitful. Therefore, very few psychologists are interested in it. It is important here to emphasize the word "contemporary," because the topic of ESP was of greater interest to psychologists some years ago, before the current bulk of negative evidence had accumulated. As history shows, research areas are not declared invalid by governing authorities; they are merely winnowed out in the competing environment of ideas.

ESP was never declared an invalid topic in psychology. The evidence of this fact is clear and publicly available (Farha, 2007; Hines, 2003; Kelly, 2005; Marks, 2001; Milton & Wiseman, 1999; Park, 2008; Wiseman, 2011). Many papers investigating ESP have appeared in legitimate psychological journals over the years. As recently as 2011, a major APA journal published a paper on a parapsychological effect (Bem, 2011). Alas, as is so often the case, the effects reported appear not to be reliable (Rouder & Morey, 2011; Wagenmakers, Wetzels, Borsboom, & van der Maas, 2011).

Parapsychologists who thrive on media exposure like to give the impression that the area is somehow new, thus implying that startling new discoveries are just around the corner. The truth is much less exciting. The study of ESP is actually as old as psychology itself. It is not a new area of investigation. It has been as well studied as many of the currently viable topics in the psychological literature. The results of the many studies that have appeared in legitimate psychological journals have been overwhelmingly negative. After more than 90 years of study, there still does not exist one example of an ESP phenomenon that is replicable under controlled conditions. This simple but basic scientific criterion has not been met despite dozens of studies conducted over many decades. Many parapsychologists and believers themselves are even in agreement on this point. In short, there is no demonstrated phenomenon that needs scientific explanation. For this reason alone, the topic is now of little interest to psychology.

And now the irony. Psychologists have played a prominent role in attempts to assess claims of paranormal abilities. The importance of their contribution is probably second only to that of the professional magicians, who have clearly done the most to expose the fraudulent nature of most purported demonstrations of paranormal abilities (Randi, 2011). Many of the most important books on the state of the evidence on paranormal abilities have been written by psychologists.

The irony, then, is obvious. Psychology, the discipline that has probably contributed most to the accurate assessment of ESP claims, is the field that is most closely associated with such pseudosciences in the public mind. Psychology suffers greatly from this guilt-by-association phenomenon. As will be discussed in greater detail later, psychology is often the victim of a "double whammy." Here is just one example. The assumption that anything goes in psychology, that it is a field without scientific mechanisms for deciding among knowledge claims, leads to its being associated with pseudosciences such as ESP. However, if psychologists ever become successful in getting the public to recognize these pseudosciences for what they really are, the pseudosciences' association with psychology will be seen as confirmation that psychology is indeed not a science!

The Self-Help Literature

The third category in the bookstore psychology section is the so-called self-help literature. There are, of course, many different genres within this category (Lilienfeld, Lynn, & Lohr, 2003; Meyers, 2008). Some books are spiritually uplifting tracts written with the purpose of generally increasing feelings of self-worth and competence. Others attempt to package familiar bromides about human behavior in new ways. A few (but all too few) are authored by responsible psychologists writing for the general public. Many that are not in the latter category vie for uniqueness by presenting new "therapies" that are usually designed not only to correct specific behavioral problems but also to help satisfy general human wants (making more money, losing more weight, and having better sex are the "big three"), thereby ensuring larger book sales. These so-called new therapies are rarely based on any type of controlled experimental investigation. They usually rest on personal experience or on a few case histories, if the author is a clinician. This is often true of the treatments of so-called alternative medicine.

The many behavioral and cognitive therapies that have emerged after painstaking psychological investigation as having demonstrated effectiveness are usually poorly represented on the bookshelves. Lilienfeld (2012) estimates that of the 3,500 self-help books that are published each year, only about 5 percent of them have any scientific validation.

The situation is even worse in the electronic media and the Internet. Radio and TV carry virtually no reports of legitimate psychology and instead present purveyors of bogus "therapies" and publicity-seeking media personalities who have no connection to the actual field of psychology. The main reason is that the legitimate psychological therapies do not claim to provide an instant cure or improvement, nor do they guarantee success or claim a vast generality for their effects ("Not only will you quit smoking, but every aspect of your life will improve!").

It is similar in the case of the Internet. The lack of peer review ensures that the therapies and cures that one finds there are often bogus. Here is one example. In 2008, Paul Offit published an important book titled *Autism's False Prophets,* in which he detailed the many treatments for autism that have been found to be bogus by actual scientific research but that have enjoyed popularity among parents desperate for a treatment to help their children. One, facilitated communication, I have discussed in Chapter 6. Offit describes many other pseudoscientific treatments that have falsely raised parents' hopes and have led them to spend thousands of dollars and to waste their time and energy chasing a bogus "cure." On January 5, 2012, I identified one of the bogus chemical "cures" for autism discussed in Offit's book (I will not name it in order not to add to its publicity) and typed it and the word "autism" into Google. Of the first ten links that appeared in the outcome of my search, three links were to websites that were *advocating* this totally bogus chemical "cure." Scientific accuracy is not guaranteed in a Web search because websites are not peer reviewed. They thus provide no consumer protection for the random searcher with no further knowledge of the scientific literature on the topic in question.

The self-help literature, which accounts for a substantial portion of the book market in the United States, has many unfortunate effects on the general perception of psychology. First, like the Freud problem, it creates confusion concerning the problems that dominate the attention of psychologists. For example, although a substantial number of psychologists are engaged in providing therapy for problems of obesity, of relationships, and of sexuality and also in researching these problems, the actual number is far less than that suggested by their representation in the self-help literature. This misrepresentation also contributes to the public's view that most psychologists are engaged in the treatment of and research on abnormal behavior. In fact, most psychological research is directed at nonpathological behavior that is typical of all humans.

Beyond the content confusion, the self-help literature creates an inaccurate impression of the methods and goals of psychology. As we showed in Chapter 4, the science of psychology does not consider a few case studies, testimonials, and personal experiences—which are the database for most of the self-help "therapies"—adequate empirical evidence to support the efficacy of a therapy. The self-help literature misleads the public by implying that this is the type of database on which most psychological conclusions rest. As illustrated in Chapter 8, the confirmation of a theory must rest on many different types of evidence, and case studies yield the weakest type of data. It is a fundamental mistake to view such data as definitive proof of a particular theory or therapy.

Recipe Knowledge

Finally, the self-help literature creates confusion about the goals of psychology and about the type of knowledge that most psychological investigations seek. It strongly implies that psychological researchers seek what has been termed "recipe knowledge." Recipe knowledge is the knowledge of how to use something without knowledge of the fundamental principles that govern its functioning. For example, most people know a lot about how to *use* a computer, but they know very little about *how* a computer actually works. This is recipe knowledge of the computer. Our knowledge of many technological products in our society is also recipe knowledge.

Of course, this is not an entirely bad thing. Indeed, most technological products have been designed to be used without knowledge of all the principles that make them work. In fact, the idea of recipe knowledge provides one way of conceptualizing the difference between basic and applied research. The basic researcher seeks to uncover the fundamental principles of nature without necessarily worrying about whether they can be turned into recipe knowledge. The applied researcher is more interested in translating basic principles into a product that requires only recipe knowledge.

Most self-help literature provides only recipe knowledge about human behavior. It usually boils down to the form "Do X and you will become more Y," or "Do Z and person A will react more B." Now, there is nothing inherently wrong here, assuming, of course, that the recipes provided are correct (which is usually not a safe assumption). Many legitimate psychotherapies also provide much recipe knowledge. However, a problem arises when people mistakenly view recipe knowledge as the ultimate goal of all psychological research. Although a number of psychological researchers do work on turning basic behavioral principles into usable psychotherapeutic techniques, health-maintaining behavior programs, or models of efficient industrial organization, psychological research is largely basic research aimed at uncovering general facts and theories about behavior. Here we have another reason why psychological research may seem strange to the outsider. Investigations of basic principles often look very different from studies focused on developing applications.

We would consider it silly to walk into a molecular biology laboratory and ask a researcher whether we should take two or three aspirins for a headache. The reason is not that molecular biology has nothing to do with pain relief. Future developments in pain relievers will probably involve knowledge from this area of science. It is silly to ask this question because the molecular biologist is simply not working at the recipe level that deals with whether to take two aspirins or three. The researcher is concerned with fundamental facts about the molecular level of biological substances. These facts could lead to recipe knowledge in any number of areas, but the transformation to recipe knowledge will probably not be accomplished by the same investigator who uncovered the basic facts at the molecular level, nor will it be accomplished by use of the same methods that led to the original discoveries.

Thus, because the self-help literature has led people to believe that most psychologists work at developing recipe knowledge, much of the basic research that psychologists conduct appears strange. What did Hecht's data (Chapter 7) about subjects looking at red lights in a dark room have to do with anything in the real world? Well, on the surface, nothing. Hecht was interested in uncovering basic laws about the way the visual system adapts to darkness. The basic principles were eventually translated into recipe knowledge of how to deal with some specific problems, such as night blindness due to vitamin deficiency. However, this translation was not done by Hecht himself, and it did not come until several years later.

Thus, the self-help literature has two unfortunate side effects on the public perception of psychology. The range of problems addressed in this literature does not necessarily represent the focus of contemporary psychology. Instead, it reflects, quite naturally, what people want to read about. The logic of television, radio, and Web-based content is the same. However, the focus of science is not determined by polling the public. In all sciences, and in psychology in particular, there is usually a gap between the ideas that are productive for scientists and those that can be packaged to sell to the public. For example, there is legitimate research on "the power of positive thinking" in psychology (Sharot, 2011), but it bears little resemblance to the self-help prescriptions to that effect that are heard on the *Oprah Show*. Instead, the real psychological research literature is full of caveats, concerns about converging evidence, and the search for connectivity across research methods—in short, all of the real research concerns discussed in this book.

Consider the area of weight loss prescriptions. Scientists have slowly accumulated evidence for some mild prescriptions that help with weight control (Brody, 2008), but they are not breakthrough remedies. It is clear that the problem of obesity is complex and is subject to our warnings about multiple causation (Bartoshuk, 2009). The problem will clearly not have a single magic-bullet solution. Many scientists have stressed, for example, how the complexities of the food environment itself (advertising, portion sizes, marketing to children) contribute to the nation's obesity problem (Brownell, 2011).

By contrast, consider the report of retired physician Harriet Hall (2008), who writes a science-based medicine blog. She describes one weight-loss product that "made the usual claims: eat all you want and still lose weight. But it had the best advertising slogan ever: 'We couldn't say it in print if it wasn't true!' I laughed out loud. Anyone can say anything in print until they get caught. These diet ads all say things that aren't true, and the Federal Trade Commission can't begin to catch them all" (p. 47). Hall's point is that there is a complete disconnect between good science and what the media (from television to print to websites) wants to publicize.

The media want quick answers to questions that are of "public interest," whereas science produces slow answers to questions that are scientifically answerable—and all the questions that the public finds interesting might not be answerable.

Psychology and Other Disciplines

Psychology, of course, does not have a monopoly on studying behavior. Many other allied disciplines, using a variety of different techniques and theoretical perspectives, also contribute to our knowledge. Many problems concerning behavior call for an interdisciplinary approach. However, a frustrating fact that most psychologists must live with is that when work on an interdisciplinary problem is publicized, the contributions of psychologists are often usurped by other fields.

There are many examples of scientific contributions by psychologists that have been ignored, minimized, or partially attributed to other disciplines. For instance, the first major survey of the evidence on television's effects on children's behavior was conducted under the aegis of the U.S. Surgeon General, so it is not surprising that the American Medical Association (AMA) passed a resolution to reaffirm the survey's findings of a suggested causal link and to bring the conclusions more publicity. Again, there is nothing wrong here, but an unintended consequence of the repeated association of the findings on televised violence with the AMA is that it has undoubtedly created the impression that the medical profession conducted the scientific research that established the results. In fact, the overwhelming majority of the research studies on the effects of television violence on children's behavior were conducted by psychologists.

One of the reasons that the work of psychologists is often ascribed to other disciplines is that the word *psychologist* has, over the years, become ambiguous. Many research psychologists commonly append their research specialty to the word *psychologist* when labeling themselves, calling themselves, for example, physiological psychologists, cognitive psychologists, industrial psychologists, evolutionary psychologists, or neuropsychologists. Some use a label that does not contain a derivative of the word "psychology" at all, for example, neuroscientist, cognitive scientist, artificial intelligence specialist, and ethologist. Both of these practices—in conjunction with the media's bias that "psychology isn't a science"—lead to the misattribution of the accomplishments of psychologists: The work of physiological psychologists is attributed to biology, the work of cognitive psychologists is attributed to computer science and neuroscience, the work of industrial psychologists is attributed to engineering and business, and so on. Psychology won't be helped by the fact that one of its most brilliant contemporary researchers, Daniel Kahneman, received the 2002

Nobel Prize in economics! Of course, no Nobel Prize is given in psychology (Benjamin, 2004; MacCoun, 2002).

In fact, here is how ridiculous the tendency to overlook psychology can get. In its April 17, 2008, issue, the *New York Review of Books* published the following correction on page 86: "In Sue Halperin's review of books about happiness [*NYR*, April 3], the field in which economist Daniel Kahneman has done pioneering research should have been referred to as hedonic psychology, not hedonistic psychology." At first we might give the magazine some points for accuracy—they corrected the mistaken use of the word hedonistic with the word hedonic. However, the editors did not notice, before printing this correction, that they had introduced *another* error—Daniel Kahneman is a cognitive psychologist, not an economist!

Psychologist Frederick King (1993), the director of the Yerkes Primate Research Center at Emory University, told of taking time to explain to a reporter the importance of animal models in the study of human neurological disorders. After listening to the long explanation by King, who had contributed for years to the research literature on the neurological and behavioral problems of epilepsy, the reporter asked, "How do you know anything about epilepsy? You're just a psychologist."

Finally, consider what happened at the trial of former White House aide Lewis (Scooter) Libby in 2007. Expert testimony from a renowned research psychologist was disallowed because the judge ruled that it was well known that memory was fallible and that juries can safely rely on their common sense to ascertain how memory works. In fact, studies show that almost 30 percent of the population believe that human memory "operates like a tape recorder" (Lilienfeld, 2012). Contrary to what the judge thought, 30 percent of his jury badly needed to hear from the expert!

Our Own Worst Enemies

Lest it appear that we are blaming everyone else for psychology's image problems, it is about time that we acknowledge the contribution of psychologists themselves to confusion about their field. Most research psychologists do very little public communication. This is because there are very few rewards for the legitimate psychologist who tries to communicate actual psychology to the public.

Nevertheless, the APA and the APS are making more efforts to facilitate public communication (West, 2007). The APS has started a new journal for this purpose: *Psychological Science in the Public Interest*. The APS also sponsors a blog called "We're Only Human" for this purpose (http://www.psychologicalscience.org/onlyhuman/). Psychology needs to make much more of an effort in this area. Otherwise, we will have only ourselves to blame for the misunderstanding of our discipline.

Past APA president Ronald Fox (1996) spoke of psychology's communication problems in a presidential address and how we have brought some of these communication problems on ourselves:

> Some practitioners who are appearing in the mass media are behaving in ways that are unprofessional, marginally ethical at best, and downright embarrassing to a majority of their peers....Our discipline lacks effective measures for responding to irresponsible and outrageous public claims....Too often in today's world, the public is treated to the views and opinions of charlatans (as observed on a recent TV talk show in which a psychologist claimed to have helped dozens of patients remember traumas suffered in past lives), rather than rational practitioners. (pp. 779–780)

And, finally, there is the phenomenon of antiscientific attitudes within parts of psychology itself. For example, some groups of psychotherapists have traditionally resisted scientific evaluations of their treatments. Columnist and psychotherapist Charles Krauthammer (1985) wrote of how this attitude presents a serious threat to the integrity of psychotherapy. First, there is the proliferation of therapies that has occurred because of a reluctance to winnow out those that do not work. Such a proliferation not only removes a critical consumer protection but also promotes confusion in the field. Krauthammer was correctly seeing that the failure to use the falsification strategy prevents scientific progress.

Finally, Krauthammer pointed to the inconsistency of a therapeutic community that, on the one hand, argues against scientific evaluation because it is "more art than science," in the common phrase, but is still greatly concerned about what he called the 800-pound gorilla: reimbursement for services by government and private health insurers. Krauthammer exposed the inconsistency of these attitudes within the psychotherapy community, pointing out that if psychotherapy is an art rather than a science, then it should be supported by the National Endowment for the Humanities, rather than by Medicare.

Some readers of the first few editions of this book commented that they thought I had "let psychologists get off too easily" by not emphasizing more strongly that unprofessional behavior and antiscientific attitudes among psychologists themselves contribute greatly to the discipline's image problem. In trying to provide more balance here, I have relied heavily upon the work of Robyn Dawes (1994) and Scott Lilienfeld (2012). If anyone doubts that psychologists themselves have contributed greatly to the field's dilemmas, they need only read the work of these two scholars. Dawes does not hesitate to air psychology's dirty linen and, at the same time, to argue that the scientific attitude toward human problems that is at the heart of the true discipline of psychology is of great utility to society (although its potential is still largely untapped). For example, Dawes argued that "there really is a science of psychology that has been developed with much work by many people over many years, but it is being increasingly ignored, derogated, and contradicted by the behavior of professionals—who, of course, give lip service to its existence" (1994, p. vii). Likewise, Lilienfeld (2012) argues that "psychologists should curb the facile temptation to place all of the blame for their field's tarnished image on widespread public misunderstanding. At least some of psychology's negative reputation appears to be deserved, as large pockets of the field, especially those pertaining to psychotherapy, remain mired in unscientific practices" (pp. 122–123).

What Dawes and Lilienfeld are objecting to is that the field of psychology justifies licensure requirements based on the scientific status of psychology and then uses licensure to protect the unscientific behavior of psychological practitioners. For example, one thing that a well-trained psychologist should know is that we can be reasonably confident only in aggregate predictions. By contrast, predicting the behavior of particular individuals is fraught with uncertainty (see Chapters 10 and 11) and is something no competent psychologist should attempt without the strongest of caveats, if at all. As Dawes (1994) noted,

> A mental health expert who expresses a confident opinion about the proba-ble future behavior of a single individual (for example, to engage in violent acts) is by definition incompetent, because the research has demonstrated that neither a mental health expert nor anyone else can make such a prediction with accuracy sufficient to warrant much confidence. (Professionals often state that their professional role "requires" them to make such judgments, however much they personally appreciate the uncertainty involved. No, they are not required—they volunteer.) (p. vii)

In short, the American Psychological Association has fostered an ethos surrounding clinical psychology that suggests that psychologists can be trained to acquire an "intuitive insight" into the behavior of individual people that the research evidence does not support. When pushed to defend licensure requirements as anything more than restraint of trade, however, the organization uses its scientific credentials as a weapon (one president of the APA, defending the organization from attack, said "Our scientific base is what sets us apart from the social workers, the counselors, and the Gypsies"; Dawes, 1994, p. 21). But the very methods that the field holds up to justify its scientific status have revealed that the implication that licensed psycholo-gists have a unique "clinical insight" is false. It is such intellectual duplicity on the part of the APA that spawned Dawes's work and that in part led to the formation of the Association for Psychological Science in the 1980s by psychologists tired of an APA that was more concerned about Blue Cross payments than with science.

Scott Lilienfeld (1998), the winner of the David Shakow Award for early career contributions to clinical psychology, reiterated all of these points in his award acceptance speech, warning that "we in clinical psychology seem to have shown surprisingly little interest in doing much about the problem of pseudoscience that has been festering in our own backyards" (p. 3). Lilienfeld (1998) listed several categories of pseudosciences that have flourished in clinical psychology during the 1990s, including unvalidated and bizarre treatments for trauma; demonstrably ineffective treatments for autism such as facilitated communication (see Chapter 6); the continued use of inadequately validated assessment instruments (e.g., many projective tests); subliminal self-help tapes; and use of highly suggestive therapeutic techniques to unearth memories of child abuse.

Lilienfeld quoted noted clinical researcher Paul Meehl (1993), "If we do not clean up our clinical act and provide our students with role models of scientific thinking, outsiders will do it for us" (p. 728). Meehl was here referring to the tendency—discussed in Chapter 11— for clinicians to imply, contrary to the empirical evidence, that they have "special" knowledge of people that goes beyond general behavioral trends that are publicly available as replicable scientific knowledge. Arguing that the clinical psychologist must, if anything, be more concerned that knowledge be empirically and publicly verified, Meehl (1993) warns that "it is absurd, as well as arrogant, to pretend that acquiring a PhD somehow immunizes me from the errors of sampling, perception, recording, retention, retrieval, and inference to which the human mind is subject" (p. 728).

Questionable practices still plague the field of clinical psychology, however. For example, the critical-incident stress debriefing has, in many localities, become a standard procedure used to treat witnesses to catastrophic and traumatic events such as bombings, shootings, combat, terrorism, and earthquakes (Groopman, 2004; McNally, Bryant, & Ehlers, 2003). The debriefing procedure involves having the client "talk about the event and ventilate their emotions, especially in the company of peers who have experienced the same incident" (McNally et al., 2003, p. 56), and its purpose is to reduce the incidence of posttraumatic stress disorders (PTSDs). The majority of debriefed clients report that the experience was helpful. Of course, no one who has read this book will find that evidence convincing (recall the discussion of placebo effects in Chapter 4). A control group (which is not given the critical-incident stress debriefing) is obviously needed. In fact, "the vast majority trauma survivors recover from initial posttrauma reactions without professional help" (McNally et al., 2003, p. 45), so it clearly needs to be demonstrated that the recovery rate is higher when the critical-incident stress debriefing is used. Properly controlled studies have shown that this is not the case (Groopman, 2004; McNally et al., 2003), yet the procedure continues to be used.

Emery, Otto, and O'Donohue (2005), in a recent review of a large body of evidence, have shown that, likewise, the clinical psychology surrounding child custody evaluations is filled with pseudoscience (Novotney, 2008). For example, they describe several assessment instruments used by clinical psychologists purportedly to assess children's best interests in these custody disputes. After reviewing several of these instruments—for example, scales purporting to assess the perception of relationships and parental awareness skills—Emery et al. (2005) conclude that none of them have demonstrated reliability or validity. They note that "no study examining the properties of these measures has ever been published in a peer-reviewed journal—an essential criterion for science" (p. 8) and conclude that "our bottom-line evaluation of these measures is a harsh one: these measures assess ill-defined constructs, and they do so poorly, leaving no scientific justification for their use in child custody evaluations" (p. 7).

Emery et al. (2005) point out that it is not just the instruments in child custody evaluations that are often faulty, but the very concepts used by clinical psychologists. Emery et al. give as one example so-called parental alienation syndrome. It is based on the "clinical experience" of just a single person and has no validation in convergent scientific research, but it is bandied about by clinical psychologists in custody evaluations as if it were a truly scientific construct. It is likewise with some well-known measures for assessing sex offenders. Clinical psychologists continue to use them in spite of their lack of predictive validity—the measures have no demonstrated ability to differentially predict the probability of re-offense (Ewing, 2006). Similarly, the instrument most used by clinicians to predict future violence among psychopathic individuals does not actually have the accuracy that is claimed for it (Skeem, Polaschek, Patrick, & Lilienfeld, 2011; Yang, Wong, & Coid, 2010).

Things may be looking up, however. In 2002, a new journal was started: *The Scientific Review of Mental Health Practice* (Lilienfeld, 2002, 2007; see also, Lilienfeld et al., 2008). The journal is dedicated to research that tries to distinguish scientific from pseudoscientific treatments, and it has been endorsed by the Council for Scientific Mental Health Practice. Even more heartening are indications that at least some psychological organizations are showing the fortitude required to police clinical practice and to rid psychological practice of its ultimately destructive "anything goes" attitude. Lilienfeld and Lohr (2000) report on how the Arizona Board of Psychological Examiners sanctioned a psychologist who attempted to treat phobias with a pseudoscientific treatment that involved tapping body parts in a predetermined order. Needless to say, there are no controlled studies of the efficacy of this treatment, and the Arizona Board ordered the therapist to stop using it and put him on probation—an all too rare example of a psychological organization policing the pseudoscience that is practiced by its clinical members.

The Association for Psychological Science commissioned an important report on the state of clinical psychology in 2009, which concluded that "clinical psychology resembles medicine at a point in its history when practitioners were operating in a largely prescientific manner. Prior to the scientific reform of medicine in the early 1900s, physicians typically shared the attitudes of many of today's clinical psychologists, such as valuing personal experience over scientific research.…Substantial evidence shows that many clinical psychology doctoral training programs, especially PsyD and for-profit programs, do not uphold high standards for graduate admission, have high student–faculty ratios, de-emphasize science in their training, and produce students who fail to apply or generate scientific knowledge" (Baker, McFall, & Shoham, 2009, p. 67). This report received considerable publicity, but some of the discussion in the general media confused the issue as much as clarified it. An otherwise accurate report in *Newsweek* magazine was unfortunately titled "Ignoring the Evidence: Why Do Psychologists Reject Science?" (Begley, 2009). The title mistakenly implies that it is *all* psychology that rejects science, rather than the problematic subfield of clinical psychology. This confusing title is bitterly ironic given that the logic of the APS report was that of all the rest of psychology, which *does* adhere to the scientific method, speaking in distress to just *one* of its many subfields that does not (clinical psychology).

In short, psychology has a kind of Jekyll and Hyde personality. Extremely rigorous science exists right alongside pseudoscientific and antiscientific attitudes. This Jekyll and Hyde aspect of the discipline was clearly apparent in the recovered-memory–false-memory debate of the last two decades (Brainerd & Reyna, 2005; Gardner, 2006; Lilienfeld, 2007; Loftus & Guyer, 2002; McHugh, 2008). Many cases were reported of individuals who had claimed to remember instances of child abuse that had taken place decades earlier but had been forgotten. Many of these memories occurred in the context of therapeutic interventions. It is clear that some of these memories were induced by the therapy itself (Gardner, 2006; Lilienfeld, 2007; Loftus & Guyer, 2002; Lynn, Loftus, Lilienfeld, & Lock, 2003). Some people insisted that such memories were never to be trusted; others insisted that they were always to be trusted. In the emotionally charged atmosphere of such an explosive social issue, psychologists provided some of the more balanced commentary and, most important, some of the more dispassionate empirical evidence on the issue of recovered or false memories (Brainerd & Reyna, 2005; McNally & Geraerts, 2009; Moore & Zoellner, 2007).

Here we have the Jekyll and Hyde feature of psychology in full-blown form. Some of the cases of therapeutically induced false memories—and, hence, of the controversial phenomenon itself—were caused by incompetent and scientifically ignorant therapists who were psychologists. On the other hand, whatever partial resolution of the controversy we do have is in large part due to the painstaking efforts of research psychologists who studied the relevant phenomena empirically. Finally, I must make clear that I do not wish to imply that it is only psychology that is beset with such problems. Indeed, medicine has had to dragged—kicking and screaming—toward a fully evidence-based approach, and it is not there yet (Gawande, 2010; Kenney, 2008).

I hope this section has helped to dispel the notion that I wish to "let psychology off the hook" with the use of my Rodney Dangerfield joke to title this chapter. In his book on research methods, psychologist Douglas Mook (2001) referred to my use of the Dangerfield joke and commented that "often indeed, psychology gets no respect; but sometimes, too, it is respected more than is warranted and for the wrong reasons" (p. 473). I agree completely with this sentiment. Mook is right that the student of psychology needs to understand the paradoxes that surround the discipline. As I have presented it in this book, as the science of human behavior, the discipline of psychology often gets too little respect. But the face that psychology often presents to the public—that of a clinician claiming "unique" insight into people that is not grounded in research evidence—often gets too much respect. The discipline is often represented to the public by segments of psychology that do not respect its unique defining feature—that it validates statements about human behavior by employing the methods of science.

Isn't Everyone a Psychologist? Implicit Theories of Behavior

We all have theories about human behavior. It is hard to see how we could get through life if we did not. In this sense, we are all psychologists. It is very important, though, to distinguish between this individual psychology and the type of knowledge produced by the science of psychology. The distinction is critical because the two are often deliberately confused in popular writings about psychology, as we shall see.

In what ways is our personal psychological knowledge different from the knowledge gained from a scientific study of behavior? We have already discussed several. Much of our personal psychological knowledge is recipe knowledge. We do certain things because we think they will lead others to behave in a certain way. We behave in particular ways because we think that certain behavior will help us achieve our goals. But it is not the mere presence of recipe knowledge that distinguishes personal psychology from scientific psychology (which also contains recipe knowledge). The main difference here is that the science of psychology seeks to validate its recipe knowledge empirically.

Scientific evaluation is systematic and controlled in ways that individual validation procedures can never be. Indeed, psychological research on decision making has indicated that humans have difficulty detecting correlations in their behavioral environment that run counter to their accepted beliefs (see Baron, 2008; Stanovich, 2009). We see what we want to see. Psychologists have uncovered many of the reasons why, but they need not concern us here. Even if we wanted to evaluate personal recipe knowledge on an individual basis, built-in biases that make us less than adequate observers of behavioral phenomena would make it extremely difficult. The scientific method has evolved to avoid the biases of any single human observer. The implication here is a simple one. The recipe knowledge generated by the science of psychology is more likely to be accurate because it has undergone validation procedures more stringent than those to which personal recipe knowledge is exposed.

As discussed throughout this book, the differences between personal and scientific psychologies go beyond the validation of recipe knowledge. Science always aspires to more than recipe knowledge of the natural world. Scientists seek more general, underlying principles that explain why the recipes work. However, the personal psychologies of some people *are* similar to scientific psychology in seeking more basic psychological principles and theories. These personal theories, though, often depart from scientific theories in important ways. We have already mentioned that they are often unfalsifiable. Rather than being coherently constructed, many people's personal psychological theories are merely a mixture of platitudes and clichés, often mutually contradictory, that are used on the appropriate occasion. They reassure people that an explanation does exist and, furthermore, that the danger of a seriously contradictory event—one that would deeply shake the foundations of a person's beliefs—is unlikely to occur. As discussed in Chapter 2, although these theories may indeed be comforting, comfort is all that theories constructed in this way provide. In explaining everything post hoc, these theories predict nothing. By making no predictions, they tell us nothing. Theories in the discipline of psychology must meet the falsifiability criterion, and in doing so, they depart from the personal psychological theories of many laypeople. Theories in psychology can be proved wrong, and, therefore, they contain a mechanism for growth and advancement that is missing from many personal theories.

The Source of Resistance to Scientific Psychology

For the reasons we just discussed, it is important not to confuse the idea of a personal psychological theory with the knowledge generated by the science of psychology. Such a confusion is often deliberately fostered to undermine the status of psychology in the public mind. The idea that "everyone's a psychologist" is true if it is understood to mean simply that we all have implicit psychological theories. But it is often subtly distorted to imply that psychology is not a science.

We discussed in Chapter 1 why the idea of a scientific psychology is threatening to some people. A maturing science of behavior will change the kinds of individuals, groups, and organizations that serve as sources of psychological information. It is natural that individuals who have long served as commentators on human psychology and behavior will resist any threatened reduction in their authoritative role. Chapter 1 described how the advance of science has continually usurped the authority of other groups to make claims about the nature of the world. The movement of the planets, the nature of matter, and the causes of disease were all once the provinces of theologians, philosophers, and generalist writers. Astronomy, physics, medicine, genetics, and other sciences have gradually wrested these topics away and placed them squarely within the domain of the scientific specialist.

Many religions, for example, have gradually evolved away from claiming special knowledge of the structure of the universe. The titanic battles between science and religion have passed into history, with the exception of some localized flare-ups such as the creationism issue. Scientists uncover the structure of the natural world. Many religions provide commentary on the implications of the uses of these discoveries, but they no longer contest with scientists for the right to determine what the discoveries are. The right to adjudicate claims about the nature of the world has unquestionably passed to scientists.

Writer Natalie Angier (2007) reminds us that many years ago when lightening would hit the wooden towers of churches and burn them down, the clergy and the populace would engage in an intense debate about whether this was a sign of "the vengeance of God." However, she reminds us that "in the eighteenth century, Benjamin Franklin determined that lightening was an electric rather than an ecclesiastic phenomenon. He recommended that conducting rods be installed on all spires and rooftops, and the debates over the lightening bolts vanished" (p. 26).

The issue, then, is the changing criteria of belief evaluation. Few newspaper editorials ever come out with strong stands on the composition of the rings of Saturn. Why? No censor would prevent such an editorial. Clearly the reason it is not written is that it would be futile. Society knows that scientists, not editorial writers, determine such things. Only a hundred years ago, newspapers and preachers in the pulpit did comment vociferously on the origins of species in the animal kingdom. These comments have largely disappeared because science has destroyed the conditions that would allow them to be believed by rational thinkers. Psychology threatens to destroy those conditions in another large domain of nature.

Some people find it difficult to accept such a state of affairs when it comes to psychology. They cling tenaciously to their right to declare their own opinions about human behavior even when these opinions contradict the facts. Of course, the correct term here is really not "right," because, obviously, in a free society, everyone has the *right* to voice opinions, regardless of their accuracy. It is important to understand that what many people want is much *more* than simply the right to declare their opinions about human behavior. What they really want is *the conditions that are necessary for what they say to be believed.* When they make a statement about human psychology, they want the environment to be conducive to the acceptance of their beliefs. This is the reason that there are always proponents of the "anything-goes" view of psychology, that is, the idea that psychological claims cannot be decided by empirical means and are simply a matter of opinion. But science is always a threat to the "anything-goes" view, because it has a set of strict requirements for determining whether a knowledge claim is to be believed. Anything does not go in science. This ability to rule out false theories and facts accounts for scientific progress.

In short, a lot of the resistance to scientific psychology is due to what might be termed "conflict of interest." As discussed in earlier chapters, many pseudosciences are multimillion-dollar industries that thrive on the fact that the public is unaware that statements about behavior can be empirically tested (there are 20 times more astrologers in the United States than astronomers; Gilovich, 1991, p. 2). The public is also unaware that many of the claims that are the basis of these industries (such as astrological prediction, subliminal weight loss, biorhythms, facilitated communication, and psychic surgery) have been tested and found to be false. Medical quackery costs the public more than is spent on legitimate medical research (Eisenberg et al., 1993; Mielczarek & Engler, 2012).

How do we recognize pseudoscientific claims? Clinical psychologist Scott Lilienfeld (2005, p. 40) gives us a list of things to watch for that could serve as a summary of many of the things that have covered in this book. Pseudoscientific claims tend to be characterized by

- A tendency to invoke ad hoc hypotheses as a means of immunizing claims from falsification
- An emphasis on confirmation rather than refutation
- A tendency to place the burden of proof on skeptics, not proponents, of claims
- Excessive reliance on anecdotal and testimonial evidence to substantiate claims
- Evasion of the scrutiny afforded by peer review
- Failure to build on existing scientific knowledge (lack of connectivity)

True scientists are at pains to emphasize these criteria rather than to avoid them. For example, three of the scientists who had major roles in introducing the concept of emotional intelligence (EI) into psychology became worried about the media, clinicians, and even other researchers at times using the concept in unscientific ways. They wrote an article specifically directing others to invoke the types of scientific criteria listed above and discussed in this book: "In our opinion, the journalistic popularizations of EI frequently employ inadequate and overly broad definitions of EI, implausible claims, and misunderstandings of the concepts and research more generally. We urge researchers and practitioners alike to refer to the scientific literature on emotions, intelligence, and emotional intelligence to guide their thinking. Simply put, researchers need to cite the research literature rather than journalistic renderings of scientific concepts, which serve a different purpose" (Mayer, Salovey, & Caruso, 2008, pp. 513–514).

By contrast, many purveyors of pseudosciences and bogus therapies depend on an atmosphere of "anything goes" surrounding psychology.

It provides a perfect environment for feeding on public gullibility, because the public has no consumer protection if anything goes. As attorney Peter Huber (1990) argued, "[At] the fringes of science and beyond...assorted believers in homeopathic medicine and the curative powers of crystals and pyramids...must discredit orthodox science to build their own cases for unorthodox nostrums" (p. 97). Those selling pseudoscience have a vested interest in obscuring the fact that there are mechanisms for testing behavioral claims.

As biologist Michael Ghiselin (1989) warned, "What is going on here is quite straightforward. People are trying to sell a given point of view. Those who know how to evaluate the product are not the same as those to whom it is being marketed" (p. 139). In the domain of behavioral claims and therapies, psychologists are the ones who "know how to evaluate the product." This is why the pseudoscience industry continues to oppose the authority of scientific psychology to evaluate behavioral claims. However, the purveyors of pseudoscience often do not need to do direct battle with psychology. They simply do an end run around psychology and go straight to the media with their claims. The media make it very easy for cranks, quacks, and pseudoscientists to do an end run around scientific psychology. The talk shows that have inundated the airwaves do not ask the guests to produce their bibliographies of scientific research. If these guests are "interesting," they are simply put on the show. And the Internet is no better. Anyone can put up a website claiming—and selling—anything. Websites are not peer reviewed, to say the least!

Folk wisdom often contains a lot of wishful thinking: People want to believe that the world is the way they wish it to be rather than the way it is. Science often has the unenviable task of having to tell the public that the nature of the world is somewhat different from how they wish it to be ("No, that fast-food lunch is *not* good for your health"). The media, which could help in this situation (by telling people what is true rather than what they want to hear), only make it worse with their focus on what will "entertain" rather than on what will inform.

Science, then, does rule out the special-knowledge claims of those proposing statements that do not meet the necessary tests. The courts rule out claims of special knowledge too. In ruling on a famous case known as *Daubert vs. Merrell Dow*, the Supreme Court established when expert testimony could be presented in court—that is, what makes expert testimony *expert!* The Court identified four factors that judges should consider when deliberating about whether to allow expert testimony: (a) the "testability" of the theoretical basis for the opinion; (b) the error rates associated with the approach, if known; (c) whether the technique or approach on which the opinion is based has been subjected to peer review; and (d) whether the technique or approach is generally accepted in the relevant scientific community (Emery et al., 2005; Michaels, 2008). The four criteria map into major topics in this book: (a) falsifiability; (b) probabilistic prediction; (c) public knowledge subjected to peer review; and (d) scientific knowledge based on convergence and consensus. The courts are like science in ruling out claims of special knowledge, intuition, and testimonials as adequate evidence.

In this book, we have briefly touched on what are considered adequate and inadequate tests in science. Introspection, personal experience, and testimonials are all considered inadequate tests of claims about the nature of human behavior. Thus, it should not be surprising that conflict arises because these are precisely the types of evidence that nonpsychologist commentators have been using to support their statements about human behavior since long before a discipline of psychology existed.

However, it should not be thought that I am recommending a sour, spoilsport role for the science of psychology. Quite the contrary. The actual findings of legitimate psychology are vastly more interesting and exciting than the repetitious gee-whiz pseudoscience of the media. Furthermore, it should not be thought that scientists are against fantasy and imagination. However, we want fancy and fantasy when we go to the movies or the theater—not when we go to the doctor's office, buy insurance, register our children for child care, fly in an airplane, or have our car serviced. We could add to this list going to a psychotherapist, having our learning-disabled child tested by a school psychologist, or taking a friend to suicide-prevention counseling at the university psychology clinic. Psychology, like other sciences, must remove fantasy, unfounded opinion, "common sense," commercial advertising claims, the advice of gurus, testimonials, and wishful thinking from its search for the truth.

It is difficult for a science to have to tell parts of society that their thoughts and opinions are needed—but not here. Psychology is the latest of the sciences to be in this delicate position. The difference in time period for psychology, however, is relevant. Most sciences came of age during periods of elite control of the structures of society, when the opinion of the ordinary person made no difference. Psychology, on the other hand, is emerging in a media age of democracy and ignores public opinion at its own peril. Many psychologists are now taking greater pains to remedy the discipline's lamentable record in public communication. As more psychologists take on a public communication role, the conflicts with those who confuse a personal psychology with scientific psychology are bound to increase.

Not everyone is a physicist, even though we all hold intuitive physical theories. But in giving up the claim that our personal physical theories must usurp scientific physics, we make way for a true science of the physical universe whose theories, because science is public, will be available to us all. Likewise, everyone is not a psychologist. But the facts and theories uncovered by the science of psychology are available to be put to practical ends and to enrich the understanding of all of us.

The Final Word

We are now at the end of our sketch of how to think straight about psychology. It is a rough sketch, but it can be of considerable help in comprehending how the discipline of psychology works and in evaluating new psychological claims. Our sketch has revealed the following:

1. Psychology progresses by investigating solvable empirical problems. This progress is uneven because psychology is composed of many different subareas, and the problems in some areas are more difficult than in others.
2. Psychologists propose falsifiable theories to explain the findings that they uncover.
3. The concepts in the theories are operationally defined, and these definitions evolve as evidence accumulates.
4. These theories are tested by means of systematic empiricism, and the data obtained are in the public domain, in the sense that they are presented in a manner that allows replication and criticism by other scientists.
5. The data and theories of psychologists are in the public domain only after publication in peer-reviewed scientific journals.
6. What makes empiricism systematic is that it strives for the logic of control and manipulation that characterizes a true experiment.
7. Psychologists use many different methods to arrive at their conclusions, and the strengths and weaknesses of these methods vary.
8. The behavioral principles that are eventually uncovered are almost always probabilistic relationships.
9. Most often, knowledge is acquired only after a slow accumulation of data from many experiments each containing flaws but nonetheless converging on a common conclusion.

The most exciting endeavor in science today is the quest to understand the nature of human behavior. By learning the concepts in this book you become able to follow this quest and perhaps, indeed, become a part of it.

References

Abrami, P., Bernard, R., Borokhovski, E., Wade, A., Surkes, M., Tamim, R., & Zhang, D. (2008). Instructional interventions affecting critical thinking skills and dispositions: A stage 1 meta-analysis. *Review of Educational Research, 78,* 1102–1134.

Adler, D. (2009). *Snap judgment.* New York: Financial Times Press.

Adler, J. (2006, November 6). Plotting Pluto's comeback. *Newsweek,* pp. 60–61.

American Psychiatric Association. (2000). *Diagnostic and statistical manual of mental disorders* (4th ed.; Text Revision). Washington, DC: Author.

Anderson, C. A., & Anderson, K. B. (1996). Violent crime rate studies in philosophical context: A destructive testing approach to heat and Southern culture of violence effects. *Journal of Personality and Social Psychology, 70,* 740–756.

Anderson, C. A., & Huesmann, L. R. (2005). The evidence that media violence stimulates aggression in young viewers remains 'unequivocal.' *APS Observer, 18*(10), 7.

Angell, M., & Kassirer, J. P. (1998). Alternative medicine: The risks of untested and unregulated remedies. *The New England Journal of Medicine, 339*(12), 839–841.

Angier, N. (2007). *The canon: A whirligig tour of the beautiful basics of science.* New York: Mariner Books.

Ariely, D. (2008). *Predictably irrational.* New York: HarperCollins.

Asimov, I. (1989). The relativity of wrong. *Skeptical Inquirer, 14,* 35–44.

Associated Press. (2007, April 24). *Can aspirin prevent cancer? The answer is not clear.*

Associated Press. (2010, September 7). Safety board renews call for young to fly in own seats. *Wall Street Journal,* A14.

Attari, S. Z., DeKay, M. L., Davidson, C. I., & Bruine de Bruin, W. (2010). Public perceptions of energy consumption and savings. *Proceedings of the National Academy of Sciences, 107,* 16054–16059.

Ayres, I. (2007). *Super crunchers: Why thinking by numbers is the new way to be smart.* New York: Bantam Books.

Azar, B. (1999, November). Crowder mixes theories with humility. *APA Monitor,* p. 18.

Baker, T. B., McFall, R. M., & Shoham, V. (2009). Current status and future prospects of clinical psychology: Toward a scientifically principled approach to mental and behavioral health care. *Psychological Science in the Public Interest, 9,* 67–103.

Baker, T. B., & Velez, W. (1996). Access to and opportunity in postsecondary education in the united states: A review. *Sociology of Education, 69,* 82–101.

Banerjee, A., & Duflo, E. (2009). The experimental approach to development economics. *Annual Review of Economics, 1,* 151–178.

Barnes, R., Keilholtz, L., & Alberstadt, A. (2008). Creationism and evolution beliefs among college students. *Skeptic, 14*(3), 13–16.

Barnett, A. (2011, December 20). Is 27 really a dangerous age for famous musicians? A retrospective cohort study. *British Medical Journal.* Retrieved December 28, 2011, from http://www.bmj.com/press-releases/2011/12/20/27-really-dangerous-age-famous-musicians-retrospective-cohort-study

Baron, J. (1998). *Judgment misguided: Intuition and error in public decision making.* New York: Oxford University Press.

Baron, J. (2008). *Thinking and deciding* (4th ed.). Cambridge, MA: Cambridge University Press.

Baron-Cohen, S. (2005). *Autism: The facts.* Oxford: Oxford University Press.

Bartels, L. M. (2008). *Unequal democracy: The political economy of the new gilded age.* Princeton, NJ: Princeton University Press.

Bartoshuk, L. (2009, September). Spicing up psychological science. *APS Observer, 22,* 3–4.

Baumeister, R. F., Campbell, J. D., Krueger, J. I., & Vohs, K. D. (2003). Does high self-esteem cause better performance, interpersonal success, happiness, or healthier lifestyles? *Psychological Science in the Public Interest, 4,* 1–44.

Baumeister, R. F., Campbell, J. D., Krueger, J. I., & Vohs, K. D. (2005). Exploding the self-esteem myth. *Scientific American, 292*(1), 84–91.

Baumeister, R. F., Vohs, K. D., & Funder, D. C. (2007). Psychology as the science of self-reports and finger movements. *Perspectives on Psychological Science, 2,* 396–403.

Beck, D. M. (2010). The appeal of the brain in the popular press. *Perspectives on Psychological Science, 5,* 762–766.

Beck, M. (2008, November 4). And you thought the debate over fluoridation was settled. *Wall Street Journal,* p. D1.

Begley, S. (2008, November 3). Why we believe. *Newsweek,* pp. 56–60.

Begley, S. (2009, October 12). Ignoring the evidence: Why do psychologists reject science? *Newsweek,* p. 30.

Begley, S. (2010, February 8). The depressing news about antidepressants. *Newsweek,* pp. 34–42.

Bem, D. (2011). Feeling the future: Experimental evidence for anomalous retroactive influences on cognition and affect. *Journal of Personality and Social Psychology, 100,* 1–19.

Benedetti, F., Carlino, E., & Pollo, A. (2011). How placebos change the patient's brain. *Neuropsychopharmacology, 36,* 339–354.

Benjamin, L. T. (2004). Behavioral science and the Nobel Prize: A history. *American Psychologist, 58,* 731–741.

Benson, E. S. (2006a, June). All that's gold does not glitter: How the Golden Fleece tarnished psychological science. *APS Observer, 19,* 12–19.

Benson, E. S. (2006b, January). Emotion, perception, cognition—it's all part of really intelligent design. *APS Observer, 19,* 22–24.

Benson, H., et al. (2006). Study of the therapeutic effects of intercessory prayer in cardiac bypass patients. *American Heart Journal, 151,* 934–942.

Berkowitz, L., & Donnerstein, E. (1982). External validity is more than skin deep. *American Psychologist, 37,* 245–257.

Berliner, D. C., & Biddle, B. (1995). *The manufactured crisis: Myths, fraud, and the attack on America's public schools.* Reading, MA: Addison-Wesley.

Bernstein, L. (2009, November 4). Stretching debate continues. *The Oregonian,* p. C2.

Bilmes, L. J., & Stiglitz, J. E. (2009, January). The $10 trillion hangover. *Harper's Magazine, 318,* 31–35.

Binga, T. (2009). Skeptical books for children and young adults. *Skeptical Inquirer, 33*(6), 43–44.

Birnbaum, M. H. (1999). Testing critical properties of decision making on the Internet. *Psychological Science, 10,* 399–407.

Birnbaum, M. H. (2004). Human research and data collection via the internet. *Annual Review of Psychology, 55,* 803–832.

Bjorklund, D. F. (2011). *Children's thinking: Cognitive development and individual differences* (5th ed.). Stamford, CT: Wadsworth.

Blass, T. (2004). *The man who shocked the world: The life and legacy of Stanley Milgram.* New York: Basic Books.

Blastland, M., & Dilnot, A. (2009). *The numbers game: The commonsense guide to understanding numbers in the news, in politics, and in life.* New York: Gotham Books.

Bloom, P., & Weisberg, D. S. (2007). Childhood origins of adult resistance to science. *Science, 306,* 996–997.

Bluming, A., & Tavris, C. (2009). Hormone replacement therapy: Real concerns and false alarms. *The Cancer Journal, 15,* 93–104.

Bogle, J. C. (2010). *Common sense on mutual funds.* Hoboken, NJ: John Wiley.

Borenstein, M., Hedges, L. V., Higgins, J., & Rothstein, H. (2009). *Introduction to meta-analysis* (Vol. 1). Hoboken, NJ: Wiley.

Bower, B. (2009, June 20). Think like a scientist. *Science News, 175,* 20–23.

Boyd, R. (2008, February 7). Do people only use 10 percent of their brains? *Scientific American.* Retrieved November 17, 2009, from http://www.sciam.com/article.cfm?id=people-only-use-10-percent-of-brain on

Boyer, P. (2010, September 6). The covenant. *The New Yorker,* pp. 60–69.

Brainerd, C. J., & Reyna, V. F. (2005). *The science of false memory.* Oxford: Oxford University Press.

Breitmeyer, B. J., & Ramey, C. T. (1986). Biological nonoptimality and quality of postnatal environment as codeterminants of intellectual development. *Child Development, 57,* 1151–1165.

Broadbent, D. E. (1958). *Perception and communication.* New York: Pergamon Press.

Broadbent, D. E. (1973). *In defense of empirical psychology.* London: Methuen.

Brody, J. E. (2008, December 10). Weight-loss guides without gimmicks. *New York Times,* p. D7.

Brody, J. E. (2011, September 13). Attacking the obesity epidemic by first figuring out its cause. *New York Times,* p. D7.

Brody, J. E. (2012, January 24). Dental exam went well? Thank fluoride. *New York Times,* p. D7.

Bronfenbrenner, U., & Mahoney, M. (1975). The structure and verification of hypotheses. In U. Bronfenbrenner & M. Mahoney (Eds.), *Influence on human development.* Hinsdale, IL: Dryden.

Bronowski, J. (1956). *Science and human values.* New York: Harper & Row.

Bronowski, J. (1973). *The ascent of man.* Boston: Little, Brown.

Bronowski, J. (1974). Science, poetry, and human specificity. *American Scholar, 43,* 386–404.

Bronowski, J. (1977). *A sense of the future.* Cambridge, MA: MIT Press.

Bronowski, J. (1978a). *The common sense of science.* Cambridge, MA: Harvard University Press.

Bronowski, J. (1978b). *Magic, science, and civilization.* New York: Columbia University Press.

Bronson, P., & Merryman, A. (2009). *Nurtureshock.* New York: Twelve.

Brooks, A. C. (2008). *Gross national happiness.* New York: Basic Books.

Brown, M. (2010). *How I killed Pluto and why it had it coming.* New York: Spiegel & Grau.

Brownell, K. D. (2011, July). Is there the courage to change America's diet? *APS Observer, 24,* 15–16.

Bruck, M., & Ceci, S. (2004). Forensic developmental psychology: Unveiling four common misconceptions. *Current Directions in Psychological Science, 13,* 229–232.

Bryan, C., Walton, G. M., Rogers, T., & Dweck, C. S. (2011). Motivating voter turnout by invoking the self. *Proceedings of the National Academy of Sciences,* 12653–12656.

Buchtel, E. E., & Norenzayan, A. (2009). Thinking across cultures: Implications for dual processes. In J. S. B. T. Evans & K. Frankish (Eds.), *In two minds: Dual processes and beyond.* Oxford: Oxford University Press.

Buckley, C. (2010, December 9). To test housing program, some are denied aid. *New York Times,* pp. A1–A4.

Buhle, J., Stevens, B., Friedman, J., & Wager, T. (2012). Distraction and placebo: Two separate routes to pain control. *Psychological Science, 23,* 1–8.

Burton, R. (2008). *On being certain.* New York: St. Martin's Press.

Buss, D. M. (Ed.). (2005). *The handbook of evolutionary psychology.* Hoboken, NJ: John Wiley.

Buss, D. M. (2011). *Evolutionary psychology: The new science of the mind* (4th ed.). Boston: Allyn and Bacon.

Cacioppo, J. T. (2007a). Psychology is a hub science. *APS Observer, 20,* 5, 42.

Cacioppo, J. T. (2007b). The structure of psychology. *APS Observer, 20,* 3, 50.

Card, N. A. (2011). *Applied meta-analysis for social science research.* New York: Guilford.

Carnagey, N. L., Anderson, C. A., & Bartholow, B. D. (2007). Media violence and social neuroscience: New questions and new opportunities. *Current Directions in Psychological Science, 16,* 178–182.

Carnoy, M., Jacobsen, R., Mishel, L., & Rothstein, R. (2005). *The charter school dust-up: Examining the evidence on enrollment and achievement.* New York: Teachers College Press.

Cartwright, J. (2008). *Evolution and human behavior* (2nd ed.). Cambridge, MA: MIT Press.

Chamberlin, J. (2010, November). Type cast. *APA Monitor,* pp. 28–30.

Chernev, A. (2011). The dieter's paradox. *Journal of Consumer Psychology, 21,* 178–183.

Chida, Y., & Hamer, M. (2008). Chronic psychosocial factors and acute physiological responses to laboratory-induced stress in healthy populations: A quantitative review of 30 years of investigations. *Psychological Bulletin, 134,* 829–885.

Cho, H. J., Hotopf, M., & Wessely, S. (2005). The placebo response in the treatment of chronic fatigue syndrome: A systematic review and meta-analysis. *Psychosomatic Medicine, 67,* 301–313.

Churchland, P. M. (1988). *Matter and consciousness* (Rev. ed.). Cambridge, MA: MIT Press.

Claridge, G., Clark, K., Powney, E., & Hassan, E. (2008). Schizotypy and the Barnum Effect. *Personality and Individual Differences, 44,* 436–444.

Claypool, H., Hall, C., Mackie, D., & Garcia-Marques, T. (2008). Positive mood, attribution, and the illusion of familiarity. *Journal of Experimental Social Psychology, 44,* 721–728.

Cleeremans, A. (2010). The grand challenge for psychology: Integrate and fire! *APS Observer, 23*(8), 15–17.

CNN.com (2004, May 1). Nightline airs war dead amid controversy. Retrieved December 30, 2005, from http://www.cnn.com/2004/SHOWBIZ/TV/05/01/abc.nightline/

Cohen, A. (2008, December 29). Four decades after Milgram, we're still willing to inflict pain. *New York Times,* p. A22.

Cohen, P. (2009, October 20). Field study: Just how relevant is political science? *New York Times,* pp. C1–C7.

Conkle, A., & West, C. (2008, June). Psychology on the road. *APS Observer, 21,* pp. 18–23.

Cozby, P. C. (2012). *Methods in behavioral research* (11th ed.). New York: McGraw-Hill.

Croswell, J., et al. (2009). Cumulative incidence of false-positive results in repeated, multimodal cancer screening. *Annals of Family Medicine, 7,* 212–222.

Currier, J. M., Neimeyer, R., & Berman, J. (2008). The effectiveness of psychotherapeutic interventions for bereaved persons: A comprehensive quantitative review. *Psychological Bulletin, 134,* 648–661.

Dacey, A. (2008). *The secular conscience.* Amherst, NY: Prometheus Books.

Dawes, R. M. (1994). *House of cards: Psychology and psychotherapy built on myth.* New York: Free Press.

Dawes, R. M., Faust, D., & Meehl, P. E. (1989). Clinical versus actuarial judgment. *Science, 243,* 1668–1673.

Dawkins, R. (2010). *The greatest show on earth.* New York: Free Press.

Dawkins, R. (2012). *The magic of reality: How we know what's really true.* New York: Free Press.

Deangelis, T. (2010, November). Getting research into the real world. *APA Monitor,* 60–65.

Deary, I. J., Penke, L., & Johnson, W. (2010). The neuroscience of human intelligence differences. *Nature Neuroscience, 11,* 201–211.

deCharms, R. C., Maeda, F., Glover, G., Ludlow, D., Pauly, J., Soneji, D., Gabrieli, J., & Mackey, S. (2005). Control over brain activation and pain learned by using real-time functional MRI. *Proceedings of the National Academy of Sciences, 102,* 18626–18631.

De Craen, S., Twisk, D., Hagenzieker, M., Elffers, H., & Brookhuis, K. (2011). Do young novice drivers overestimate their driving skills more than experienced drivers? *Accident Analysis and Prevention, 43,* 1660–1665.

Deer, B. (2011, January 5). How the case against the MMR vaccine was fixed. *British Medical Journal, 342,* c5347.

de la Cruz, D. (2007, January 5). FTC fines diet-drug marketers. *The Oregonian* (from Associated Press), p. A10.

DeLoache, J., Chiong, C., Sherman, K., Islam, N., Vanderborght, M., Troseth, G. L., Strouse, G., & ODoherty, K. (2010). Do babies learn from baby media? *Psychological Science, 21,* 1570–1574.

Demetriou, A., Kui, Z. X., Spanoudis, G., Christou, C., Kyriakides, L., & Platsidou, M. (2005). The architecture, dynamics, and development of mental processing: Greek, Chinese, or universal? *Intelligence, 33*, 109–141.

Dennett, D. C. (1995). *Darwin's dangerous idea: Evolution and the meanings of life.* New York: Simon & Schuster.

Dennett, D. C. (2000). Why getting it right matters: Postmodernism and truth. *Free Inquiry, 20*(1), 40–43.

Dickinson, D. K., & Neuman, S. B. (Eds.). (2005). *Handbook of early literacy research* (Vol. 2). New York: Guilford Press.

Dietrich, A., & Kanso, R. (2010). A review of EEG, ERP, and neuroimaging studies of creativity and insight. *Psychological Bulletin, 136*, 822–848.

Dingfelder, S. F. (2006, December). Nix the tics. *APA Monitor*, 18–20.

Dingfelder, S. F. (2007, April). Introduction to science. *APA Monitor, 38*, 24–26.

Dobzhansky, T. (1973). Nothing in biology makes sense except in the light of evolution. *American Biology Teacher, 35*, 125–129.

Dodes, J. E. (1997). The mysterious placebo. *Skeptical Inquirer, 21*(1), 44–45.

Dodge, K. A., & Rutter, M. (2011). *Gene-environment interactions in developmental psychopathology.* New York: Guilford Press.

Dokoupil, T. (2007, July 16). Trouble in a black box: Did effort to reduce teen suicides backfire? *Newsweek*, p. 48.

Dufresne, T. (Ed.). (2007). *Against Freud: Critics talk back.* Stanford, CA: Stanford University Press.

Duncan, J., Parr, A., Woolgar, A., Thompson, R., Bright, P., Cox, S., Bishop, S., & Nimmo-Smith, I. (2008). Goal neglect and Spearman's g: Competing parts of a complex task. *Journal of Experimental Psychology: General, 137*, 131–148.

Durso, F. T., Nickerson, R. S., Dumais, S., Lewandowsky, S., & Perfect, T. (2007). *Handbook of applied cognition.* Hoboken, NJ: Wiley.

Ehrenberg, R. G., Brewer, D. J., Gamoran, A., & Williams, J. D. (2001). Class size and student achievement. *Psychological Science in the Public Interest, 2*, 1–27.

Ehri, L. C., Nunes, S., Stahl, S., & Willows, D. (2001). Systematic phonics instruction helps students learn to read: Evidence from the national reading Panel's meta-analysis. *Review of Educational Research, 71*, 393–447.

Einhorn, H. J. (1986). Accepting error to make less error. *Journal of Personality Assessment, 50*, 387–395.

Eisenberg, L. (1977). The social imperatives of medical research. *Science, 198*, 1105–1110.

Eisenberg, D. M., Kessler, R., Foster, C., Norlock, F., Calkins, D., & Delbanco, T. (1993). Unconventional medicine in the United States. *The New England Journal of Medicine, 328*(4), 246–252.

Ellis, B. J., & Bjorklund, D. F. (Eds.). (2005). *Origins of the social mind: Evolutionary psychology and child development.* New York: Guilford.

Emery, R. E., Otto, R. K., & O'Donohue, W. T. (2005). A critical assessment of child custody evaluations. *Psychological Science in the Public Interest, 6*(1), 1–29.

Engel, J. (2008). *American therapy.* New York: Gotham Books.

Epstein, A. S. (2008). An early start on thinking. *Educational Leadership, 65*(5), 38–42.

Ernst, E., & Abbot, N. C. (1999). I shall please: The mysterious power of placebos. In S. Della Sala (Ed.), *Mind myths: Exploring popular assumptions about the mind and brain* (pp. 209–213). Chichester, England: John Wiley & Sons.

Estes, W. (1979). Experimental psychology: An overview. In E. Hearst (Eds.), *The first century of experimental psychology* (pp. 12–38). Hillsdale, NJ: Erlbaum.

Evans, J. St. B. T. (2005). *How to do research: A psychologist's guide.* Hove, England: Psychology Press.

Ewing, C. P. (2006, January). Testing tool in question. *APA Monitor,* p. 61.

Fackelman, K. (1996, November 9). Gastrointestinal blues. *Science News, 150,* 302–303.

Fancher, R. (1985). *The intelligence men.* New York: W. W. Norton.

Farber, I. B., & Churchland, P. S. (1995). Consciousness and the neurosciences: Philosophical and theoretical issues. In M. S. Gazzaniga (Ed.), *The cognitive neurosciences* (pp. 1295–1306). Cambridge, MA: MIT Press.

Farha, B. (2007). *Paranormal claims: A critical analysis.* Lanham, MD: University Press of America.

Farha, B., & Steward, G. (2006). Paranormal beliefs: An analysis of college students. *Skeptical Inquirer, 30*(1), 37–40.

Ferguson, C. J. (2009). Is psychological research really as good as medical research? *Review of General Psychology, 13,* 130–136.

Fernald, D. (1984). *The Hans legacy.* Hillsdale, NJ: Erlbaum.

Feshbach, S., & Tangney, J. (2008). Television viewing and aggression. *Perspectives on Psychological Science, 3,* 387–389.

Finkel, A. M. (1996, May). Who's exaggerating? *Discover, 17*(5), 48–54.

Fischer, P. et al. (2011a). The bystander-effect: A meta-analytic review on bystander intervention in dangerous and non-dangerous emergencies. *Psychological Bulletin, 137,* 517–537.

Fischer, P., Greitemeyer, T., Kastenmüller, A., Vogrincic, C., & Sauer, A. (2011b). The effects of risk-glorifying media exposure on risk-positive cognitions, emotions, and behaviors: A meta-analytic review. *Psychological Bulletin, 137,* 367–390.

Flynn, J. R. (2007). *What is intelligence?* Cambridge: Cambridge University Press.

Foster, E. A., Jobling, M. A., Taylor, P. G., Donnelly, P., Deknijff, P., Renemieremet, J., Zerjal, T., & Tyler-Smith, C. (1998). Jefferson fathered slave's last child. *Nature, 396,* 27–28.

Foster, R. G., & Roenneberg, T. (2008). Human responses to the geophysical daily, annual and lunar cycles. *Current Biology, 18,* R784–R794.

Fountain, H. (2006, January 15). On not wanting to know what hurts you. *New York Times,* p. WK14.

Fox, R. E. (1996). Charlatanism, scientism, and psychology's social contract. *American Psychologist, 51,* 777–784.

Frank, R. H. (2007). *The economic naturalist.* New York: Basic Books.

Frazier, K. (2009). Pew/AAAS poll. *Skeptical Inquirer, 33*(6), 11–13.

Frazier, K. (2010). Three-country evolution poll. *Skeptical Inquirer, 34*(6), 5–6.

Funder, D. C. (2009). Naive and obvious questions. *Perspectives on Psychological Science, 4,* 340–344.

Galovski, T. E., Malta, L. S., & Blanchard, E. B. (2006). *Road rage: Assessment and treatment of the angry, aggressive driver.* Washington, DC: American Psychological Association.

Gardner, D. (2008). *The science of fear.* New York: Dutton.

Gardner, M. (1972, April). Mathematical games: Why the long arm of coincidence is usually not as long as it seems. *Scientific American, 227*(4), 110–112.

Gardner, M. (2006). The memory wars. *Skeptical Inquirer, 30*(1), 28–31.

Gardner, M. (2010). Oprah Winfrey: Bright (but gullible) billionaire. *Skeptical Inquirer, 34*(2), 54–56.

Gaunt, R. (2006). Couple similarity and marital satisfaction: Are similar spouses happier? *Journal of Personality, 74,* 1401–1420.

Gawande, A. (2010). *The checklist manifesto: How to get things right.* New York: Metropolitan Books.

Gaynor, S. T. (2004). Skepticism and caricatures: B. F. Skinner turns 100. *Skeptical Inquirer, 28*(1), 26–29.

Geary, D. C. (2005). *The origin of the mind: Evolution of brain, cognition, and general intelligence.* Washington, DC: American Psychological Association.

Geary, D. C. (2008). An evolutionarily informed education science. *Educational Psychologist, 28,* 179–195.

Gelman, A. (2008). *Red state, blue state, rich state, poor state.* Princeton, NJ: Princeton University Press.

Gernsbacher, M. A. (2007, May). The value of undergraduate training in psychological science. *APS Observer, 20,* 5–6.

Ghiselin, M. T. (1989). *Intellectual compromise.* New York: Paragon House.

Gigerenzer, G. (2002). *Calculated risks: How to know when numbers deceive you.* New York: Simon & Schuster.

Gigerenzer, G. (2004). Dread risk, September 11, and fatal traffic accidents. *Psychological Science, 15,* 286–287.

Gigerenzer, G. (2006). Out of the frying pan into the fire: Behavioral reactions to terrorist attacks. *Risk Analysis, 26,* 347–351.

Gigerenzer, G., Gaissmaier, W., Kurz-Milcke, E., Schwartz, L. M., & Woloshin, S. (2007). Helping doctors and patients make sense of health statistics. *Psychological Science in the Public Interest, 8,* 53–96.

Gilbert, D. (2006). *Stumbling on happiness.* New York: Alfred A. Knopf.

Gilovich, T. (1991). *How we know what isn't so: The fallibility of human reason in everyday life.* New York: Free Press.

Gilovich, T., Griffin, D., & Kahneman, D. (Eds.). (2002). *Heuristics and biases: The psychology of intuitive judgment.* New York: Cambridge University Press.

Gladwell, M. (2004, December 13). The picture problem. *The New Yorker,* pp. 74–81.

Gladwell, M. (2010, May 17). The treatment. *The New Yorker,* pp. 69–77.

Gleitman, H. (1981). *Psychology.* New York: W. W. Norton.

Goldacre, B. (2008). *Bad science.* London: Fourth Estate.

Gorchoff, S., John, O. P., & Helson, R. (2008). Contextualizing change in marital satisfaction during middle age. *Psychological Science, 19,* 1194–1200.

Gosling, S. D. (2001). From mice to men: What can we learn about personality from animal research? *Psychological Bulletin, 127,* 45–86.

Gosling, S. D., Simine, V., Srivastava, S., & John, O. P. (2004). Should we trust web-based studies? A comparative analysis of six preconceptions about Internet questionnaires. *American Psychologist, 59,* 93–104.

Goswami, U. (Ed.). (2008). *Cognitive development: The learning brain.* London: Psychology Press.

Gould, S. J. (1987). Justice Scalia's misunderstanding. *Natural History, 96,* 14–21.

Grady, D. (2008, June 24). From a prominent death, some painful truths. *New York Times,* p. D5.

Grady, D. (2009, January 6). Should patients be told of better care elsewhere? *New York Times,* p. D1.

Grant, J. (2011). *Denying science.* Amherst, NY: Prometheus Books.

Gray, P. (2008). The value of Psychology 101 in liberal arts education: A psychocentric theory of the university. *APS Observer, 21,* 29–32.

Grice, G. (2001, July 30). Slice of life: How a convicted killer's corpse brought anatomy into the digital age. *The New Yorker,* pp. 36–41.

Griffin, S., Regnier, E., Griffin, P., & Huntley, V. (2007). Effectiveness of fluoride in preventing cares in adults. *Journal of Dental Research, 86,* 410–415.

Griggs, R. A., Proctor, D. L., & Bujak-Johnson, A. (2002). The nonexistent common core. *American Psychologist, 57,* 452–453.

Grissmer, D. (2000). The continuing use and misuse of SAT scores. *Psychology, Public Policy, and Law, 6,* 223–232.

Groopman, J. (2004, January 26). The grief industry: How much does crisis counselling help—or hurt? *The New Yorker,* pp. 30–38.

Groopman, J. (2007). *How doctors think.* Boston: Houghton Mifflin.

Groopman, J. (2009, November 5). Diagnosis: What doctors are missing. *New York Review of Books,* pp. 26–28.

Haack, S. (2007). *Defending science—within reason: Between scientism and cynicism.* Buffalo, NY: Prometheus Books.

Hacohen, M. C. (2000). *Karl Popper: The formative years, 1902–1945.* Cambridge, England: Cambridge University Press.

Hafer, C. L., & Begue, L. (2005). Experimental research on just-world theory: Problems, developments, and future challenges. *Psychological Bulletin, 131,* 128–167.

Haidt, J. (2006). *The happiness hypothesis.* New York: Basic Books.

Hall, H. (2008). 'We couldn't say it in print if it wasn't true': Akavar's version of truth in advertising. *Skeptical Inquirer, 32*(5), 45–49.

Hariri, A. R., & Holmes, A. (2006). Genetics of emotional regulation: The role of the serotonin transporter in neural function. *Trends in Cognitive Sciences, 10,* 182–191.

Harlow, H. F. (1958). The nature of love. *American Psychologist, 13,* 673–685.

Harlow, H. F., & Suomi, S. J. (1970). The nature of love—Simplified. *American Psychologist, 25,* 161–168.

Harriet, H. (2008, September/October). 'We couldn't say it in print if it wasn't true'. *Skeptical Inquirer, 32,* 46–49.

Harrington, A. (2008). *The cure within.* New York: Norton.

Hastie, R., & Dawes, R. M. (2010). *Rational choice in an uncertain world.* Thousand Oaks, CA: Sage.

Hearst, E. (1979). *The first century of experimental psychology.* Hillsdale, NJ: Erlbaum.

Hendrie, C. (2005). Book faults achievement in charter schools. *Education Week,* p. 3.

Henrich, J., Heine, S. J., & Norenzayan, A. (2010). The weirdest people in the world? *Behavioral and Brain Sciences, 33,* 1–75.

Henriques, G. (2011). *A new unified theory of psychology.* New York: Springer.

Herman, C. P., & Polivy, J. (2005). Normative influences on food intake. *Physiology & Behavior, 86,* 762–772.

Hill, C. A. (2010). What cognitive psychologists should find interesting about tax. *Psychonomic Bulletin & Review, 17,* 180–185.

Hilton, D. J. (2003). Psychology and the financial markets: Applications to understanding and remedying irrational decision-making. In I. Brocas & J. D. Carrillo (Eds.), *The psychology of economic decisions: Rationality and well-being* (Vol. 1, pp. 273–297). Oxford: Oxford University Press.

Hines, T. M. (1998). Comprehensive review of biorhythm theory. *Psychological Reports, 83,* 19–64.

Hines, T. M. (2003). *Pseudoscience and the paranormal* (2nd ed.). Buffalo, NY: Prometheus Books.

Hitsch, G., Hortacsu, A., & Ariely, D. (2010). Matching and sorting in online dating. *American Economic Review, 100,* 130–163.

Holton, G., & Roller, D. (1958). *Foundations of modern physical science*. Reading, MA: Addison-Wesley.

Honda, H., Shimizu, Y., & Rutter, M. (2005). No effect of MMR withdrawal on the incidence of autism: A total population study. *Journal of Child Psychology and Psychiatry, 46*, 572–579.

Huber, P. W. (1990). Pathological science in court. *Daedalus, 119*, 97–118.

Hulme, C., & Snowling, M. J. (2011). Children's reading comprehension difficulties: Nature, causes, and treatments. *Current Directions in Psychological Science, 20*, 139–142.

Humphrey, N. (1996). *Leaps of faith*. New York: Copernicus.

Immen, W. (1996, August 8). Could you repeat that in Klingon? *Globe & Mail (Toronto)*.

Insurance Institute for Highway Safety (2005, July 16). If you drive while phoning you're far more likely to get into a crash in which you'll be injured. *Status Report, 40*(6), 1–3.

Ioannidis, J. (2004). Contradicted and initially stronger effects in highly cited clinical research. *JAMA, 294*, 218–228.

Isaacson, W. (2011). *Steve jobs*. New York: Simon & Schuster.

Jacobson, J. W., Foxx, R. M., & Mulick, J. A. (Eds.). (2004). *Controversial therapies for developmental disabilities: Fads, fashion, and science in professional practice*. Mahwah, NJ: Erlbaum.

Jaffe, E. (2005). How random is that? Students are convenient research subjects but they're not a simple sample. *APS Observer, 18*(9), 20–30.

Jaffe, E. (2011, September). Identity shift. *APS Observer, 24*, 12–16.

Johnson, S. (2007). *The ghost map*. New York: Riverhead Books.

Jordan, S. D. (2007, May). Global climate change triggered by global warming. *Skeptical Inquirer, 31*, 32–45.

Joyce, N. (2010, March). Spotting the enemy. *APA Monitor*, pp. 24–25.

Judelsohn, R. G. (2007, November/December). Vaccine safety: Vaccines are one of public health's great accomplishments. *Skeptical Inquirer, 31*(6), 32–35.

Kagan, J. (2006). *An argument for mind*. New Haven, CT: Yale University Press.

Kahneman, D. (1973). *Attention and effort*. Englewood Cliffs, NJ: Prentice Hall.

Kahneman, D. (2011). *Thinking, fast and slow*. New York: Farrar, Straus & Giroux.

Kalat, J. W. (2007). *Biological psychology* (9th ed.). Belmont, CA: Wadsworth.

Kalb, C., & White, E. (2010, May 24). What should you really be afraid of? *Newsweek*, p. 64.

Kantrowitz, B., & Kalb, C. (2006, March 13). Food news blues. *Newsweek*, 44–54.

Kaplan, M., & Kaplan, E. (2007). *Chances are: Adventures in probability*. New York: Penguin Books.

Keating, D. P. (2007). Understanding adolescent development: Implications for driving safety. *Journal of Safety Research, 38*, 147–157.

Keith, K. D., & Beins, B. C. (2008, August). *My students believe what? Psychological myths and sound science in the undergraduate classroom*. Paper presented at the meeting of the American Psychological Association, Boston.

Keizer, K., Lindenberg, S., & Steg, L. (2008, November 20). The spreading of disorder. *Science, 322*, 1681–1685.

Kelly, I. W. (1997). Modern astrology: A critique. *Psychological Reports, 81*, 931–962.

Kelly, I. W. (1998). Why astrology doesn't work. *Psychological Reports, 82*, 527–546.

Kelly, L. (2005). *The skeptic's guide to the paranormal*. New York: Thunder's Mouth Press.

Kenney, C. (2008). *The best practice: How the new quality movement is transforming medicine*. New York: PublicAffairs Books.

Kida, T. (2006). *Don't believe everything you think: The 6 basic mistakes we make in thinking*. Amherst, NY: Prometheus Books.

King, F. (1993, March). Science literacy and public support of science. *APS Observer, 6*(2), 2–11.

Klein, D. N. (2010). Chronic depression: Diagnosis and classification. *Current Directions in Psychological Science, 19*, 96–100.

Knight, G. P., Johnson, L., Carlo, G., & Eisenberg, N. (1994). A multiplicative model of the dispositional antecedents of a prosocial behavior: Predicting more of the people more of the time. *Journal of Personality and Social Psychology, 66*, 178–183.

Kolata, G. (2009, August 20). One injured hamstring, a string of treatments. *New York Times*, p. E8.

Kolata, G. (2011, June 21). When running up mileage, 10 percent isn't the cap. *New York Times*, p. D5.

Kolbert, E. (2005, September 19). Storm warnings. *The New Yorker*, pp. 35–36.

Koocher, G. P. (2006, October). Psychological science is not politically correct. *APA Monitor*, p. 5.

Kosova, W., & Wingert, P. (2009, June 8). Crazy talk. *Newsweek*, pp. 54–62.

Kowalski, P., & Taylor, A. K. (2009). The effect of refuting misconceptions in the introductory psychology class. *Teaching of Psychology, 36*, 153–159.

Krauss, L. M. (2008, October 28). McCain's science earmark error. *Los Angeles Times*. Retrieved November 5, 2008, from http://genesis1.asu.edu/~krauss/latimesoct28.html

Krauthammer, C. (1985, December 29). The twilight of psychotherapy? *Detroit News*.

Kristof, N. (2009, November 29). How can we help? *New York Times Book Review*, p. 27.

Krueger, J. I., Vohs, K. D., & Baumeister, R. F. (2008). Is the allure of self-esteem a mirage after all? *American Psychologist, 63*, 64–65.

Kruger, J., Wirtz, D., & Miller, D. T. (2005). Counterfactual thinking and the first instinct fallacy. *Journal of Personality and Social Psychology, 88*, 725–735.

Kruglanski, A. W., Crenshaw, M., Post, J. M., & Victoroff, J. (2007). What should this fight be called? *Psychological Science in the Public Interest, 8*, 97–133.

Kruglanski, A. W., Gelfand, M., & Gunaratna, R. (2010, January). Detainee deradicalization: A challenge for psychological science. *APS Observer*, 19–22.

Kunar, M. A., Carter, R., Cohen, M., & Horowitz, T. S. (2008). Telephone conversation impairs sustained visual attention via a central bottleneck. *Psychonomic Bulletin & Review, 15*, 1135–1140.

Kushner, H. I. (1999). *A cursing brain? The histories of Tourette Syndrome*. Cambridge, MA: Harvard University Press.

Laden, G. (2008). Likely voters prefer evolution over creationism. *Skeptical Inquirer, 32*(4), 13–14.

Landsburg, S. E. (2007). *More sex is safer sex: The unconventional wisdom of economics*. New York: Free Press.

Larrick, R. P., Timmerman, T. A., Carton, A. M., & Abrevaya, J. (2011). Temper, temperature, and temptation: Heat-related retaliation in baseball. *Psychological Science, 22,* 423–428.

Lazarsfeld, P. (1949). The American Soldier—an expository review. *Public Opinion Quarterly, 13,* 377–404.

Lehrer, J. (2010, December 13). The truth wears off. *The New Yorker,* 52–57.

Leibowitz, H. W. (1996). The symbiosis between basic and applied research. *American Psychologist, 51,* 366–370.

Levy, E. (2009. February 13). The maggots in your mushrooms. *New York Times,* p. A25.

Levy, J., Pashler, H., & Boer, E. (2006). Central interference in driving: Is there any stopping the psychological refractory period? *Psychological Science, 17,* 228–235.

Levy, S. (2005, January 31). Does your iPod play favorites? *Newsweek,* p. 10.

Lewis, M. (2004). *Moneyball.* New York: Norton.

Li, C. (1975). *Path analysis: A primer.* Pacific Grove, CA: Boxwood Press.

Li, M., & Chapman, G. B. (2009). "100% of anything looks good": The appeal of one hundred percent. *Psychonomic Bulletin & Review, 16,* 156–162.

Lilienfeld, S. O. (1998). Pseudoscience in contemporary clinical psychology: What it is and what we can do about it. *The Clinical Psychologist, 51*(4), 3–9.

Lilienfeld, S. O. (2002). New journal dedicated to distinguishing science from pseudoscience in mental health. *Skeptical Inquirer, 26*(3), 7–8.

Lilienfeld, S. O. (2005). The 10 commandments of helping students distinguish science from pseudoscience in psychology. *APS Observer, 18*(9), 39–51.

Lilienfeld, S. O. (2006, February). Correlation still isn't causation. *APS Observer, 19,* 9.

Lilienfeld, S. O. (2007). Psychological treatments that cause harm. *Perspectives on Psychological Science, 2,* 53–70.

Lilienfeld, S. O. (2010). Can psychology become a science? *Personality and Individual Differences, 49,* 281–288.

Lilienfeld, S. O. (2012). Public skepticism of psychology: Why many people perceive the study of human behavior as unscientific. *American Psychologist, 67,* 111–129.

Lilienfeld, S. O., & Lohr, J. M. (2000). Thought field therapy practitioners and educators sanctioned. *Skeptical Inquirer, 24*(2), 5.

Lilienfeld, S. O., Lynn, S. J., & Lohr, J. M. (Eds.). (2003). *Science and pseudoscience in clinical psychology.* New York: Guilford Press.

Lilienfeld, S. O., Lynn, S. J., Ruscio, J., & Beyerstein, B. L. (2010). *50 great myths of popular psychology.* Malden, MA: Wiley-Blackwell.

Lilienfeld, S. O., Ruscio, J., & Lynn, S. J. (Eds.). (2008). *Navigating the mindfield: A guide to separating science from pseudoscience in mental health.* Buffalo, NY: Prometheus Books.

Loftus, E. F., & Guyer, M. J. (2002, May/June). Who abused Jane Doe: The hazards of the single case history. *Skeptical Inquirer, 26*(3), 24–32.

Long, B. (2007). The contributions of economics to the study of college access and success. *Teachers College Record, 109,* 2367–2443.

Lutsky, N. (2006, March). Teaching quantitative reasoning. *APS Observer, 19,* 35–36.

Lynn, S. J., Loftus, E. F., Lilienfeld, S. O., & Lock, T. (2003). Memory recovery techniques in psychotherapy: Problems and pitfalls. *Skeptical Inquirer, 27*(4), 40–46.

Lyubomirsky, S., & Boehm, J. K. (2010). Human motives, happiness, and the puzzle of parenthood. *Perspectives on Psychological Science, 5,* 327–334.

MacCoun, R. (2002, December). Why a psychologist won the Nobel Prize in economics. *APS Observer, 15*(10), 1–8.

Madrick, J. (2006, January 12). The way to a fair deal. *New York Review of Books*, pp. 37–40.

Magee, B. (1985). *Philosophy and the real world: An introduction to Karl Popper.* LaSalle, IL: Open Court.

Maizels, M. (2005). Why should physicians care about behavioral research? *Headache, 45,* 411–413.

Malabre, A. (1994). *Lost prophets: An insider's history of the modern economists.* Cambridge, MA: Harvard Business Press.

Malkiel, B. G. (2011). *A random walk down Wall Street.* New York: Norton.

Mamudi, S. (2009, October 8). Active management loses in risk study. *Wall Street Journal,* p. C9.

Manjoo, F. (2008). *True enough: Learning to live in a post-fact society.* Hoboken, NJ: John Wiley.

Marks, D. F. (2001). *The psychology of the psychic.* Buffalo, NY: Prometheus Books.

Martin, L. et al. (2011). The "distressed" personality, coping and cardiovascular risk. *Stress and Health, 27,* 64–72.

Martin, R., & Hull, R. (2006). The case study perspective on psychological research. In R. J. Sternberg, H. L. Roediger & D. F. Halpern (Eds.), *Critical thinking in psychology* (pp. 90–109). New York: Cambridge University Press.

Matthews, K. A. (2005). Psychological perspectives on the development of coronary heart disease. *American Psychologist, 60,* 783–796.

Matute, H., Yarritu, I., & Vadillo, M. (2011). Illusions of causality at the heart of pseudoscience. *British Journal of Psychology, 102,* 392–405.

Mayer, J. D., Salovey, P., & Caruso, D. R. (2008). Emotional intelligence: New ability or eclectic traits? *American Psychologist, 63,* 503–517.

Mazur, J. E. (2010). *What's luck got to do with it?* Princeton, NJ: Princeton University Press.

McBride-Chang, C., & Kail, R. V. (2002). Cross-cultural similarities in the predictors of reading acquisition. *Child Development, 73,* 1392–1407.

McCabe, D. P., & Castel, A. D. (2008). Seeing is believing: The effect of brain images on judgments of scientific reasoning. *Cognition, 107,* 343–352.

McCloskey, M. (1983, April). Intuitive physics. *Scientific American, 248*(4), 122–130.

McEvoy, S. P., Stevenson, M. R., McCartt, A. T., Woodword, M., Haworth, C., Palamara, P., & Cercarelli, R. (2005, August 20). Role of mobile phones in motor vehicle crashes resulting in hospital attendance: A case-crossover study. *British Medical Journal, 331*(7514), 428.

McHugh, P. (2008). *The memory wars: Psychiatry's clash over meaning, memory, and mind.* Washington, DC: The Dana Foundation.

McNally, R. J., Bryant, R. A., & Ehlers, A. (2003). Does early psychological intervention promote recovery from posttraumatic stress? *Psychological Science in the Public Interest, 4*(2), 45–79.

McNally, R. J., & Geraerts, E. (2009). A new solution to the recovered memory debate. *Perspectives on Psychological Science, 4,* 126–134.

Medawar, P. B. (1967). *The art of the soluble.* London: Methuen.

Medawar, P. B. (1979). *Advice to a young scientist.* New York: Harper & Row.

Medawar, P. B. (1984). *The limits of science.* New York: Harper & Row.

Medawar, P. B. (1990). *The threat and the glory.* New York: HarperCollins.

Medawar, P. B., & Medawar, J. S. (1983). *Aristotle to zoos: A philosophical dictionary of biology.* Cambridge, MA: Harvard University Press.

Medin, D. L., & Atran, S. (2004). The native mind: Biological categorization and reasoning in development and across cultures. *Psychological Review, 111*, 960–983.

Meehl, P. E. (1954). *Clinical versus statistical prediction: A theoretical analysis and review of the literature.* Minneapolis: University of Minnesota Press.

Meehl, P. E. (1986). Causes and effects of my disturbing little book. *Journal of Personality Assessment, 50*, 370–375.

Meehl, P. E. (1993). Philosophy of science: Help or hindrance? *Psychological Reports, 72*, 707–733.

Meier, B., Robinson, M., & Wilkowski, B. (2007). Aggressive primes activate hostile information in memory: Who is most susceptible? *Basic and Applied Social Psychology, 29*, 23–34.

Meyers, L. (2008, January). Recommended reading: Psychologists share the contents of their self-help shelves. *APA Monitor*, pp. 26–27.

Michaels, D. (2008). *Doubt is their product: How industry's assault on science threatens your health.* New York: Oxford University Press.

Mielczarek, E., & Engler, B. (2012). Measuring mythology: Startling concepts in NCCAM grants. *Skeptical Inquirer, 36*(1), 35–43.

Miller, K. R. (2008). *Only a theory: Evolution and the battle for America's soul.* New York: Viking.

Milton, J., & Wiseman, R. (1999). Does psi exist? Lack of replication of an anomalous process of information transfer. *Psychological Bulletin, 125,* 387–391.

Mineka, S., & Zinbarg, R. (2006). A contemporary learning theory perspective on the etiology of anxiety disorders. *American Psychologist, 61*, 10–26.

Mischel, W. (2008, December). The toothbrush problem. *APS Observer, 21*, 5.

Mlodinow, L. (2008). *The drunkard's walk: How randomness rules our lives.* New York: Pantheon.

Monk, R. (1990). *Ludwig Wittgenstein: The duty of genius.* New York: Free Press.

Mook, D. G. (1982). *Psychological research: Strategies and tactics.* New York: Harper & Row.

Mook, D. G. (1983). In defense of external invalidity. *American Psychologist, 38*, 379–387.

Mook, D. G. (1989). The myth of external validity. In L. W. Poon, D. C. Rubin, & B. A. Wilson (Eds.), *Everyday cognition in adulthood and late life* (pp. 25–43). Cambridge, England: Cambridge University Press.

Mook, D. G. (2001). *Psychological research: The ideas behind the methods.* New York: Norton.

Moore, S. A., & Zoellner, L. (2007). Overgeneral autobiographical memory and traumatic events: An evaluative review. *Psychological Bulletin, 133*, 419–437.

Morera, O. F., & Dawes, R. M. (2006). Clinical and statistical prediction after 50 years: A dedication to Paul Meehl. *Journal of Behavioral Decision Making, 19*, 409–412.

Moskowitz, T., & Wertheim, L. (2011). *Scorecasting.* New York: Crown.

Mulick, J., Jacobson, J., & Kobe, F. (1993, Spring). Anguished silence and helping hands: Autism and facilitated communication. *Skeptical Inquirer, 17,* 270–280.

Munro, G. (2010). The scientific impotence excuse: Discounting belief-threatening scientific abstracts. *Journal of Applied Social Psychology, 40,* 579–600.

Murchison, C. (1934). *Handbook of general experimental psychology.* Worcester, MA: Clark University Press.

Myers, D. G. (2006). *Social psychology.* Columbus, OH: McGraw-Hill.

National Reading Panel: Reports of the Subgroups. (2000). *Teaching children to read: An evidence-based assessment of the scientific research literature on reading and its implications for reading instruction.* Washington, DC.

National Safety Council. (2001). *Report on Injuries in America, 2001.* Retrieved March 29, 2002, from www.nsc.org/library/rept2000.htm

Nickerson, R. S. (1998). Confirmation bias: A ubiquitous phenomenon in many guises. *Review of General Psychology, 2,* 175–220.

Nickerson, R. S. (2004). *Cognition and chance: The psychology of probabilistic reasoning.* Mahwah, NJ: Erlbaum.

Nijhuis, M. (2008, June/July). The doubt makers. *Miller-McCune,* pp. 26–35.

Nolen-Hoeksema, S., Wisco, B., & Lyubomirsky, S. (2008). Rethinking rumination. *Perspectives on Psychological Science, 3,* 400–424.

Novella, S. (2007, November/December). The anti-vaccine movement. *Skeptical Inquirer, 31*(6), 25–31.

Novella, S. (2010, November). The poor, misunderstood placebo. *Skeptical Inquirer, 34*(6), 33–34.

Novotney, A. (2008, July). Custody collaborations. *APA Monitor,* pp. 49–51.

Novotney, A. (2009, February). Dangerous distraction. *APA Monitor,* pp. 32–36.

Oberman, L. M., & Ramachandran, V. S. (2007). The simulating social mind: The role of the mirror neuron system and simulation in the social and communicative deficits of autism spectrum disorders. *Psychological Bulletin, 133,* 310–327.

Obrecht, N. A., Chapman, G. B., & Gelman, R. (2009). An encounter frequency account of how experience affects likelihood estimation. *Memory & Cognition, 37,* 632–643.

O'Connor, A. (2011, December 27). Really? *New York Times,* p. D5.

Offit, P. A. (2008). *Autism's false prophets.* New York: Columbia University Press.

Olivola, C. Y., & Oppenheimer, D. M. (2008). Randomness in retrospect: Exploring the interactions between memory and randomness cognition.

Psychonomic Bulletin & Review, 15, 991–996.

Olson, R. K. (2004). SSSR, environment, and genes. *Scientific Studies of Reading, 8,* 111–124.

Oreskes, N. (2004). Beyond the ivory tower: The scientific consensus on climate change. *Science, 306,* 1686.

Oreskes, N., & Conway, E. (2011). *Merchants of doubt.* London: Bloomsbury.

Overskeid, G. (2007). Looking for Skinner and finding Freud. *American Psychologist, 62,* 590–595.

Paloutzian, R. F., & Park, C. L. (Eds.). (2005). *Handbook of the psychology of religion and spirituality.* New York: Guilford Press.

Park, R. L. (2008). *Superstition: Belief in the age of science.* Princeton, NJ: Princeton University Press.

Parker, I. (2010, May 17). The poverty lab. *The New Yorker,* pp. 79–89.

Parker-Pope, T. (2009, January 13). A problem of the brain, not the hands. *New York Times,* p. D5.

Parker-Pope, T. (2011, October 10). Prostate test finding leaves a swirl of confusion. *New York Times Wellness Blog,* pp. 1–4. Retrieved October 12, 2011, from, http://well.blogs.nytimes.com/2011/10/10/prostate-test-finding-leaves-a-swirl-of-confusion/

Pashler, H., McDaniel, M., Rohrer, D., & Bjork, R. (2009). Learning styles: Concepts and evidence. *Psychological Science in the Public Interest, 9,* 105–119.

Paulos, J. A. (2001). *Innumeracy: Mathematical illiteracy and its consequences.* New York: Hill and Wang.

Pennington, B. F., & Olson, R. K. (2005). Genetics of dyslexia. In M. J. Snowling & C. Hulme (Eds.), *The science of reading: A handbook* (pp. 453–472). Malden, MA: Blackwell.

Peterson, C. (2009). Minimally sufficient research. *Perspectives on Psychological Science, 4,* 7–9.

Petry, N. M. (2005). *Pathological gambling: Etiology, comorbidity, and treatment*. Washington, DC: American Psychological Association.

Pigliucci, M. (2010). *Nonsense on stilts*. Chicago: University of Chicago Press.

Pinker, S. (1997). *How the mind works*. New York: W. W. Norton.

Pohl, R. (Ed.). (2004). *Cognitive illusions: A handbook on fallacies and biases in thinking, judgment and memory*. Hove, England: Psychology Press.

Popper, K. R. (1959). *The logic of scientific discovery*. New York: Harper & Row.

Popper, K. R. (1963). *Conjectures and refutations*. New York: Harper & Row.

Popper, K. R. (1972). *Objective knowledge*. Oxford, England: Oxford University Press.

Popper, K. R. (1976). *Unended quest: An intellectual biography*. La Salle, IL: Open Court.

Postman, N. (1988). *Conscientious Objections*. New York: Vintage Books.

Powell, B. (1993, December). Sloppy reasoning, misused data. *Phi Delta Kappan, 75*(4), 283, 352.

Powell, B., & Steelman, L. C. (1996). Bewitched, bothered, and bewildering: The use and misuse of state SAT and ACT scores. *Harvard Educational Review, 66,* 27–59.

Pressley, M. (2005). *Reading instruction that works: The case for balanced teaching* (3rd ed.). New York: Guilford Press.

Price, E. (2009, July). Behavioral research can help curb swine flu. *APA Monitor*, p. 11.

Rabin, R. (2009, June 16). Alcohol's good for you? Some scientists doubt it. *New York Times*, p. D1.

Radcliffe Richards, J. (2000). *Human nature after Darwin: A philosophical introduction*. London: Routledge.

Radford, B. (2005). Ringing false alarms: Skepticism and media scares. *Skeptical Inquirer, 29*(2), 34–39.

Radford, B. (2006). Geller revisited. *Skeptical Inquirer, 30*(1), 27.

Radford, B. (2009). Psychic exploits horrific abduction case. *Skeptical Inquirer, 33*(6), 6–7.

Radford, B. (2010). The psychic and the serial killer. *Skeptical Inquirer, 34*(2), 32–37.

Radford, B. (2011). Left brained or right brained. *Skeptical Inquirer, 35*(1), 22.

Raine, A. (2008). From genes to brain to antisocial behavior. *Current Directions in Psychological Science, 17,* 323–328.

Rajendran, G., & Mitchell, P. (2007). Cognitive theories of autism. *Developmental Review, 27,* 224–260.

Randall, L. (2005, September 18). Dangling particles. *New York Times*, p. WK13.

Randi, J. (1995). *An encyclopedia of claims, frauds, and hoaxes of the occult and supernatural exposed by James Randi*. New York: St. Martin's Press.

Randi, J. (2005). Fakers and innocents: The one million dollar challenge and those who try for it. *Skeptical Inquirer, 29*(4), 45–50.

Randi, J. (2011). Twas brillig: Trying to give away a million dollars. *Skeptic Magazine, 16*(4), 8–9.

Redberg, R. (2011, May 26). Squandering Medicare's money. *New York Times*, p. A27.

Redelmeier, D. A., & Tibshirani, R. J. (2001). Car phones and car crashes: Some popular misconceptions. *Canadian Medical Association Journal, 164*(11), 1581–1582.

Regnier, P. (2010, January). Can you outsmart the market? *Money*, pp. 86–91.

Reis, H. T., Maniaci, M. R., Caprariello, P. A., Eastwick, P. W., & Finkel, E. J. (2011). Familiarity does indeed promote attraction in live interaction. *Journal of Personality and Social Psychology, 101,* 557–570.

Riener, C., Proffitt, D. R., & Salthouse, T. (2005). A psychometric approach to intuitive physics. *Psychonomic Bulletin and Review, 12,* 740–745.

Rind, B. (2008). The Bailey affair: Political correctness and attacks on sex research. *Archives of Sexual Behavior, 37,* 481–484.

Robins, R. W., Gosling, S. D., & Craik, K. H. (1999). An empirical analysis of trends in psychology. *American Psychologist, 54,* 117–128.

Rosenthal, R. (1990). How are we doing in soft psychology? *American Psychologist, 46,* 775–776.

Ross, L., & Nisbett, R. E. (1991). *The person and the situation: Perspectives of social psychology.* Philadelphia: Temple University Press.

Rouder, J., & Morey, R. (2011). A Bayes factor meta-analysis of Bem's ESP claim. *Psychonomic Bulletin & Review, 18,* 682–687.

Rozin, P. (2006). Domain denigration and process preference in academic psychology. *Perspectives on Psychological Science, 1,* 365–376.

Rozin, P. (2007). Exploring the landscape of modern academic psychology: Finding and filling the holes. *American Psychologist, 62,* 754–765.

Rozin, P. (2009). What kind of empirical research should we publish, fund, and reward? *Perspectives on Psychological Science, 4,* 435–439.

Ruse, M. (1999). *Mystery of mysteries: Is evolution a social construction?* Cambridge, MA: Harvard University Press.

Russo, F. (1999, May). The clinical-trials bottleneck. *The Atlantic Monthly,* pp. 30–36.

Rutter, M. (1979). Maternal deprivation, 1972–1978: New findings, new concepts, and new approaches. *Child Development, 50,* 283–305.

Sagan, C. (1996). *The demon-haunted world: Science as a candle in the dark.* New York: Random House.

Salthouse, T. A. (2012). Consequences of age-related cognitive declines. *Annual Review of Psychology, 63,* 201–226.

Saul, S. (2010, July 20). Prone to error: Earliest steps to find cancer. *New York Times,* pp. A1–A14.

Scahill, L., et al. (2006). Contemporary assessment and pharmacotherapy of Tourette syndrome. *NeuroRx, 3,* 192–206.

Schaie, K. W., & Willis, S. (Eds.). (2010). *Handbook of the psychology of aging* (7th ed.). San Diego: Academic Press.

Scholl, S. G., & Greifeneder, R. (2011). Disentangling the effects of alternation rate and maximum run length on judgments of randomness. *Judgment and Decision Making, 6,* 531–541.

Schwartz, M. (2008, December). The golden touch. *Harper's Magazine, 317,* pp. 71–78.

Scott, E. C. (2005). *Evolution vs. creationism.* Berkeley, CA: University of California Press.

Scott, S. (1999, January 2). Risking all on alternative cancer therapies. *National Post (Toronto),* p. B1.

See, J. (2006, May). When 007 meets Ph.D. *APS Observer, 19*(5), 15.

Seethaler, S. (2009). *Lies, damned lies, and science.* Upper Saddle River, NJ: Pearson Education.

Seife, C. (2010). *Proofiness: The dark arts of mathematical deception.* New York: Viking.

Senechal, M. (2006). Testing the home literacy model: Parent involvement in kindergarten is differentially related to Grade 4 reading comprehension, fluency, spelling, and reading for pleasure. *Scientific Studies of Reading, 10,* 59–88.

Seppa, N. (2006, January 14). Put down that fork: Studies document hazards of obesity. *Science News, 169,* 21.

Shadish, W. R., & Baldwin, S. A. (2005). Effects of behavioral marital therapy: A meta-analysis of randomized controlled trials. *Journal of Consulting and Clinical Psychology, 73,* 6–14.

Shaffer, R., & Jadwiszczok, A. (2010). Psychic defective: Sylvia Browne's history of failure. *Skeptical Inquirer, 34*(2), 38–42.

Shapin, S. (2006, November 6). Sick city: Maps and mortality in the time of cholera. *The New Yorker,* pp. 110–115.

Shapiro, A., Shapiro, E., Bruun, R., & Sweet, R. (1978). *Gilles de la Tourette syndrome.* New York: Raven Press.

Sharot, T. (2011). *Optimism bias.* New York: Pantheon.

Shaywitz, S. E., & Shaywitz, B. A. (2004). Neurobiologic basis for reading and reading disability. In P. McCardle & V. Chhabra (Eds.), *The voice of evidence in reading research* (pp. 417–442). Baltimore: Paul Brookes.

Sheese, B. E., & Graziano, W. G. (2005). Deciding to defect: The effects of video-game violence on cooperative behavior. *Psychological Science, 16,* 354–357.

Shepard, R. (1983). "Idealized" figures in textbooks versus psychology as an empirical science. *American Psychologist, 38,* 855.

Shermer, M. (2005). *Science friction: Where the known meets the unknown.* New York: Times Books.

Shermer, M. (2006). *Why Darwin matters: The case against intelligent design.* New York: Times Books.

Shermer, M. (2011). *The believing brain.* New York: Times Books.

Sielski, M. (2010, November 17). Rethinking quarterback stats. *Wall Street Journal,* p. D6.

Simmons, J., Nelson, L., & Simonsohn, U. (2011). False-positive psychology. *Psychological Science, 22,* 1359–1366.

Simmons, R., Burgeson, R., Carlton-Ford, S., & Blyth, D. (1987). The impact of cumulative change in early adolescence. *Child Development, 58,* 1220–1234.

Simonton, D. K. (2004). Psychology's status as a scientific discipline: Its empirical placement within an implicit hierarchy of the sciences. *Review of General Psychology, 8,* 59–67.

Sinaceur, M., Heath, C., & Cole, S. (2005). Emotional and deliberative reactions to a public crisis: Mad cow disease in France. *Psychological Science, 16,* 247–254.

Singer, P. (2008). The tragic cost of being unscientific. *Project Syndicate.* Retrieved December 31, 2008, from http://www.project-syndicate.org/commentary/singer

Singh, K., Spencer, A., & Brennan, D. (2007). Effects of water fluoride exposure at crown completion and maturation on caries of permanent first molars. *Caries Research, 41,* 34–42.

Sivak, M., & Flannagan, M. J. (2003). Flying and driving after the September 11 attacks. *American Scientist, 91,* 6–7.

Skeem, J. L., Polaschek, D., Patrick, C. J., & Lilienfeld, S. O. (2011). Psychopathic personality: Bridging the gap between scientific evidence and public policy. *Psychological Science in the Public Interest, 12,* 93–162.

Skenazy, L. (2009). *Free-range kids.* San Francisco: Jossey-Bass.

Skenazy, L. (2010, October 27). 'Stranger danger' and the decline of Halloween. *Wall Street Journal,* p. A19.

Skitka, L., & Sargis, E. (2006). The internet as psychological laboratory. *Annual Review of Psychology, 57,* 529–555.

Slovic, P. (2007). "If I look at the mass I will never act": Psychic numbing and genocide. *Judgment and Decision Making, 2,* 79–95.

Smith, T., Polloway, E., Patton, J., & Dowdy, C. (2008). *Teaching students* with special needs in inclusive settings (5th ed.). Boston: Allyn & Bacon.

Snowling, M. J., & Hulme, C. (Eds.). (2005). *The science of reading: A handbook.* Malden, MA: Blackwell.

Spellman, B. A., & Busey, T. A. (2010). Emerging trends in psychology and law research. *Psychonomic Bulletin & Review, 17,* 141–142.

Spitz, H. H. (1997). *Nonconscious movements: From mystical messages to facilitated communication.* Mahwah, NJ: Erlbaum.

Stahl, S. A., & Kuhn, M. (1995). Does whole language or instruction matched to learning styles help children learn to read? *School Psychology Review, 24,* 393–404.

Standing, L. G., & Huber, H. (2003). Do psychology courses reduce belief in psychological myths? *Social Behavior and Personality, 31,* 585–592.

Stanovich, K. E. (2000). *Progress in understanding reading.* New York: Guilford Press.

Stanovich, K. E. (2004). *The robot's rebellion: Finding meaning in the age of Darwin.* Chicago: University of Chicago Press.

Stanovich, K. E. (2009). *What intelligence tests miss: The psychology of rational thought.* New Haven, CT: Yale University Press.

Stanovich, K. E. (2010). *Decision making and rationality in the modern world.* New York: Oxford University Press.

Stanovich, K. E. (2011). *Rationality and the reflective mind.* New York: Oxford University Press.

Sternberg, R. J. (Ed.). (2005). *Unity in psychology: Possibility or pipedream?* Washington, DC: American Psychological Association.

Sternberg, R. J. & Kaufman, S. B. (Eds.). (2011). *Cambridge handbook of intelligence.* New York: Cambridge University Press.

Sternberg, R. J., Roediger, H. L., & Halpern, D. F. (Eds.). (2006). *Critical thinking in psychology.* New York: Cambridge University Press.

Strayer, D. L., & Drews, F. A. (2007). Cellphone-induced driver distraction. *Current Directions in Psychological Science, 16,* 128–131.

Strayer, D. L., & Johnston, W. A. (2001). Driven to distraction: Dual-task studies of simulated driving and conversing on a cellular telephone. *Psychological Science, 12,* 462–466.

Suls, J., & Bunde, J. (2005). Anger, anxiety, and depression as risk factors for cardiovascular disease: The problems and implications of overlapping affective dispositions. *Psychological Bulletin, 131,* 260–300.

Surowiecki, J. (2010, August 16). Soak the very, very rich. *The New Yorker,* p. 33.

Swanson, D. (2001). *Nibbling on Einstein's brain: The good, the bad & the bogus in science.* Toronto: Annick Press.

Swanson, D. (2004). *Turn it loose: The scientist in absolutely everybody.* Toronto: Annick Press.

Swets, J. A., Dawes, R. M., & Monahan, J. (2000). Psychological science can improve diagnostic decisions. *Psychological Science in the Public Interest, 1,* 1–26.

Tager-Flusberg, H. (2007). Evaluating the theory-of-mind hypothesis of autism. *Current Directions in Psychological Science, 16,* 311–315.

Tait, R., Chibnall, J., & Kalauokalani, D. (2009). Provider judgments of patients in pain: Seeking symptom certainty. *Pain Medicine, 10,* 11–34.

Talbot, M. (2005, December 5). Darwin in the dock. *The New Yorker,* pp. 66–77.

Taleb, N. (2007). *The black swan: The impact of the highly improbable.* New York: Random House.

Tanaka, H., et al. (2011). The brain basis of the phonological deficit in dyslexia is independent of IQ. *Psychological Science, 22,* 1442–1451.

Taylor, A. K., & Kowalski, P. (2004). Naive psychological science: The prevalence, strength, and sources of misconceptions. *Psychological Record, 54,* 15–25.

Taylor, B. (2006). Vaccines and the changing epidemiology of autism. *Child Care, Health, and Development, 32,* 511–519.

Tetlock, P. E. (2005). *Expert political judgment.* Princeton, NJ: Princeton University Press.

Thaler, R. H., & Sunstein, C. R. (2008). *Nudge: Improving decisions about health, wealth, and happiness.* New Haven, CT: Yale University Press.

Thornton, E. (1986). *The Freudian fallacy.* London: Paladin Books.

Tilburt, J. C., Emanuel, E. J., Kaptchuk, T. J., Curlin, F. A., & Miller, F. G. (2008, October 23). Prescribing placebo treatments: Results of national survey of US internists and rheumatologists. *BMJ, 337,* a1938 (doi:10.1136/bmj.a1938).

Todd, A. (2010, May). Behavioral science is the new green. *APS Observer,* pp. 23–24.

Toplak, M., Liu, E., Macpherson, R., Toneatto, T., & Stanovich, K. E. (2007). The reasoning skills and thinking dispositions of problem gamblers: A dual-process taxonomy. *Journal of Behavioral Decision Making, 20,* 103–124.

Trout, J. D. (2008). Seduction without cause: Uncovering explanatory necrophilia. *Trends in Cognitive Science, 12,* 281–282.

Tuerkheimer, D. (2010, September 20). Anatomy of a misdiagnosis. *New York Times.* Retrieved November 22, 2010, from http://www.nytimes.com/2010/2009/2021/opinion/2021tuerkheimer.html

Tversky, A., & Kahneman, D. (1974). Judgment under uncertainty: Heuristics and biases. *Science, 185,* 1124–1131.

Twachtman-Cullen, D. (1997). *A passion to believe.* Boulder, CO: Westview.

University of California, Berkeley. (1991, January). The 18-year gap. *Berkeley Wellness Letter,* p. 2.

Vanderbilt, T. (2008). *Traffic: Why we drive the way we do (and what it says about us).* New York: Knopf.

Vazire, S., & Gosling, S. D. (2003). Bridging psychology and biology with animal research. *American Psychologist, 58,* 407–408.

Vellutino, F., Fletcher, J. M., Snowling, M., & Scanlon, D. M. (2004). Specific reading disability (dyslexia): What have we learned in the past four decades? *Journal of Child Psychology and Psychiatry, 45,* 2–40.

Waber, R., Shiv, B., Carmon, Z., & Ariely, D. (2008). Commercial features of placebo and therapeutic efficacy. *JAMA, 299,* 1016–1017.

Wachs, T. D. (2000). *Necessary but not sufficient: The respective roles of single and multiple influences on individual development.* Washington, DC: American Psychological Association.

Wade, C., & Tavris, C. (2008). *Psychology* (9th ed.). Upper Saddle River, NJ: Pearson Education.

Wagenaar, W. A. (1988). *Paradoxes of gambling behavior.* Hove, England: Erlbaum.

Wagenaar, W. A., & Keren, G. (1986). The seat belt paradox: Effect of adopted roles on information seeking. *Organizational Behavior and Human Decision Processes, 38,* 1–6.

Wagenmakers, E. J., Wetzels, R., Borsboom, D., & van der Maas, H. (2011). Why psychologists must change the way they analyze their data. *Journal of Personality and Social Psychology, 100,* 426–432.

Wagner, R. K., & Kantor, P. (2010). Dyslexia deciphered. In D. Preiss & R. J. Sternberg (Eds.), *Innovations in educational psychology* (pp. 25–47). New York: Springer.

Wainer, H. (1999). The most dangerous profession: A note on nonsampling error. *Psychological Methods, 4,* 250–256.

Wang, L. (2009). Money and fame: Vividness effects in the National Basketball Association. *Journal of Behavioral Decision Making, 22,* 20–44.

Wargo, E. (2007). Aiming at happiness and shooting ourselves in the foot. *APS Observer, 20,* 13–15.

Wargo, E. (2008, October). The many lives of superstition. *APS Observer, 21,* 18–24.

Wargo, E. (2011, November). From the lab to the courtroom. *APS Observer, 21,* 10–33.

Watts, D. J. (2011). *Everything is obvious— once you know the answer.* New York: Crown Business.

Wegner, D. M., Fuller, V. A., & Sparrow, B. (2003). Clever hands: Uncontrolled intelligence in facilitated communication. *Journal of Personality and Social Psychology, 85,* 5–19.

Weisberg, D. S., Keil, F. C., Goodstein, J., Rawson, E., & Gray, J. R. (2008). The seductive allure of neuroscience explanations. *Journal of Cognitive Neuroscience, 20,* 470–477.

Welch, H. G., Schwartz, L. M., & Woloshin, S. (2012). *Overdiagnosed: Making people sick in the pursuit of health.* Boston: Beacon Press.

Wellman, H. M., Fang, F., & Peterson, C. C. (2011). Sequential progressions in a theory of mind scale: Longitudinal perspectives. *Child Development, 82,* 780–782.

Wells, G. L., Memon, A., & Penrod, S. D. (2006). Eyewitness evidence: Improving its probative value. *Psychological Science in the Public Interest, 7,* 45–75.

West, C. (2007, May). From findings to front page: APS engages the public in psychological science. *APS Observer, 20,* 15–19.

West, S. G. (2009). Alternatives to randomized experiments. *Current Directions in Psychological Science, 18,* 299–304.

Whitson, J. A., & Galinsky, A. D. (2008). Lacking control increases illusory pattern perception. *Science, 322,* 115–117.

Wickens, C. D., Lee, J., Liu, Y., & Gordon-Becker, S. (2003). *Introduction to human factors engineering* (2nd ed.). Upper Saddle River, NJ: Prentice Hall.

Wilkinson, L. (1999). Statistical methods in psychology journals: Guidelines and explanations. *American Psychologist, 54,* 595–604.

Wilkowski, B., & Robinson, M. (2008). The cognitive basis of trait anger and reactive aggression: An integrative analysis. *Personality and Social Psychology Review, 12,* 3–21.

Willingham, D. T. (2009). *Why don't students like school?* San Francisco: Jossey-Bass.

Wilson, D. S. (2007). *Evolution for everyone: How Darwin's theory can change the way we think about our lives.* New York: Delacorte Press.

Wiseman, R. (2011). *Paranormality: Why we see what isn't there.* London: Macmillan.

Wolf, M. (2007). *Proust and the squid.* New York: Harper.

Wolff, C. (2011, August 2). Baseballs' weight problem. *Wall Street Journal,* p. D6.

Wood, J. M., Nezworski, M. T., Lilienfeld, S. O., & Garb, H. N. (2003). *What's wrong with the Rorschach?* San Francisco: Jossey-Bass.

Woodcock, R. W. (2011). *Woodcock Reading Mastery Tests, revised-normative update.* San Antonio, TX: Pearson Education.

Wright, R. (1988). *Three scientists and their gods.* New York: Harper & Row.

Yang, M., Wong, S. C. P., & Coid, J. (2010). The efficacy of violence prediction: A meta-analytic comparison of nine risk assessment tools. *Psychological Bulletin, 136,* 740–767.

Zebrowitz, L. A., White, B., & Wieneke, K. (2008). Mere exposure and racial prejudice: Exposure to other-race faces increases liking for strangers of that race. *Social Cognition, 26,* 259–275.

Zill, N., & Winglee, M. (1990). *Who reads literature?* Cabin John, MD: Seven Locks Press.

Zimbardo, P. G. (2004). Does psychology make a significant difference in our lives? *American Psychologist, 59,* 339–351.

Zimmer, B. (2010, October 10). Truthiness: The fifth anniversary of Stephen Colbert's introduction of a zeitgeisty word. *New York Times Magazine,* p. 22.

Zvolensky, M. J., Vujanovic, A. A., Bernstein, A., & Leyro, T. (2010). Distress tolerance: Theory, measurement, and relations to psychopathology. *Current Directions in Psychological Science, 19,* 406–410.

Zweig, M. (2008). *Your money and your brain.* New York: Simon & Schuster.

Credits

Chapter 2: p. 32, ©2000 Council for Secular Humanism.

Chapter 4: p. 59, Copyright The New England Journal of Medicine.

Chapter 10: p. 156, Copyright © 2005 Condè Nast. All rights reserved. Originally published in The New Yorker. Reprinted by permission.

Name Index

Subject Index